W9-DHT-943

CONTENTS

CAREER OPPORTUNITIES FOR WRITERS

FOURTH EDITION

Rosemary Ellen Guiley

with
Janet Frick

✓® **Checkmark Books**®
An imprint of Facts On File, Inc.

CAREER OPPORTUNITIES FOR WRITERS, FOURTH EDITION

Checkmark Books
An imprint of Facts On File, Inc.
11 Penn Plaza
New York, NY 10001

Library of Congress Cataloging-in-Publication Data

Guiley, Rosemary.
  Career opportunities for writers.—4th ed./Rosemary Ellen Guiley, Janet Frick.
    p. cm. — (Career opportunities series)
  Includes bibliographical references and index.
  ISBN 0-8160-4143-1 (hc; alk. paper)—ISBN 0-8160-4144-X (pbk; alk. paper)
  1. Authorship—Vocational guidance. I. Frick, Janet. II. Title.
III. Facts on File's career opportunities series.
PN151.G84   2000
808′.02—dc21   99-087738

Checkmark Books are available at special discounts when purchased in bulk quantities for businesses, associations, institutions or sales promotions. Please call our Special Sales Department in New York at (212) 967-8800 or (800) 322-8755.

You can find Facts On File on the World Wide Web at http://www.factsonfile.com

Cover design by Nora Wertz

Printed in the United States of America

VB Hermitage 10 9 8 7 6 5 4 3 2 1
        (pbk) 10 9 8 7 6 5 4 3 2 1

This book is printed on acid-free paper.

PREFACE
How to Use This Book

Purpose

Career Opportunities for Writers presents one of the most comprehensive catalogs of writing jobs available in a single volume. It does not focus on a single field of writing, but covers numerous jobs in eight major fields. Jobs are not merely summarized in a paragraph or two but described in detail, including duties, salaries, prerequisites, employment and advancement opportunities, organizations to join, and opportunities for women and minorities. It is intended to help both aspiring writers who are seeking entry-level jobs as well as experienced writers who are interested in making career changes.

Generally the jobs included in this book are open to persons with appropriate educational credentials (usually a bachelor's degree) and up to five or so years of experience. These are predominantly entry- and middle-level positions, those that are available to the largest number of candidates.

Sources of Information

Research for this book included the author's own experience, interviews with numerous professionals in various fields, and surveys, reports, facts, and other information obtained from professional associations, trade unions, the federal government, and universities. The author has worked as a writer, journalist, or editor, either on staff or on a freelance basis, in newspaper and magazine journalism, advertising trade news and sales promotion, corporate communications, ghostwriting and collaboration, and scriptwriting.

The job descriptions are based on representative samples of actual job positions. In general, writing jobs are broad in their responsibilities, and they can vary greatly from one employer to another. In many cases, a writing job is what the employee makes of it. Jobs at small firms tend to be broader in scope than those in large, structured companies and organizations. The descriptions in this book note some of the wide ranges of duties and responsibilities for various types of jobs.

Organization of Material

This book has nine parts: eight cover different fields and industries that employ many writers; the last section consists of appendixes listing educational institutions, helpful web sites for writers, associations and unions, periodicals, and a bibliography of additional sources, all pertinent to writing careers. While most of the jobs listed are based solely on writing and editing skills, a few are writing-related; that is, in addition to substantial writing and editing skills, they require other skills or education. Some of the jobs that fall into this category are sales-oriented positions, research positions, and jobs requiring technical, legal, academic, or foreign-language training. The Introduction gives an overview of job opportunities for writers, as well as explaining employment trends for the next decade or so.

The Internet has brought about an explosion of information that has revolutionized writers' jobs in every medium and specialty. It is essential for anyone in the information field to know how to use computers and navigate the Internet. As more information is transmitted electronically, the ability to conduct research using computers and distribute information to specialized audiences via the Internet will become increasingly important to writers. Advances in technology have also made it possible for freelancers to provide for more sophisticated services.

Explanation of Job Descriptions

Each job description follows a basic format and is complete unto itself; the reader does not have to consult another section of the book to get a complete picture of a particular job. Therefore, readers may encounter some repetition from job to job within a given industry.

Jobs are listed by their predominant title, followed by a Career Profile, which summarizes main duties, alternate titles, salary ranges, employment prospects, advancement prospects, and prerequisites of education, experience, and special skills. A Career Ladder diagram shows a typical career path, including the positions above and below each job. If a job is entry level, school or other related positions are listed as preceding it.

The Position Description is a narrative that describes typical job duties and responsibilities, working hours and conditions, and optional duties that may or may not be part of an individual job. It covers peers and superiors, and it indicates the frequency of overtime or travel, wherever pertinent.

Salaries explains income ranges and the factors, such as individual skills, size of employer, or geographic location, that affect how much a particular job may pay. Salary ranges are based on averages, and readers may find positions that pay less or more than the figures cited in this book.

Readers will find particularly helpful the sections on Employment Prospects and Advancement Prospects. Some jobs may sound terrific or be very glamorous, but they also may be extremely difficult to obtain. Others may prove to be dead ends, with advancement difficult or impossible. These are important factors to weigh in any job search.

Education describes academic requirements for various jobs. In most cases, writers who have earned undergraduate degrees in liberal arts or communications will qualify; some jobs require other educational backgrounds. Graduate degrees are not often required but are increasingly advantageous for many jobs. At the opposite end of the spectrum, some writing jobs require only high school diplomas.

In addition to education, many jobs require prior experience. The Experience/Skills section describes what background is essential or helpful in competing for a job. Previous experience may not be required for many entry-level positions, but candidates who have had some kind of related experience—even on collegiate, volunteer, or community levels—often have significant competitive advantages. In addition, this section spells out the skills and qualities employers look for, attributes which enhance prospects for success in particular fields.

Most communicators—a generic term that includes writers, editors, and others in various communications jobs—do not belong to a union. Those who do, work for organized fields such as print and broadcast journalism, film and television entertainment, schools, and government. Even in those areas, unionization is not uniform throughout. Many do, however, belong to one or more professional associations, where they meet others who have similar jobs, exchange information and ideas, and make contacts. The Unions/Associations section, which ends each job description, lists the major associations of interest to professionals in a particular field, as well as the most likely unions, if any, that would represent them in wage negotiations. Please bear in mind that the associations listed for each job are only a small sampling of the possible organizations to which people in that field might belong. Readers are encouraged to browse through Appendix III to look for organizations that interest them, and to contact those organizations to obtain more information about membership eligibility. You would not guess from its title, for example, that membership in the Association for Women in Communications is also open to men—but you will find this out by visiting the web site listed in Appendix III.

Appendixes

Appendix I, "Educational Institutions," lists colleges, universities, and educational institutions, in every state and the District of Columbia, which offer undergraduate degrees in major areas of communications—broadcasting, advertising, public relations, education, technical and specialized journalism, newspaper and magazine journalism, as well as courses in publishing. The list does not include every institution which offers courses or degrees in communications. The list also does not include two-year colleges, since most jobs require or give preference to degree-holders from four-year institutions.

The list gives each institution's address, telephone number, fax number, E-mail address, and web site, as well as the major programs, specialties, and courses of interest to writers.

Appendix II, "Useful Web Sites for Writers," is reproduced courtesy of *Writer's Digest* magazine. It gives 101 web sites that the editors of that magazine highly recommend for writers, and these sites are divided into useful subcategories. Please check the actual site at http://www.writersdigest.com/101sites/ to make sure you get the most up-to-date version, since the site is periodically updated.

Appendix III, "Professional, Industry and Trade Associations and Unions," lists major organizations for writers, editors, and those in the writing-related fields included in this book. Unlike earlier editions of this book, this edition gives fax numbers, E-mail addresses and web sites for these organizations as well. (Sometimes specific information is deliberately omitted, however. For example, if the web site lists multiple E-mail addresses to contact for different purposes, no E-mail address is listed in the appendix.)

Appendix IV, "Major Trade Periodicals," groups such periodicals according to field or industry.

Finally, Appendix V is a bibliography of sources that give additional career and salary information. Some of this information is from the Internet. Again, you may wish to check the web sites yourself, since most are updated frequently.

ACKNOWLEDGMENTS

I would like to thank the Newspaper Association of America, which granted me generous access to its library at the Newspaper Center and supplied several helpful salary surveys. The Newspaper Guild also provided me with salary information; Professor Lee B. Becker of the School of Journalism at Ohio State University provided a copy of his survey of journalism school graduates, done with Gerald M. Kosicki.

Thanks also to Joe Pinder, press secretary to Rep. Jim Leach of Iowa; Elizabeth Stoloff Vehse of the University of Chicago alumni office; Anne Hinman Diffily, editor of the *Brown Alumni Monthly;* Helene Redmond, a graphic artist and freelance desktop publisher; Gary Craig, manager of Thomas Online at the Thomas Publishing Company; and Kathy Christensen of the Cable News Network library.

Thanks also to Jewel Bradstreet Heldman, who researched part of this book.

For this fourth edition I am indebted to the Newspaper Guild-Communications Workers of America for providing updated salary surveys once again; and to Melanie Rigney, editor of *Writer's Digest* magazine, for permission to include its 101 Top Web Sites for Writers as Appendix II. I would like to thank James Chambers at Facts On File and Bert Holtje at James Peter Associates for their astute guidance and support. Finally, I am grateful to the reference librarians at all the libraries where I did research, especially Helen Beckert at the Glen Ridge Free Public Library in New Jersey. Her assistance has been invaluable on this and many other projects.

INTRODUCTION

The Job Outlook for Writers and Other Communicators

So you want to be a writer. Or maybe you write already, but want to try something new.

Perhaps you want to crouch in a musty newsroom, ear tuned to a police scanner. Or maybe you want to speak indirectly to voters, telling them why the country should pass a bill, or wage a war, or vote for your boss.

You can extol the virtues of consumer goods. Or write a screenplay someone else will rewrite and someone else will change again, until finally an actor mouths words something like yours on the big screen.

Or maybe your prose will become pixels of light instantaneously flashed across the screen of someone else's computer, halfway around the world.

Whatever it is you want to do, can afford to do, or have the talent to do, the jobs are there. You can probably make a better-than-average living, but unless you write that bestseller or Oscar-winning screenplay, don't plan on a fortune. And the more familiar you are with finance, economics, health care, computers, or technical subjects, the better you will do. During the next 10 years, job prospects for writers and communicators should continue to grow in the service sector. Health, environmental-related areas, leisure, travel, and international trade should all grow.

The Information Technology Revolution

Since the first edition of this book was published in 1983, the fields covered here have been revolutionized by computer technology and the ability to transmit information with E-mail, increasingly fast fax-modems, and the Internet. It's now possible to research any subject you're writing about without leaving home, even if you're a night owl working at 3:00 A.M., and then send the finished article to your publisher with the click of a mouse.

Traditional forms of the printed word—books, newspapers, and magazines—are scrambling to keep up with the new technology and assess how it helps or hurts them.

Increasingly specialized information can now be made available to smaller audiences at low cost. This has spawned thousands of specialized magazines; small publishing houses that, through desktop publishing, can produce titles for a small segment of the market; and computerized data-

bases targeting financial investors or other small but sophisticated audiences.

No longer does the cost of printing information on paper force companies solely to seek mainstream audiences. And no longer do workers need to be tied to a central geographic location if they are equipped with a computer, modem, and fax.

In the past 15 years, the number of new computerized databases has multiplied rapidly. During that same time, the number of consumer magazines has greatly increased, and thousands of small publishing companies have sprung up all over the country.

The public relations industry has become more prominent. Although public relations budgets suffer in poor economic times, the need for professional public relations services to polish images has been recognized by most institutions and is expected only to grow.

There has also been an increase in demand for people with skills to perform computer-aided research—librarians, researchers, and information managers. Some newspapers are becoming information brokers on the side, selling their news articles to electronic databases and providing research services for a fee.

The Internet has become an absolutely invaluable research tool for writers and communicators of all kinds, whether they work in an office or at home. Virtually every single job in this book now requires use of computer, E-mail, and the Internet. A survey done by *Publishers Weekly* found that 97 percent of respondents in the book publishing industry had access to the Internet in 1998 and used it slightly less than five hours per week.

The Internet is also blurring the traditional boundaries among media, as pointed out in a report for a 1998 Newspaper Guild conference. Work created for one medium is easily transferred into another. Some old-time professionals who are all thumbs at technology yearn for the days when manuscripts were typed on typewriters and edited with pencils. However, anyone who has written or edited a lengthy manuscript on a computer must appreciate the merits of a computer for making extensive revisions easily. Search and replace is a godsend for making last-minute adjustments to style, tracking down the first occurrence of terms defined in the glossary, and so on. It is also wonderful to be able to E-mail or fax a finished job to a client rather than having to send hard copy.

Writing Jobs for the Twenty-First Century

The Bureau of Labor Statistics estimates that there were about 286,000 employed writers and editors in the United States in 1996, and that the number will increase to 347,000 by the year 2006: an increase of 21.2 percent. This means an excellent outlook for the field as a whole.

Several of the specific jobs within this book have a very promising outlook for growth:

Job	Number Employed (in 000s)		% increase
	1996	2006	
Desktop publishing specialists	30	53	73.5%
Marketing, advertising, PR managers	482	620	28.5%
Public relations specialists and publicity writers	110	140	27.2%
College and university faculty	864	1,026	18.8%
Professional librarians	154	162	7%

Nearly a third of salaried writers and editors work for newspapers, magazines, and book publishers. Substantial numbers also work in advertising agencies, in radio and television broadcasting, in public relations firms, and on journals and newsletters published by business and nonprofit organizations, such as professional associations, labor unions, and religious organizations. Others develop publications for government agencies or write for motion picture companies. And a rapidly growing number work on the Internet.

Many technical writers work for computer software firms or manufacturers of aircraft, chemicals, pharmaceuticals, and computers and other electronic equipment.

Jobs with major book publishers, magazines, broadcasting companies, advertising agencies and public relations firms, and the federal government are concentrated in New York, Chicago, Los Angeles, Boston, Philadelphia, San Francisco, and Washington, D.C. Jobs with newspapers and professional, religious, business, technical, and trade union magazines or journals are more widely dispersed throughout the country. Technical writers are employed throughout the country as well, but the largest concentrations are found in the Northeast, Texas, and California.

Thousands of other writers and editors work as freelancers, earning some income from their articles, books, and (less commonly) television and movie scripts. Most freelancers support themselves primarily with income derived from other sources, although it is possible to earn a comfortable living by working hard as a full-time freelancer. Many freelancers work at home. Others do freelance work in offices, as on-site consultants. Workers in this situation generally receive no paid vacation, health insurance, or other benefits, particularly if they work fewer than 21 hours per week, but they have more freedom over their schedules than do full-time employees. In some cases hourly pay is better for working at the employer's office than for working at home.

The Internet: A Hot New Field for Writers

A burgeoning job scene for writers in the new millennium is the World Wide Web. This is a relatively new field, so job descriptions and titles vary widely: various sources refer to content manager, web site developer, web site writer or editor. Some people who write for the Internet work for one corporation and continually update its web site. These employees may have some completely different job title and many other unrelated job responsibilities. Others are freelancers or work for consulting or advertising firms that specialize solely in web site development.

U.S. News & World Report chose web site developer as one of 20 hot career tracks in its 1999 annual guide to the best jobs for the future. Average salary for a chief copywriter working on the web was $48,400 in 1998, according to that article. For content manager the average was $63,200. Other studies in 1997 through 1999 have reported that salaries for web site workers are increasing because their skills are in demand. The 2000 edition of *Writer's Market* says that freelance web page writing/editing pays $50 low, $85 mid, $500 high per hour.

Writers who develop web sites must make sure that the information is clearly presented, that it scans well to the eye on the screen (which is different from the printed page), and that it is accessible to people with disabilities or those possessing older computers. Hyperlinks should be used well to organize all the material clearly and make it easy to access each page.

E-zines (electronic magazines) offer writers a promising new medium for their talents. There are e-zines out there on every conceivable topic, and many feature the work of new writers. Try typing "writing e-zines" into your favorite search engine to get a good up-to-date list and see which ones appeal to you. Also check out the excellent article entitled "Write for the Web—and Sell!" by Michael Ray Taylor in the 2000 edition of *Writer's Market*. Remember that writing for web-based media is different from writing for the printed page. Writers must understand their medium well in order to succeed at it.

Job-Hunting: Getting a Foot in the Door

It used to be that if you had a knack for grammar and spelling and could type 60 words per minute, you could get an entry-level job as an editorial assistant or administrative assistant with most publishers. This is no longer true. Job applicants should be well versed in software programs and the Internet. Microsoft Word is one of the most popular word processing programs, and knowledge of spreadsheet software such as Excel gives an applicant a competitive edge.

To land that first entry-level job, there are several strategies that will help you. Work on a college newspaper or radio station is good experience that will look great on your resume. Internships during college are also helpful in any aspect of publishing, broadcasting, and communications. A 1997 study by the Career Services Department at Seton Hall University found that students who had been interns found jobs sooner after they graduated and earned higher starting salaries than students who had not. Eighty percent of interns were offered permanent employment by the organization where they held the internship.

For useful information about using the Internet as a job-hunting tool for any writing (or other) field, see Richard Nelson Bolles's 1999 book, *Job-Hunting on the Internet* or other books on the same topic. Here are a few web sites that job-hunters may find especially useful:

For journalism jobs:

http://ajr.newslink.org/newjoblink.html

For salary information:

http://jobsmart.org/tools/salary/sal-prof.htm

For freelancers:

http://www.FreelanceOnline.com/wwwboard.html

To compare living costs in different cities:

http://pathfinder.com/money/bestplaces
http://www.datamasters.com
http://www.aboutwork.com

Factors Affecting Salaries

Many of the salary ranges in this book are very wide, but this reflects the real world out there. Here are several key factors that affect where, within a broad salary range, a given job may fall:

1. *Location, location, location.* Richard Nelson Bolles, in his 1999 book, *Job-Hunting on the Internet,* pointed out that location is just as important in job-hunting as in real estate. For example, a 1998 study published by the Society for Technical Communication found that the median salary for technical writers in some parts of California is $61,500, but in Idaho and Wyoming it is only $30,000. *American Salaries & Wages Survey,* 5th edition (1999), offers a highly detailed look at how salaries for comparable work vary by location.

However, before you pull up stakes to move to the city with the highest salary, take into account that it probably has a higher cost of living as well. For example, *Money* magazine found in 1998 that a salary of $50,000 in New York gave the same buying power as only $19,448.03 in New Orleans.

If you have no desire to move from your current location, you might look into doing freelance work for a client in a higher-paying city. This way, your location doesn't have to match your employer's. However, it is usually easiest to market yourself as a freelancer to clients who already know your work.

2. *Length of experience in the field.* A worker who has years of experience in a particular job or field naturally earns more than one who's just been hired right out of school. Employers are seeking specific sets of skills, most of which are learned on the job rather than in school.

3. *Size of company.* As a general rule, the larger the company, the higher the salaries. *Publishers Weekly* found this to be true in book publishing both in 1998 and 1999.

4. *Size of its market.* Magazines and newspapers with higher circulation pay higher salaries. TV and radio stations with larger audiences pay higher salaries also.

5. *Level of formal education.* Study after study has shown that education pays, and that the earnings gap between those with a college degree and those without one is widening in the United States. The Census Bureau determined that college graduates earned an average of $40,478 in 1997. This was 76 percent more than the $22,895 average earned by high school graduates that year. In 1975 the gap was only 57 percent.

In unusual cases—through connections, luck, and talent—it is sometimes possible to get a job without the educational background recommended for it in this book. However, you may not be paid as well or get promoted to the next level. On the other hand, *Money* magazine reported in 1998 that although getting a graduate degree does increase salary in technical fields by 18 to 28 percent at first, the difference shrinks to only 5 percent after four years. Experience on the job is considered more important by many employers.

6. *Gender and race.* Unfortunately, statistics show that white males still earn more than women and minorities in many of the jobs described in this book. This is partly because there are more white men in top managerial positions, and partly because men are still sometimes paid more for doing the same job as women.

But both these factors are gradually changing. A 1998 *Business Week* article suggested that technology has become a great equalizer. It is easier for women to compete equally with men at high-tech jobs than at jobs requiring a lot of upper body strength. A majority of associate, bachelor's, and master's degrees are now earned by women.

A 1997 study by Vernon Stone of the Missouri School of Journalism found that the glass ceiling has been shattered for women in TV news. In 1972 only 0.5 percent of news director positions were held by women; in 1996 it was 14.1 percent, and indicators suggest that by the year 2001, a third of all TV news directors will be women.

Progress is slower for minorities. One study sponsored by the Freedom Forum revealed that 37 percent of black journalists felt that their race had hurt their careers; 14 percent of Hispanic news staffs felt the same way.

The American workforce is becoming more and more ethnically diverse, so the communications field will have to come up with ways to deal with these challenges in the new century.

General Trends

In the past, traditional jobs offered enough comforts that people were not willing to leave their positions. Today benefits packages are less generous, and long-term job security is not guaranteed in most places, making it easier for people to decide to leave. In fact, in some areas of the industry, people typically get bigger raises if they move to another job than if they stay in one place too long.

The Bureau of Labor Statistics classifies most jobs in this book in the service sector. Although wages have increased in that sector, as in the overall U.S. economy since the early 1980s, that increase is deceptive. For example, the average hourly wage in the service sector in June 1999 was $13.23, but when measured in constant (1982) dollars, that amounts to only $7.88. Despite the booming economy of the late 1990s, many employers are laying off permanent full-time staff and hiring freelancers instead in a growing movement to save costs and benefits. Some social researchers have written about a growing unrest and anger in the country during the 1990s, largely due to this decline in real wages and job security. Many Americans feel that the gap between the rich and the poor is increasing.

A Princeton University study cited in *Business Week* in 1998 attributed 30 to 50 percent of the increased demand for skilled workers over the preceding 25 years to the computer. Those who do not have the technical skills that will be required to meet the new century will be left behind. However, according to a 1998 *Business Week* article, the skill level of the American workforce is increasing and will continue to do so. Most working- and middle-class Americans—particularly the younger generations—are learning what it will take to prosper in the years ahead.

One trend in book publishing, reported by the *New York Times* in 1998, was that publishing houses are downsizing and reducing their editorial staffs, often as the result of mergers and acquisitions. During the 1990s the number of editors working in New York City declined by approximately 16 percent, according to the Federal Equal Employment Opportunity Commission. Yet simultaneously, more books are being published each year. The Book Industry Study Group reported in 1998 that consumer expenditures on all books are expected to increase to $32.8 billion by the year 2002. This is an increase from approximately $21.2 billion in 1992. Book production methods have changed with computerization, and schedules are tight in order to save money and beat the competition to the market. As a result of this paradoxical combination, fewer book editors are on staff, but they are under increasing pressure to produce more books in less time. The *New York Times* pointed out that more errors are finding their way into finished books as a result. Many editors find their jobs increasingly pressured and less satisfying than they were ten years ago. Still, according to a *Publishers Weekly* survey, 87 percent of respondents said they were satisfied with their jobs in 1998. It is not surprising that those who were least satisfied were in the lowest-paying editorial jobs; only 22.5 percent of them were satisfied with their work.

Competition remains stiff in the more glamorous fields of author, playwright, and screenwriter. Advances were high in the 1990s for celebrity books or books by well-known authors, but in most other cases publishers were playing it safe. "Midlist authors" were finding it difficult to get their next book published.

Salaries remain low at many small newspapers. The *Mississippi Business Journal* reported in 1996 that more print journalism graduates are entering corporate public relations because of low salaries in the print journalism field.

Median annual entry-level pay remains lower in television and radio broadcasting than in print journalism, partly because of the higher demand for these positions.

Editors at business-to-business magazines are usually paid less than those at consumer magazines, but in 1999 the gap narrowed, according to a survey by *Folio*. Some editors were unhappy with their jobs because they felt they were expected to take on new responsibilities, such as managing web sites and advertorials (advertising sections prepared by the magazine), without being paid extra. However, others enjoyed the new challenges involved.

Another important trend is on-line bookselling. More and more books, CDs, videos, and so on are now being sold via such services as Amazon.com. The Book Industry Study Group, in its study entitled "Book Industry Trends 1998: Covering the Years 1992–2002," called on-line bookselling the issue of the year in 1998.

Opportunities continue to be good for freelancers, especially those who offer multiple services. Freelancers in writing and communications specialties still do not make tremendous amounts of money, but many enjoy the freedom and flexibility of the lifestyle. Freelance income and workloads are often irregular—"feast or famine"—and the uncertainty of work and pay require good sales skills, perseverance, self-discipline, organization, and financial management. Freelancers also have to invest in office equipment and bear the cost of running an office.

Even as recently as the late 1980s, it was possible to set up shop as a freelance copy editor with just a desk and chair, a telephone, a few reference books, a typewriter and some blank paper, and a bunch of pencils. As we enter the twenty-first century, freelancers are expected to have quite a lot of sophisticated equipment in addition to these basics: a fast computer with sufficient memory, a disk drive, a printer, a fax/modem, and reliable access to the Internet. Depending on the nature of their work, they may also need extra items like scanners and photocopiers. Also, electronic equipment goes obsolete dismayingly fast. You can't just buy a computer once and keep using it till it finally dies fifteen years later, as you can with, say, a refrigerator. It must be compatible with your clients' equipment so that you can read each other's disks. This means that freelancers have considerably higher overhead than before.

Most freelancers are versatile and don't bank on a single market or type of work, as market needs can shift and contacts can be lost. Several years of experience in staff positions can provide a good background for a freelancer.

More than 75 percent of the Editorial Freelancers Association members are women; more than half said they would not take a full-time permanent job if one was offered. More than half of the membership also said they were overloaded with work some months and too idle in others. One in five had an appropriate amount of work each month; one in ten was swamped every month; and almost one in six needed more work every month.

Although salaries might not be high in most writing or communications jobs, they are above average. The smaller the company, the lower the pay scale. In some parts of the country, some entry-level jobs can pay as little as $12,000 a year. Average salaries for experienced communications professionals are generally in the $30,000 to $50,000 range. Women continue to experience pay gaps in most fields, especially at the senior levels. Salaries are more equal in journalism, where women and men make roughly the same in entry-level jobs; in higher-level jobs a pay gap develops, but remains smaller than in other sectors.

Whether you find your destiny in a cramped, messy newspaper office in some far-flung city, the ivy-covered halls of a distinguished university, or the buttoned-down boardrooms of corporate America, chances are you will find yourself in the company of creative, interesting people who influence the way other people think and feel.

The persuasive art of advertising, the clearheaded presentation of news, the loathed and loved business of image creation, and the lovely cadence of a poem all rely on the skillful manipulation of words for success.

Whatever kind of writing you find yourself doing, you may enjoy using your own creative skills and imagination to produce a work that informs, sells, entertains, or perhaps even changes the world.

NEWSPAPERS AND NEWS SERVICES

COPY AIDE

CAREER PROFILE

Duties: Assist reporters and editors in minor news-gathering and editing tasks

Alternate Title(s): Editorial Assistant; Newsroom Assistant; Copy Assistant; Intern; Copy Person

Salary Range: $8,000 to $37,000+

Employment Prospects: Fair

Advancement Prospects: Good

Prerequisites:
  Education—Undergraduate degree in journalism, communications, English, or liberal arts
  Experience—None
  Special Skills—Organization; writing; dealing with public

CAREER LADDER

```
┌─────────────────────────────┐
│   Journalist; Copy Editor   │
└─────────────────────────────┘

┌─────────────────────────────┐
│          Copy Aide          │
└─────────────────────────────┘

┌─────────────────────────────┐
│           College           │
└─────────────────────────────┘
```

Position Description

Copy aides, the lowest rung on the newsroom ladder, are jacks-of-all-trades. Most of them are journalism or communications students who are working at newspapers while enrolled in college; a few are graduates who've been unable to find jobs as reporters.

At one time, it was customary for all reporters to start out as copy aides. The job consisted primarily of running copy from reporters to editors, doing errands, and disseminating materials throughout the newsroom.

Today, with most copy transmitted electronically, the job of the copy aide has changed. Copy aides monitor the wire machines of news services and see that the right editors get the appropriate stories (called "ripping the wire"), act as newsroom receptionists, and perform general news-related tasks. The job can provide excellent entry-level training. For example, a copy aide may help a reporter with research by going through clips in the news library, may make routine phone calls to police and weather sources, and may write up obituaries and other small news items. Copy aides may work under the supervision of journalists or editors.

Enterprising copy aides can turn their jobs into full-fledged internships, accompanying reporters on assignments and eventually writing their own stories. Copy aides can also learn the duties of the copy desk, doing minor editing and headline writing.

Salaries

On unionized papers, top minimums for copy aides range from $8,320 to about $37,254, with even higher top minimums at some Canadian papers. Most aides make toward the lower end of the scale, however.

The *Mississippi Business Journal* reported in 1996 that more print journalism graduates are entering corporate public relations because of low salaries in the print journalism field.

Employment Prospects

College programs and internships can lead to part- and full-time jobs as copy aides, though it is possible to get hired without help from a school. Many larger papers hire copy aides for evening and weekend work, which fits in with student schedules.

Advancement Prospects

Experience as a copy aide, particularly if the job involves research, writing, or editing tasks, can count heavily toward promotion to journalist or copy editor.

Education

Many copy aides are undergraduates in schools of journalism, communications, or liberal arts. Journalism study or background is desirable.

Experience/Skills

No experience is required to be a copy aide.

Unions/Associations

Students may join the Quill and Scroll Society; the collegiate chapters of the Society of Professional Journalists; and Association for Women in Communications.

REPORTER SPECIALIST

Duties: Gather and report information about a specific area of expertise or "beat"; keep abreast of new developments in that area in an effort to become the newspaper's expert on the subject

Alternate Title(s): Beat Reporter, Journalist

Salary Range: $15,000 to $60,000+

Employment Prospects: Good

Advancement Prospects: Fair

Prerequisites:

Education—Undergraduate degree in journalism, communications, English, or liberal arts; a graduate degree or some advanced courses in the area of specialization may also be required

Experience—Several years as a general assignment reporter for a daily paper, with work displaying some expertise in the chosen specialization

Special Skills—Ability to write longer, in-depth "enterprise" stories; good writing skills; aggressiveness; persistence; good interpersonal relations; good research habits; organizational ability; self-discipline

```
┌──────────────────────────────────────┐
│         Reporter Specialist          │
└──────────────────────────────────────┘

┌──────────────────────────────────────┐
│     General Assignment Reporter      │
└──────────────────────────────────────┘

┌──────────────────────────────────────┐
│         Copy Aide; College           │
└──────────────────────────────────────┘
```

Position Description

Unlike a general assignment reporter, who covers a wide range of stories at the discretion of an editor, a specialist covers a single area of expertise. A specialist also tries to stay abreast of developments in his or her field by developing sources, reading trade magazines, and taking courses.

For some specialties, larger papers may require a graduate degree. A business reporter may be asked to get a master's of business administration, or an education reporter may need a master's in education.

Reporters also cover geographic beats from outlying bureaus, but these jobs are generally given to less experienced reporters and resemble general assignment positions, in that a wide range of topics can be included. Bureau reporters often generate their own story ideas or field assignments from an editor.

Traditional "beats" or areas of specialization include courts, city hall, education, and police. However, as newspa-pers seek ways to remain interesting and relevant to a younger market that, as studies show, relies more on TV news to keep informed, beats such as health, environmental issues, ethics, and the family have started to appear.

Some newspapers expanded beat coverage into such areas as transportation, shopping, pets, and hobbies. The Orange County (California) *Register* created a position for a shopping mall reporter. The *Star Tribune* of Minneapolis added an ethics beat to its coverage, and other newspapers now have reporters covering traffic issues. In addition, a broad beat such as business may be broken down into smaller categories, such as insurance, banking, biotechnology, manufacturing, computer companies, etc.

Some of these specialty positions, usually added at the expense of general assignment positions, may not have survived the cutbacks brought by the recession in the early 1990s. But others, such as business, the environment, health, and science, have become standard at larger newspapers.

Beat reporters need to manage the beat—become acquainted with important news sources, monitor events, cover meetings, and look for stories of interest to the public. The reporter must keep editors informed of his or her activities and upcoming stories.

Beats are also generally long-term assignments, so journalists can build sources and expertise. Beat reporters work against deadlines on breaking stories. The number of deadlines varies with the size of the newspaper and the number of editions being put out, with larger papers having five or six deadlines per day, and smaller newspapers one or two.

Beat reporters are generally required to write longer, in-depth articles that require more research and interviewing. Work schedules change according to the demands of the business, but beat reporters are more likely to have regular hours.

But when a beat really heats up, that reporter could find him or herself working around the clock, on weekends or traveling to keep up with unfolding news. In sports, reporters often travel with the local teams during the season, working weeks without any days off and making up the extra time in the off-season.

Beat reporters sometimes still need to fill some less popular shifts, such as nights or weekends, or fill in as general assignment reporters if the newspaper is short of staff.

Salaries

Because specialists generally have more experience and training, they usually make more than entry-level journalists. Even the smallest papers employ sports reporters (often at the entry level) and possibly business reporters, and often have low pay scales.

Even in a strong economy, many small newspapers and TV stations continue to pay painfully low salaries. Entry-level pay for television reporters is less than for newspaper reporters. A 1999 study by Kosicki and Becker found that median annual first-year pay was $18,200 for television reporters and $22,600 for daily newspaper reporters. In fact, the same study found, the gap had doubled between 1989 and 1999. This is partly because the demand for television jobs is higher: 10 applicants for each television job versus only four for each newspaper job.

Newspaper reporters' pay is negotiated by the Newspaper Guild-CWA when they start a new job at a Guild paper, and again after a specified number of years, which varies from one paper to another. The Newspaper Guild often treats reporter specialists and general assignment reporters as one group for salary bargaining purposes. Specialists might get a differential to make their pay higher, especially if they're truly specialists (such as medical reporters) rather than reporters simply assigned to a beat.

Pay still varies widely. According to a Newspaper Guild survey, the starting minimum weekly salary for reporters at the *New York Times* (N.Y.) was $1,332.77 as of April 1999, whereas the starting minimum for the *Scranton Times and Tribune* (Pa.) was $360.91. The average top minimum annual salary for all Guild reporters as of August 1999 was $40,872.

One 1998 study found that starting newspaper salaries ranged from the low $20,000s to nearly $40,000, with most around $30,000. In the West, salaries are generally higher, starting from $26,000 to $31,000 and rising in range from $47,000 to $52,000 after six years at larger, unionized papers.

Employment Prospects

Employment of reporters is expected to grow about as fast as average for all occupations; however, much of this growth will come at the bottom—from an increase in small town and suburban daily and weekly newspapers. Small newspapers typically offer low salaries.

Other job openings will come from journalists leaving the field. The number of big city dailies is expected to be static, and the competition for jobs on them keen. Some reporters are switching over to the Internet field. Print reporters are usually more prepared for Internet journalism than are TV reporters, so it is easier for them to make the switch.

Advancement Prospects

Advancement prospects are fair. Specialists have more chances to move to larger newspapers than general assignment reporters. In addition, they may have good shots at becoming section editors or columnists, depending on their area of expertise. Those who handle highly specialized scientific or technical subjects will be at an advantage in the job market.

Education

This job generally requires an undergraduate degree in journalism, communications, English, or liberal arts at a minimum. Specialists also often hold advanced degrees in subjects related to their area of expertise. An education reporter may need a master's degree in education, for example.

Experience/Skills

Good basic reporting skills are essential. Beat reporters must have a keen curiosity and sharp observational skills. They should feel comfortable dealing with and interviewing persons in positions of authority. They should know how to research and organize information and be able to explain complicated topics in a simple way. Speed, clarity, and accuracy are essential.

In addition, most specialized positions require several years of general reporting experience and some additional training in the area of specialization.

Unions/Associations

The Newspaper Guild is the primary union for print journalists. Professional associations include the Society of Professional Journalists; Newspaper Association of America; American Society of Journalists and Authors, Inc.; Associated Business Writers of America, Inc.; Asian American Journalists Association; Association of Earth Science Editors; Construction Writers Association; Council of Biology Editors; Investigative Reporters and Editors; National Association of Hispanic Journalists; Outdoor Writers Association of America; National Turf Writers Association; Religion Newswriters Association; Society of American Travel Writers; and many others.

GENERAL ASSIGNMENT REPORTER

CAREER PROFILE

Duties: Gather and report information for news and feature stories on a wide variety of topics

Alternate Title(s): Bureau Reporter; Journalist

Salary Range: $15,000 to $60,000+

Employment Prospects: Good

Advancement Prospects: Fair

Prerequisites:

    Education—Undergraduate degree in journalism, communications, English, or liberal arts

    Experience—Work on a college publication or internship for small daily or weekly newspapers; minimum one to two years of experience for large dailies

    Special Skills—Aggressiveness; persistence; good interpersonal relations; good research habits; organizational ability; self-discipline

CAREER LADDER

```
┌─────────────────────────────────────┐
│   Assistant Editor; Section Editor;  │
│        Reporter Specialist           │
└─────────────────────────────────────┘

┌─────────────────────────────────────┐
│     General Assignment Reporter      │
└─────────────────────────────────────┘

┌─────────────────────────────────────┐
│          Copy Aide; College          │
└─────────────────────────────────────┘
```

Position Description

General assignment reporters go to work not knowing exactly what they will be doing that day. If they work in the main newsroom, they find out from an assignment editor.

If they work in an outlying bureau covering a geographic territory or another city, they field assignments from a bureau chief, generate their own story ideas after making the rounds of their sources, or develop some combination of the two.

General assignment reporters need to work fast, meet deadlines, and switch gears smoothly as they move from one assignment to the next. Assignments may vary from covering a fire to a governmental meeting to interviewing a visiting celebrity. General assignment reporters often report on topics last covered by someone else. They need to quickly find and read through other stories on the topic and to follow all major stories appearing in the newspaper, even on days they don't work, so they can fill in at a moment's notice. On smaller newspapers or in bureaus, general assignment reporters may also take their own photographs, give assignments to freelance reporters (called stringers), and edit the resulting stories—or file from the scene of a breaking story with a portable computer or by dictating over the phone.

Because a general assignment reporter's wide-ranging duties help build skills in many areas, many newspapers require inexperienced reporters to work as general assignment reporters before considering them for a specialty or beat position.

Even plans to work on a long-range project can be disrupted by breaking news, making it hard to plan ahead. Night and weekend shifts are common. Deadline frequency depends on how many editions the newspaper prints, with deadlines around the clock at some large newspapers and one or two times a day on smaller dailies.

Salaries

One 1998 study found that starting newspaper salaries ranged from the low $20,000s to nearly $40,000, with most around $30,000. In the West, salaries are generally higher, starting from $26,000 to $31,000 and rising in range from $47,000 to $52,000 after six years at larger, unionized papers.

A December 1997 survey by *Advertising Age* found that beginning salaries for reporters ranged between $17,500 and $22,500. The same survey found that the reporter's level and quality of education, and previous industry experience, such as an internship, influenced starting position and salary considerably.

Even in a strong economy, many small newspapers and TV stations continue to pay painfully low salaries. Entry-level pay for television reporters is less than for newspaper reporters. A 1999 study by Kosicki and Becker found that median annual first-year pay was $18,200 for television reporters and $22,600 for daily newspaper reporters. In fact, the same study found, the gap had doubled between 1989 and 1999. This is partly because the demand for television jobs is higher: 10 applicants for each television job versus only four for each newspaper job.

Newspaper reporters' pay is negotiated by the Newspaper Guild-CWA when they start a new job at a Guild paper, and again after a specified number of years, which varies from one paper to another. Pay still varies widely. According to a Newspaper Guild survey, the starting minimum weekly salary for reporters at the *New York Times* (N.Y.) was $1,332.77 as of April 1999, whereas the starting minimum for the *Scranton Times and Tribune* (Pa.) was $360.91. The average top minimum annual salary for all Guild reporters as of August 1999 was $40,872.

Employment Prospects

Most of the growth in newspapers is expected to come from small local newspapers. The number of large daily newspapers is expected to remain static, and competition for jobs on them is keen.

Other job openings are expected to be created by journalists leaving the field.

Advancement Prospects

Advancement prospects are fair. Bureau reporters generally move into city room jobs, starting as general assignment reporters and working their way into more specialized reporting jobs or management. The first promotion into management is likely to be either section editor or assistant editor.

Some reporters are switching over to the Internet field. Print reporters are usually more prepared for Internet journalism than are TV reporters, so it is easier for them to make the switch.

Education

Most newspapers require an undergraduate degree in journalism, communications, English, or liberal arts. A survey done by the Center for Survey Research at Indiana University's Bloomington campus showed that 82 percent of journalists had bachelor's degrees; of those, 61 percent did not major in journalism. Some employers believe a general, well-rounded education prepares journalists best for the wide variety of topics they need to cover; others prefer the practical instruction offered by programs at journalism school.

Experience/Skills

General assignment reporter is generally an entry-level position. However, with more journalists losing jobs during the recession, newspapers that once hired inexperienced reporters can now choose from a more experienced field. Collegiate writing experience or internships help distinguish newcomers from the pack.

Journalists in these jobs need to be versatile, good listeners, and attentive to detail. They should not be intimidated easily and must be willing to ask questions.

They must be able to perform research and explain complex topics in a clear, simple way. Speed, accuracy, and clarity in writing are of the utmost importance.

Unions/Associations

The Newspaper Guild is the primary union for print journalists. Professional associations include the Society of Professional Journalists, and the American Society of Journalists and Authors, Inc. In addition, there are a number of associations that represent reporters in a wide variety of specialties or reporters of different racial or ethnic backgrounds.

WIRE SERVICE REPORTER

CAREER PROFILE

Duties: Report events quickly under constant deadline pressure; write summaries of stories for news digests; edit stories from local newspapers and broadcast stations for wire release

Alternate Title(s): none

Salary Range: $25,000 to $75,000+

Employment Prospects: Good

Advancement Prospects: Fair

Prerequisites:

Education—Undergraduate degree in journalism, communications, English, or liberal arts

Experience—None for a temporary position; 18 months or more at a newspaper or other news organization for a permanent job with some wire services

Special Skills—Ability to work fast and accurately under great deadline pressure; aggressiveness; good news judgment

CAREER LADDER

Assistant Editor; Assistant Bureau Chief; Foreign Correspondent

Wire Service Reporter

Temporary Reporter; Intern

Position Description

For years, the traditional wire service job involved working for one of several worldwide services that supplied general news to newspapers. Because most newspapers do not have overseas or national bureaus, they rely on wire services for international and national news.

Now, with the advent of on-line computer services, people interested in a specific topic can subscribe to news services or "real-time" databases devoted to that field. Some of these services also provide copy to newspapers; others are strictly for subscribers.

Wire services differ from newspapers in that they are not restricted by printing deadlines. By providing news without relying on paper, stories can be continuously updated 24 hours a day.

At a general news wire service, reporters cover a wider scope of news than at most newspapers. When an event breaks, wire service reporters battle to be first to phone in a deadline. Sometimes this means actually racing to a phone; other times, the reporters may carry cellular phones or portable computers to do the job. Then they race to provide a story. The pressure to be first is intense and constant. For specialized business wires providing information to investors on Wall Street, for example, a delay in getting the news out can mean a lost opportunity for financial gain for their subscribers.

Wire services maintain bureaus throughout the world. For general news wire services, such as the Associated Press, bureau reporters may be expected to generate routine copy, arrests, weather reports, commodity market prices, and the like, in addition to major news. Hours can be erratic, with night and weekend hours common.

Wire service reporters must be able to work both in the field, reporting stories, and at a desk, editing copy submitted by other reporters and member newspapers and broadcast stations.

Wire service reporters face great pressure, but they also can have the satisfaction of seeing their work reach a worldwide audience. The trade-off is that they may not get the time to write in-depth pieces or features.

Salaries

Salaries at wire services on the whole are higher than those at newspapers, according to the Newspaper Guild. The Guild negotiates wire service reporters' salaries when they begin a new job in a unionized wire service and again when they have attained several years of experience. Salaries vary with the size of the organization and the experience of the journalist, with high salaries for high profile, knowledgeable stars.

Salaries may also depend on the city in which a reporter works. Most wire services, such as the Associated Press (AP), have city differentials depending on the cost of living; for example, it's much more expensive to live in Honolulu than in Rochester, N.Y., so wire service reporters are paid more in Honolulu. According to the Newspaper Guild, unionized wire reporter salaries range from a top minimum of $35,244 at United Press International to a top minimum of $71,121.96 at Reuters News Service as of April 1999.

Employment Prospects

Established wires maintain hundreds of bureaus around the world. In addition, new wires specializing in business and other topics have emerged, creating jobs. These jobs may be somewhat harder to obtain now than five years ago; some wires that maintained in-house training programs have abandoned them because the pool of experienced applicants is now so large.

A new wire reporter can expect to work on the desk, taking dictation from reporters in the field, editing stories submitted by member newspapers or broadcast stations, and performing clerical tasks.

Advancement Prospects

Experience on a wire service was once regarded as excellent training for those aspiring to work on larger dailies. In addition, reporters can move within a wire service to become news editors, bureau chiefs, assistant bureau chiefs, or work in foreign bureaus, capital bureaus, or the national capital.

Education

Wire service reporters are generally required to have a bachelor's degree in journalism or liberal arts. In addition, some services require applicants to take a vocabulary and news writing test.

Experience/Skills

Wire service reporters must be able to work under extreme deadline pressure. They must be both accurate and fast. Often, a wire service reporter must know what news has already been reported so he or she can make a split-second decision about an event's news value.

Wire service reporters may also be called upon to compose stories in their heads from notes, which they then dictate to an editor over the phone. They must be tenacious, aggressive, level-headed, and have good news judgment.

Wire services frequently require a minimum of 18 months full-time news experience on a daily newspaper or broadcast station. Those with less experience may qualify for temporary openings, which sometimes lead to full-time employment.

Proficiency in a foreign language can help if your goal is to work in a bureau overseas.

Unions/Associations

Employees at United Press International, Associated Press, and Reuters are represented by the Newspaper Guild. Other professional associations include the Society of Professional Journalists; Investigative Reporters and Editors, Inc.; Association for Women in Communications; National Association of Black Journalists; National Press Club; and the Software & Information Industry Association.

FINANCIAL WIRE REPORTER

CAREER PROFILE

Duties: Follow the performance of companies and report changes that might affect the economy or the stock market; report economic developments and economic indicators; provide other financial information of interest to the wire service's customers

Alternate Title(s): Real-time Financial Database Reporter

Salary Range: $20,000 to $70,000+

Employment Prospects: Fair

Advancement Prospects: Fair

Prerequisites:

Education—Undergraduate degree in journalism, liberal arts, or communications; courses in business, economics, or computers helpful

Experience—None for entry-level positions. Otherwise, experience at a newspaper, wire service, or trade publication as a journalist or at a company working in public relations is needed

Special Skills—Must be able to work fast and accurately under deadlines; aggressive; able to explain complicated information simply and clearly without distorting its meaning

CAREER LADDER

```
┌─────────────────────────────────┐
│  Newspaper Magazine Business     │
│            Reporter              │
└─────────────────────────────────┘

┌─────────────────────────────────┐
│     Financial Wire Reporter      │
└─────────────────────────────────┘

┌─────────────────────────────────┐
│       Entry-Level Position       │
└─────────────────────────────────┘
```

Position Description

Financial wire reporters exist in the growing overlap between traditional news organizations and the specialized world of computerized information.

Some business wire reporters file reports intended for use by mainstream newspapers, which take them off the wire and print them. Others send their information directly to subscribers electronically, so the words never see print. This information helps money managers decide what investments to make, and when.

Because of this highly specialized audience, the pressure on financial wire reporters can be even more acute than it is for general wire reporters. Investors on Wall Street need information as soon as it becomes available. Any delay can mean a lost opportunity for them, and it could cost the wire service subscribers.

Any information that might affect the stock of a company must be put out immediately, even if only in the briefest headline form. Details follow as soon as possible as reporters race to be first with the news.

Financial wire reporters often work regular hours because so much of what they do is tied to the stock market. However, when a particular business or specialty topic becomes hot, a reporter can expect to put in the hours necessary to see that the news gets covered.

Many financial wires also offer general news, so reporters may have to work weekends writing news summaries or be on call during off hours in case of breaking events.

Each reporter may cover a different industry, tracking changes within that industry, following changes in stock prices and trying to find out why a change in stock price happened.

Salaries

The Newspaper Guild negotiates wire service reporters' salaries when they begin a new job in a unionized wire service and again when they have attained several years of experience.

Salaries for financial wire reporters are in line with salaries for general wire reporters, ranging from the low $20,000s for inexperienced reporters to the $70,000s and higher for those with more experience. Pay is highest in cities with the highest cost of living.

Employment Prospects

While other news organizations suffered cutbacks during the early 90s, financial wire services and other business databases blossomed. There are several services now competing for the same clients, and conventional wires have also added business reporting resources to stay in the game. Because the target market is specific and affluent, financial wires have a ready-made audience and money to sustain growth.

Opportunities in this field are better than in general news, which has experienced cutbacks. Some insiders believe that electronic information services targeting a select audience may be the future of reporting.

Advancement Prospects

At newer companies, advancement can be more rapid because growth is continually opening up new opportuni-ties. Some financial wires maintain bureaus in major cities around the world, with large bureaus in New York and Tokyo to cover the stock markets there. Experience at such an organization may also lead to jobs at business magazines or other business or trade publications.

Education

As with most jobs in journalism, business reporters should have undergraduate degrees in journalism, communications, or liberal arts. Courses or degrees in business, computers, or economics are also desirable.

Experience/Skills

Some companies expect reporters to already possess a good understanding of the world's financial markets; others prefer to hire promising young writers and train them about the business world in-house. Previous experience as a business reporter elsewhere, or a background in business combined with good writing skills are good qualifications for this work. Proficiency in a foreign language can help land a job in a bureau overseas.

Unions/Associations

The Newspaper Guild represents employees of some companies with financial wire services. The Software & Information Industry Association is the main trade association for businesses of this type.

COPY EDITOR

Duties: Edit reporters' copy for clarity, conciseness, organization, and grammar; write headlines and photo cutlines; lay out pages

Alternate Title(s): Copy Reader

Salary Range: $15,000 to $60,000+

Employment Prospects: Good

Advancement Prospects: Poor

Prerequisites:

Education—Undergraduate degree in journalism, communications, liberal arts, or English

Experience—Often an entry-level position; experience desirable for large papers

Special Skills—Grammatical knowledge; speed; ability to spot weaknesses in articles; creativity

```
┌─────────────────────────────────┐
│       Copy Chief; Editor        │
└─────────────────────────────────┘

┌─────────────────────────────────┐
│           Copy Editor           │
└─────────────────────────────────┘

┌─────────────────────────────────┐
│   Journalist; Copy Aide; College │
└─────────────────────────────────┘
```

Position Description

Copy editors are often the unsung heroes of the newspaper. The reporters may get the bylines, but the quality of their stories often depends on the copy editor.

The copy editor is often the last person to handle a reporter's story before it is typeset, after it has been read and edited by a news editor. For all but the smallest papers, there are usually several copy editors on duty who sit in a cluster or horseshoe near the news editor and copy chief.

Copy editors check the stories for spelling, punctuation, correct newspaper style, and other points of grammar. They may question reporters about vague sentences or inconsistencies. While substantial editing is the province of the news editors, copy editors can revise stories. Often the news editor is under too much pressure at deadline to spend a lot of time meticulously editing each story; consequently the task falls to the copy editor. Copy editors also write headlines and photo cutlines for the stories they handle, and they may do page layouts as well.

The work is fast-paced at deadline, and copy editors have to make quick and correct news judgment decisions. During slow times, enterprising copy editors research and write news or feature stories for the paper. In addition, copy editors may monitor wire service terminals.

Copy editors report to the copy chief, who works in coordination with the news editor in charge. Sometimes the copy chief is also the wire editor or page-makeup editor.

Salaries

Most copy editors make more than reporters; sometimes just a few dollars a week more, sometimes more significant amounts. On some newspapers, the starting pay is the same, but copy editors, who are in greater demand, move up the salary scale more quickly.

On a small paper, median salaries for copy editors range from the low $20,000s for a novice to the high $20,000s after several years' experience. At the largest papers, those with circulations over 5,000, the least experienced editors make a median in the low to mid $40,000s, and the more experienced a median in the mid to high $50,000s.

Employment Prospects

The overall journalism market is very competitive, but sometimes it's easier to get a job as a copy editor than as a journalist. In fact, many reporters take copyediting jobs in order to get on a desired newspaper, then work their way into reporting by writing stories during slow periods or on their own time. Some papers require every journalist to spend a probationary period on the copy desk before he or she can join the reporting staff.

Advancement Prospects

Advancement for copy editors depends largely on individual career goals. Some copy editors enjoy working only with copy and have little interest in news reporting, while others aspire to move into reporter positions. Typical advanced copy editing positions are copy chief and wire editor. Copy editors with news reporting experience may be promoted to assistant news editor or assistant city editor, jobs which require supervising reporters and making decisions about news coverage. Most top level managerial jobs in the newsroom, such as executive editor or editor in chief, require news reporting experience.

Because good copy editors can be hard to come by, it may be easier to move into a copy editing position than to seek a reporting job. However, if your ultimate goal is to become a reporter, it may also be harder to make the switch to reporting later on unless you are willing to go to a smaller newspaper or move out of the main newsroom into a news bureau.

Education

An undergraduate degree in journalism or mass communications is preferred. A degree in English may be especially valuable to a copy editor. Liberal arts degrees also are acceptable.

Experience/Skills

Copy editing is often an entry-level job, although some large newspapers require experience. The copy editor must be skilled in grammar and be able to edit quickly and under pressure. Knowledge of type point sizes and column pica widths is needed for writing headlines and cutlines. The copy editor also should be creative in writing crisp headlines that influence people to read the stories. Most editing is done on a display terminal, requiring computer literacy.

Unions/Associations

The Newspaper Guild, affiliated with the AFL-CIO, represents copy editors on many newspapers. Related professional associations include Association for Women in Communications, Society of Professional Journalists, and National Association of Black Journalists.

ASSISTANT EDITOR

CAREER PROFILE

Duties: Assist news or department editor in news gathering and editing operations; assign stories to reporters

Alternate Title(s): Deputy Editor; Assistant City Editor; Assistant Metropolitan Editor

Salary Range: $20,000 to $56,000+

Employment Prospects: Fair

Advancement Prospects: Fair

Prerequisites:
  Education—Undergraduate degree in journalism, communications, English, or liberal arts
  Experience—Background as a journalist essential
  Special Skills—Editing; directing and motivating others; news judgment

CAREER LADDER

```
┌─────────────────────────────┐
│   News Editor; City Editor;  │
│        Section Editor        │
└─────────────────────────────┘

┌─────────────────────────────┐
│       Assistant Editor       │
└─────────────────────────────┘

┌─────────────────────────────┐
│          Journalist          │
└─────────────────────────────┘
```

Position Description

Most assistant editors serve on the general-news desk, while a smaller number serve section editors. Assistant editors are the front-line editors for nearly all copy, and they relieve editors of much work, giving the editors time for administrative and policy-making duties.

Assistant editors control the flow of copy through the editing process. They screen stories and do the preliminary editing. They have authority to ask reporters for changes and to decide on the importance of a story, determining its position in the newspaper. Decisions or editing that involves sensitive stories may be referred to the news editor or editor in charge.

Once assistant editors finish editing stories, they pass them along to the copy desk for additional editing and head-line writing. They inform the makeup or layout editor of the positions the stories are to occupy on various pages and their approximate lengths.

Assistant editors help execute editorial decisions, field questions from reporters, and assign coverage of breaking stories. Some assistant news editors split their time between being journalists and working on the desk. The position is often a tryout to test a promising reporter's news judgment, editing, and management abilities.

Assistant editors may be assigned to work any shift, depending on the needs of the paper. In addition, assistant editors may write news stories and write headlines and cutlines.

Salaries

Assistant editors are often excluded from Newspaper Guild contracts because they are considered managerial jobs. However, this varies from one newspaper or bargaining unit to another.

Salaries may range from $20,000 to the high $50,000s, depending on the size of the paper. Papers with larger circulations pay the most. This job is generally not found at the smallest papers.

Employment Prospects

The assistant editor position is usually a training post, with candidates chosen from the reporting staff. Small papers offer the most and best opportunities for beginning assistant editors.

Advancement Prospects

The assistant editor's job is on track to middle and upper editorial management positions. Movement to another paper as assistant editor is unlikely; however, an assistant editor on a large paper may qualify for a news editor's post on a smaller paper.

Education

Most assistant editors have undergraduate degrees in journalism, communications, English, or liberal arts. The *Mississippi Business Journal* reported in 1996 that an increasing number of the print journalism graduates who might once have sought an assistant editor job are now entering corporate public relations because of low salaries in the print journalism field.

Experience/Skills

On small papers, a journalist with one or two years' experience may be promoted to assistant editor. On larger papers, four to six years' reporting experience is necessary.

Assistant editors should have good editing skills and news judgment. They should be able to meet deadlines and be well organized, in order to avoid copy bottlenecks at the last minute. They should be able to direct and motivate others.

Unions/Associations

Major professional associations include the Society of Professional Journalists; American Society of Newspaper Editors; Association for Women in Communications; National Association of Black Journalists; International Society of Weekly Newspaper Editors; Investigative Reporters and Editors; and National Federation of Press Women, Inc.

NEWS EDITOR

CAREER PROFILE

Duties: Manage a news-gathering staff; determine the direction and content of the newspaper; make policy decisions

Alternate Title(s): City Editor; Metropolitan Editor; Executive Editor

Salary Range: $20,000 to $83,000+

Employment Prospects: Fair

Advancement Prospects: Excellent

Prerequisites:

Education—Undergraduate degree in journalism, communications, or liberal arts

Experience—Background in reporting and copy editing essential

Special Skills—Ability to direct and motivate others; news judgment; editing

CAREER LADDER

```
┌─────────────────────────────────┐
│   Assistant Managing Editor;    │
│ Managing Editor; Executive Editor │
└─────────────────────────────────┘

┌─────────────────────────────────┐
│          News Editor            │
└─────────────────────────────────┘

┌─────────────────────────────────┐
│  Assistant Editor; Section Editor │
└─────────────────────────────────┘
```

Position Description

The quality of a newspaper often falls squarely on the shoulders of the news editor, who is in charge of the day-to-day operations of a newsroom. News editors must stay abreast of all major breaking and developing news stories, decide how the paper will cover them and play them on the page, and determine who will write the stories. They keep track of reporters' activities and make split-second decisions on how to handle breaking news.

News editors make story assignments and determine which reporters will handle what beats. In addition to editing copy, they monitor the progress of stories and the flow of copy through the editing process. They meet with high-level editors to determine the content and direction of the paper and discuss problems.

News editors are also administrators. They make up work schedules for reporters and assistants, arbitrate problems, write reports to upper management, and have a voice in the promotion, hiring, and firing of subordinates. They need to be informed on all labor laws pertaining to their employees. And, most important, they must be able to work within a budget.

Finally, news editors are community liaisons. Often they are called upon to speak for or represent the paper at civic functions and in the classroom.

On a small newspaper, the news editor may be in charge of the entire newsroom operation and have no assistant editors. On larger papers, news-editor positions are broken down into geographic areas, and each editor has one or more assistants.

The job is demanding, because a typical day can encompass a wide range of news and administrative tasks. News editors work regular business hours, but days run longer if a major story breaks. The counterpart of the news editor for the nighttime shift is the night editor, who oversees the operation of a daily paper after the news editor goes home.

Salaries

News editors are often excluded from Newspaper Guild contracts because they are considered managerial jobs. However, this varies from one newspaper or bargaining unit to another.

Salaries vary widely from about $20,000 to $83,000 or more, according to the circulation of the paper. The larger the paper, the higher the salary.

Employment Prospects

Skilled news editors are always in demand on papers of all sizes, though opportunities are best with small dailies and weeklies. The pool of competitors is much smaller than for journalists, but opportunities may be greatly restricted by the size of the publication and relocation requirements.

Advancement Prospects

News editors are in an excellent position for advancement into upper management.

Education

Most news editors have undergraduate degrees in journalism, communications, English, or liberal arts. Advanced degrees are not necessary but can be helpful. News editors should have additional training in management techniques.

Experience/Skills

On a very small paper, two or three years' experience as a journalist, section editor, or assistant editor can qualify someone for news editor. Five to ten years or more are required on larger papers. News editors should be adept at editing, rewriting, and making quick decisions, and they should be smooth in handling personnel matters. They must be detail-oriented and well organized in order to handle administrative tasks. Experience and ease in public speaking helps if the job involves community liaison work.

Unions/Associations

Major professional associations include the Society of Professional Journalists; American Society of Newspaper Editors; Investigative Reporters and Editors; Association for Women in Communications; National Association of Black Journalists; International Society of Weekly Newspaper Editors; and National Federation of Press Women, Inc.

SECTION EDITOR

CAREER PROFILE

Duties: Supervise content and layout of special-interest section or page

Alternate Title(s): Business Editor; Lifestyle Editor; Sunday Magazine Editor; Sports Editor; etc.

Salary Range: $17,000 to $80,000+

Employment Prospects: Fair

Advancement Prospects: Excellent

Prerequisites:

Education—Undergraduate degree in journalism, communications, English, or liberal arts; advanced degree desirable for specialized fields

Experience—Background as journalist, copy editor, or assistant editor

Special Skills—Staff supervision ability; news judgment; editing; graphics

CAREER LADDER

```
┌─────────────────────────────┐
│       News Editor;          │
│  Assistant Managing Editor  │
└─────────────────────────────┘

┌─────────────────────────────┐
│       Section Editor        │
└─────────────────────────────┘

┌─────────────────────────────┐
│  Journalist; Assistant Editor; │
│         Copy Editor         │
└─────────────────────────────┘
```

Position Description

Section editors are responsible for specialized sections or pages of a newspaper, such as business, lifestyle, arts and entertainment, real estate, suburban news, or Sunday magazine. They are responsible for determining content, assigning reporters and photographers to stories, monitoring deadlines, editing copy, and executing or overseeing page graphics. Most are expected to write for their pages as well.

Section editors may work under the direction of the news editor in charge, who may be called the city editor, metropolitan editor, or executive editor. Some section editors may be independent and work with other editors on a coordinating or advisory basis.

The job of section editor calls for a good sense of organization as well as the ability to manage others. The editor must monitor other sources of news, such as wire stories and magazines, for story ideas; work on both short-term and long-term stories; and coordinate the work of others.

On a typical day, a section editor may meet with other editors, review wire copy to determine which stories will be used in the section or page, assign stories, edit copy, and select photos and other artwork to illustrate the text. Many section editors do their own page layouts, while others work with the newspaper's art and photo departments. An editor of a daily page, such as business, must have good news judgment and be able to react to breaking news quickly.

The job can be especially rewarding, not only for the decision-making freedom that goes with it, but also for the leeway one has to put a personal "stamp" on part of a newspaper. Section editors tend to work regular business hours and usually are not subject to shift changes or weekend or night work.

Salaries

Section editors are often excluded from Newspaper Guild contracts because they are considered managerial jobs. However, this varies from one newspaper or bargaining unit to another.

Salaries vary widely from about $17,000 to $80,000 or more, according to the size of the paper. The larger the paper's circulation, the higher the salary.

Employment Prospects

Most section editors are promoted from within. Some newspapers, however, conduct national searches for talent. Journalists and editors with advanced degrees or specialized education in certain fields, such as law, business, or science, have a hiring advantage. Jobs are highly competitive.

Advancement Prospects

Section editors are in excellent positions to be promoted to higher level jobs, but competition is keen.

Education

Section editors should have undergraduate degrees in journalism, communications, English, or liberal arts.

Experience/Skills

Background experience required depends on the size of the newspaper. A journalist with only one or two years of experience may become a section editor on a small paper, while larger papers require four or more years of experience. Many section editors have served time as copy editors or assistant news editors.

Section editors should be thoroughly knowledgeable about their subject areas and the audience they serve. They should be good writers and editors, and be able to lay out pages.

Unions/Associations

Major professional associations include the Society of Professional Journalists; Association for Women in Communications; National Association of Black Journalists; International Society of Weekly Newspaper Editors; and National Federation of Press Women.

EDITORIAL WRITER

CAREER PROFILE

Duties: Research and write editorials on issues; screen columns, letters to the editor, and other editorial articles; help decide newspaper's position

Alternate Title(s): Editorial Page Editor

Salary Range: $20,000 to $120,000+

Employment Prospects: Fair

Advancement Prospects: Fair

Prerequisites:
 Education—Undergraduate degree in journalism, communications, or liberal arts; advanced degree helpful
 Experience—Background as journalist and editor
 Special Skills—Logic; persuasiveness; excellent, clear writing; thoroughness; objectivity

CAREER LADDER

```
┌─────────────────────────────────────┐
│   Senior Editor; Managing Editor     │
└─────────────────────────────────────┘

┌─────────────────────────────────────┐
│          Editorial Writer            │
└─────────────────────────────────────┘

┌─────────────────────────────────────┐
│ News Editor; Section Editor; Journalist │
└─────────────────────────────────────┘
```

Position Description

Editorial writers work away from the daily hubbub of the newsroom; they are concerned with the issues generated by events rather than the news of the events. They are responsible for the contents of the editorial page and the page opposite, called the "op ed" page. The editorial page is a sensitive area because it represents the quality and character of the newspaper.

Editorial writers comprise an editorial board, which also includes members of senior management and the publisher. A small newspaper may have only one or two editorial writers to share all the duties, while a larger paper may allow particular editorial writers to focus on special areas of expertise. On a large paper, junior editorial writers may do research for senior members of the board.

Editorial writers examine issues that arise, research them, and decide on a position. Some editorials must be timely, reacting to the latest news. Others, on topics of current interest but not related to breaking news, may be researched and written more slowly. Editorial writers do research the same way as journalists do, by calling sources and consulting library clips and other published sources. They may ask a journalist for additional information.

In examining an issue, editorial writers must be thorough, objective, and accurate. In order to be fully informed

of local, national, and international news, most editorial writers do extensive reading of other news and commentary publications. All sides of an issue must be carefully weighed in order to arrive at a position.

In addition, editorial writers screen letters and columns for publication on the editorial pages. The "letters to the editor" column is an important public forum. Columns may be written by the newspaper's own news staff or by syndicated writers.

Smaller newspapers may only have an editorial page editor to write editorials, or the news editor may write them.

Salaries

The Newspaper Guild often bargains for editorial writers along with copy editors, but it depends how management views the job. There may be a differential that gives editorial writers a higher salary than copy editors, especially if a writer is well known.

Salaries may range from $20,000 to $120,000 or more. The larger the circulation of the paper, the higher the salary.

Employment Prospects

Several years of seasoning are required to qualify for editorial writer. Candidates have to have demonstrated their reporting and analytical abilities as journalists first; editorial ability as newsroom editor is sometimes necessary as well.

Advancement Prospects

Fair opportunities exist to rise within the editorial board structure. Most senior managers, however, are selected from editors who run the daily operations of the newsroom. Many editorial writers, however, have no wish to leave the editorial department.

Education

Editorial writers should have at least undergraduate degrees in journalism, communications, English, or liberal arts. Degrees in business, economics, law, or other graduate degrees are likely to help career advancement because of the specialized nature of many editorial-writing positions.

Experience/Skills

Editorial writers have had at least several years' seasoning as journalists and, most likely, as newsroom editors as well. They have demonstrated their ability to write balanced, clear news analyses and accurate news stories. They have good news judgment, are objective, and are good editors. They do thorough research and stay abreast of public opinion through extensive reading.

Unions/Associations

Associations include the National Conference of Editorial Writers; American Society of Newspaper Editors; Society of Professional Journalists; Association for Women in Communications; National Association of Black Journalists; International Society of Weekly Newspaper Editors; and National Federation of Press Women.

NEWS LIBRARIAN

CAREER PROFILE

Duties: Acquire, catalog, and maintain collections of information for use by journalists; perform research, including computer searches, for journalists under tight deadline pressure

Alternate Title(s): News Information Resource Manager; News Library Director; Newspaper Library Manager

Salary Range: $12,000 to $80,000

Employment Prospects: Fair to good

Advancement Prospects: Fair to good

Prerequisites:

Education—Graduate degree in library science for top jobs on larger papers; undergraduate degree needed for assistants

Experience—Newspaper experience helpful, may be required if applicant has no library science degree or library experience; computer experience, especially familiarity with computer database searches, also a plus

Special Skills—Research skills; good organizational skills; knowledge of newsroom operations; good oral and written communication skills; ability to work with journalists under deadline pressure

CAREER LADDER

```
┌─────────────────────────────┐
│   News Library Director     │
└─────────────────────────────┘

┌─────────────────────────────┐
│      News Librarian         │
└─────────────────────────────┘

┌─────────────────────────────┐
│  Library Clerk; Researcher  │
└─────────────────────────────┘
```

Position Description

Once a job filled by journalists near retirement (hence the traditional name for the library, the morgue) or newsroom managers in need of something to manage, the news librarian job earned new respect in the 1970s with the advent of on-line computer databases.

Where librarians once simply handed folders of clippings to reporters, news librarians now perform sophisticated computer searches under deadline pressure.

In addition, librarians at some papers, as the resident experts in computer technology, help put electronic versions of newspapers on-line. Some also act as the newsroom systems editors, choosing computer systems for use by reporters and editors.

Newsroom librarians, in their capacity as researchers, can even serve on Pulitzer Prize–winning investigative teams. In one case, a team of news librarians used databases to help flesh out coverage of a school bus accident that left 27 students dead. They compiled a list of all school bus accidents in the state, compared them to school bus accidents nationwide, and collected information about drunken driving laws, school bus design, and bus evacuation procedures.

News librarians can help with statistical analysis of election polls, or create a database to analyze the characteristics of a jury pool.

Marketing the information stored in newspaper libraries to the public provides a new source of revenue for companies feeling the recessionary pinch. Several newspapers around the country, including *The St. Petersburg Times, The Fort Lauderdale Sun-Sentinel, The Sacramento Bee* and *The Miami Herald,* now offer research services directly to the public for a fee.

These operations charge either by the article or by the hour and generally require full-time positions separate from the librarians serving the newsroom.

Most major newspapers also market their stories through electronic databases available to subscribers or·libraries. Newsroom librarians edit and prepare the data for public release.

Librarians code the contents of the paper for the electronic library each day. At larger papers, they also maintain archives of digital photographs within the computer system.

Newspapers with circulations of under 30,000 often do not hire librarians, instead relying on each reporter to keep his or her own files.

Salaries

Top minimums paid by newspapers represented by the Newspaper Guild in 1999 ranged from $77,889 for the chief librarian at the *New York Times* to $12,399 for a library clerk at the Terre Haute, Indiana, *Tribune-Star.*

Librarians at larger newspapers can expect to make more; non-union papers may pay less. The median salary for news librarians was about $28,600 in 1999.

Job Prospects

Employment of librarians in general is expected to grow more slowly than for all occupations through the year 2005. However, many traditional librarians work for school, public, or university libraries, which face budgetary constraints.

Librarians in nontraditional settings can expect increased job opportunities, especially in information management. With newspapers beginning to provide a variety of electronic information services, librarians can expect increased responsibility and better job prospects.

Advancement Prospects

Good for those with the right combination of skills. Assistant librarians can also use their research skills to move into freelance book research or other research jobs. More opportunities exist at larger newspapers.

Librarians may also take over systems editor positions, buying computer systems for the newsroom.

Education

Most journalism jobs require a bachelor's degree in journalism, communications, liberal arts, or English. A master's of library science (M.L.S.) is required for library management jobs at larger papers. The M.L.S. includes advanced courses in cataloging, indexing, computer automation, abstracting, and library administration. Other recommended courses include those dealing with business management, computer use, statistics, and databases.

Many large newspapers now hire library professionals from outside their ranks for top jobs, but smaller papers still often move newsroom employees into the library to be trained "in-house." Traditional library science programs generally don't offer courses in newspaper librarianship.

More specialized training can be obtained from the Special Libraries Association's News Division, which offers books, guides, newsletters, presentations, research, seminars, workshops, conferences, and consultation services.

Assistant librarian or clerk jobs are generally populated by those unable to find newsroom jobs or those who like to do research. No experience may be required for entry-level jobs. Experience in news is a plus. Those who hope to move up may want to get a MLS degree.

Experience/Skills

Knowledge of computer systems, an understanding of newsroom operations, the ability to find information fast and good organizational skills are all important. Previous news experience, preferably in newspapers but also in other media, can help.

Unions/Associations

The Special Libraries Association has a division for news libraries. News librarians are also represented by the Newspaper Guild at unionized newspapers. The American Library Association and the American Society for Information Science provide support to librarians.

COLUMNIST

CAREER PROFILE

Duties: Write daily or weekly columns

Alternate Title(s): None

Salary Range: $17,000 to $200,000+

Employment Prospects: Poor

Advancement Prospects: Poor

Prerequisites:

Education—Undergraduate degree in journalism, communications, English, or liberal arts; advanced degrees if specialized

Experience—Background as journalist

Special Skills—Good storytelling ability; creativity

CAREER LADDER

```
┌─────────────────────────────────┐
│  Assistant Editor; Section Editor  │
└─────────────────────────────────┘

┌─────────────────────────────────┐
│            Columnist            │
└─────────────────────────────────┘

┌─────────────────────────────────┐
│     Journalist; Copy Editor     │
└─────────────────────────────────┘
```

Position Description

Columnists are regarded as having plum jobs on newspapers, but their job is harder than it appears. And, because they are showcased, they are also subject to more criticism.

Most columnists have human-interest, around-the-town or social-notes beats. Their columns may be collections of short, gossipy, or newsy items, or they may each consist of a single feature story built around an interesting person or someone's dilemma. Also common on most papers are political columnists who analyze or comment on the activities of politicians. A few columnists are nationally syndicated.

Specialized columnists can write about any topic that catches the public's fancy—computers, pets, health, love and romance, plants, bridge, medicine—the list goes on and on.

Columns may be daily or weekly. Columnists are expected to generate their own material, which sometimes is not all that easy. The column goes to press regardless of material at hand.

Columnists usually operate autonomously and have a great deal of freedom. They become "personalities" and build up audiences, thus becoming promotional assets to their newspapers; consequently, some of them can negotiate higher pay than their fellow journalists. The position is usually an end goal rather than a stepping-stone to something else. Few columnists want to give up their domain and their audience for something else.

Not all columnists work at their columns full time. Many report for the general-news pages as well.

Columnists who become syndicated can earn a good deal of money—up to $200,000 or more.

Salaries

Not enough smaller newspapers hire full-time columnists for salary data to be available. At smaller newspapers, many reporters write columns in addition to their reporting duties in the hope that this experience and visibility may catapult them into full-time columnist positions later.

Columnists are sometimes grouped with reporters by the Newspaper Guild for negotiation purposes, but there may be a differential that gives columnists a higher salary, especially if they are well known.

Salaries generally range from $17,000 to $80,000. A particularly prestigious or popular columnist may command an even higher salary at a large newspaper or in syndication.

Employment Prospects

Most newspapers do not hire journalists to be columnists unless they have established a track record and audience. The best bet is to use a journalist's position as the launching point to build a local readership for one's work.

Advancement Prospects

Few columnists aspire to managerial jobs; the column is the sought-after position. A popular column, however, can establish a writer as an authority in a certain area, and that can lead to syndication.

Education

Like their fellow journalists, most columnists have undergraduate degrees in journalism, communications, English, or liberal arts. A columnist writing about a specialized area, such as economics or medicine, should have the appropriate education and credentials.

Experience/Skills

Most columnists are experienced journalists; experience varies according to the market. Columnists must be creative.

For human-interest subjects, they need to be good storytellers. Political columnists are expected to have good analytical skills. Since most columns are short, columnists must write concisely.

Unions/Associations

Many columnists are members of the Newspaper Guild union. Professional associations include the Society of Professional Journalists; Association for Women in Communications; National Association of Black Journalists; and National Federation of Press Women, Inc.

CRITIC

CAREER PROFILE

Duties: Review artistic performances, recordings, exhibits and books; write columns

Alternate Title(s): Reviewer

Salary Range: $15,000 to $55,000+

Employment Prospects: Poor

Advancement Prospects: Poor

Prerequisites:

Education—Undergraduate degree in journalism, communications, English, or liberal arts; specialization in a particular field

Experience—Background as a journalist and expertise in the area reviewed

Special Skills—Good writing ability; thorough knowledge of subject matter

CAREER LADDER

```
┌─────────────────────────────┐
│       Section Editor        │
└─────────────────────────────┘

┌─────────────────────────────┐
│           Critic            │
└─────────────────────────────┘

┌─────────────────────────────┐
│    Journalist; Copy Editor  │
└─────────────────────────────┘
```

Position Description

Critics can wield a great deal of influence with the public and can affect the success of artists, films, plays, books, and musical and/or dance productions. Bad reviews can keep an audience away and close a play or kill a film.

Critics, many of whom work evenings and weekends, review plays, films, concerts, operas, exhibits, dance productions, books, records, nightclub acts—anything connected with the arts and entertainment field—and write their opinions in columns. They may be highly specialized; for example, a music critic may not handle films or plays. Some small to medium-sized papers, however, have one or two persons who handle all reviewing.

Critics are expected to be knowledgeable about their subjects and keep abreast of trends and news. They interview performers and celebrities, and they do extensive reading, even studying in their respective areas. They must be objective and have good judgment. Like columnists, they develop audiences who trust their views.

Besides review columns, critics often write celebrity interviews, feature stories, and in-depth articles on trends or other aspects of the arts.

Salaries

Critics earn roughly the same as, or sometimes more than, their fellow experienced journalists—approximately $15,000 to $55,000 or more. High salaries depend heavily on experience, credentials, and the size of the newspaper.

The Newspaper Guild sometimes groups critics together with reporters in negotiating for their salaries, but critics (like columnists) may get a differential to increase their salaries, especially if they are popular or well known.

Employment Prospects

Many critics start out as journalists and work their way into full-time critic posts by doing occasional reviews. A position as a staff writer or assistant editor for the lifestyle or arts-and-entertainment sections is an excellent place to start. Once a critic is established, it is possible to change employers, though the job market is very small.

Advancement Prospects

Like columnists, many critics don't wish to do any other kind of news work. The most likely advancement is to become editor of the arts-and-entertainment section or book-review section.

Education

Critics are expected to have a background in their area of expertise; this may involve specialized or advanced degrees. Basic education is an undergraduate degree in journalism, communications, liberal arts, or other areas pertaining to the arts.

Experience/Skills

Critics should be thoroughly familiar with their specialization in order to give fair and objective reviews. This requires extensive reading and often periodic study. They should be good interviewers and be able to write quickly on deadline.

Unions/Associations

Professional associations include the American Theatre Critics Association, Dance Critics Association, Music Critics Association of North America, Society of Professional Journalists, Association for Women in Communications, National Association of Black Journalists, and National Federation of Press Women. The Newspaper Guild negotiates wages for many journalists, including critics.

MAGAZINES

EDITORIAL ASSISTANT

CAREER PROFILE

Duties: Clerical and receptionist duties; errands; minor editorial and production tasks; research

Alternate Title(s): None

Salary Range: $13,000 to $19,000+

Employment Prospects: Fair

Advancement Prospects: Good

Prerequisites:
Education—Undergraduate degree in communications, journalism, English, or liberal arts; courses in publishing
Experience—None, for many positions
Special Skills—Editing; proofreading; secretarial skills; writing

CAREER LADDER

```
┌─────────────────────────────────────┐
│  Associate Editor; Assistant Editor  │
└─────────────────────────────────────┘

┌─────────────────────────────────────┐
│         Editorial Assistant          │
└─────────────────────────────────────┘

┌─────────────────────────────────────┐
│         College; Secretary           │
└─────────────────────────────────────┘
```

Position Description

Editorial assistant is the entry-level position on a magazine's editorial staff. The job is more secretarial than editorial, but beginners are given a chance to learn on the job and work their way into more responsible editorial positions.

Editorial assistants report to higher-level editors, including assistant and associate editors, senior editors, and editors. They do library research for superiors who are writing articles, and they check the accuracy of facts in articles written by outside authors. They are responsible for reviewing other magazines and newspapers and clipping articles of interest for editors. Such articles may generate story ideas or provide helpful information on stories in progress.

They also proofread galleys and write headlines, photo cutlines, and "deck" copy, which consists of several lines of large type excerpted from the article to break up the gray type on a page. Secretarial functions include opening and routing the mail, answering the telephone, running errands, filing, and typing letters.

As experience is gained, editorial assistants are given more editorial responsibilities, such as editing manuscripts and suggesting article ideas. They may also be given a chance to write short bylined articles or columns for the magazine or be responsible for collecting short items for news-roundup columns.

In addition, editorial assistants may:

- handle production details, including trafficking copy, galleys, and artwork;
- give a first reading to unsolicited manuscripts;
- work with freelancers involved in writing and production;
- screen job applications.

Salaries

Most editorial assistants earn between $13,000 and $19,000. Some top magazines pay as much as $21,000. Trade publications sometimes pay more than average for those who have specialized education or experience, such as technical or computer-science backgrounds.

Employment Prospects

Competition for magazine editorial jobs is keen, even at the entry level. Beginners who have taken skill-oriented journalism or publishing classes in high school and college—writing and editing—and have had school newspaper or intern experience have an advantage.

Advancement Prospects

Editorial assistants have a good chance of working their way up the editorial ladder, though competition remains stiff at all levels.

Education

An undergraduate degree in communications, journalism, English, or liberal arts is necessary. In some cases, a master's degree in communications or publishing may be advantageous. Technical and trade journals may require specialized education in such fields as engineering, computer programming, science, law, or economics.

Experience/Skills

Although no experience is required for many editorial-assistant jobs, the candidates with the best chances of employment are those who've taken writing/editing journalism and publishing courses in school, been actively involved in school publications, and have had internships or summer jobs in the field.

Editorial assistants should demonstrate both editing and writing ability, though they may not immediately write articles. Production knowledge also is useful.

Unions/Associations

The American Society of Magazine Editors; American Society of Journalists and Authors, Inc.; and Association for Women in Communications are among the major professional associations open to magazine editors. Some editors also join specialized authors' groups or trade and industry associations. Those who work for major news and feature magazines may belong to The Newspaper Guild.

RESEARCHER

CAREER PROFILE

Duties: Read all stories and mark facts to be verified; check with author and sources; keep records of any changes and apprise editor of changes

Alternate Title(s): Fact Checker; Research Editor; Editorial Assistant

Salary Range: $12,000 to $30,000+

Employment Prospects: Poor

Advancement Prospects: Good

Prerequisites:

Education—Undergraduate degree in journalism, communications, English, or liberal arts; advanced degrees or course work for technical/scientific/business publications

Experience—Entry-level researcher does not necessarily require any previous experience; background as journalist, writer, or editor helpful

Special Skills—Meticulous attention to detail; organization; telephone skills; editing; writing

CAREER LADDER

```
┌─────────────────────────────────────┐
│  Associate Editor; Assistant Editor  │
└─────────────────────────────────────┘

┌─────────────────────────────────────┐
│             Researcher               │
└─────────────────────────────────────┘

┌─────────────────────────────────────┐
│    Editorial Assistant; College      │
└─────────────────────────────────────┘
```

Position Description

Researcher is often an entry-level position with a magazine, but one that is usually understood to lead to more editorial responsibility. Researchers must verify each piece of information in a reporter's story and make sure that all corrections are made. Both the reporter and the assistant editor should be informed of any changes the researcher makes.

Smaller publications usually do not hire researchers but depend on their own reporters to verify facts and information. At larger magazines, the researcher not only checks data but shepherds stories under his or her responsibility through the entire production process, making sure that everything remains correct at each step.

To groom them for reporting and other editorial positions, editors may assign small, bylined stories or column features to researchers. Write-ups of personnel changes or new-business columns may be the regular responsibility of a researcher. Researchers may also be responsible for proofreading galleys and writing headlines and captions.

In addition, researchers may:

- handle other production details;
- attend seminars, workshops, and trade shows to keep up with industry trends.

Salaries

Some magazine researchers are represented by the Newspaper Guild. Salaries vary widely, from about $12,000 to $30,000 and up, depending on the magazine, the employee's level of experience, and so on. Some researchers make as little as $10,000, and are often not represented by a union.

Employment Prospects

Since researcher is an entry-level job, there is more turnover at such positions than at higher ones. People who have patience and are capable of meticulous attention to detail are not always easy to come by, yet a magazine's credibility depends on the accuracy of its stories. Beginners with journalism skills and great organizational ability have less trouble breaking into the editorial staff by acquiring such researcher positions. Not all magazines employ researchers.

Advancement Prospects

Most researchers have good advancement prospects. Often a researcher is hired with the understanding that, if everything works out all right, promotion to assistant or associate editor is quite likely in about two years. On smaller publications, a researcher may move up even sooner. As with all editorial jobs, however, competition is stiff.

Education

An undergraduate degree in journalism, English, communications, or liberal arts is essential. Any secretarial training that gives the researcher organizational skills is also a boon. Advanced course work, sometimes even an advanced degree, is necessary for researcher jobs on specialized publications, such as those for law, medicine, or high technology.

Experience/Skills

While no formal experience in journalism is necessary, aspiring researchers who have taken writing and editing courses, have been involved in school publications, and who have had summer jobs or internships have a leg up on other applicants. Many editors think a good researcher should have a background in liberal arts and have a strong interest in reading in general. Attendance at summer seminars or workshops is also advantageous.

Researchers should demonstrate good organizational skills, plus editing and writing abilities. Knowledge of magazine production is very helpful.

Unions/Associations

Researchers are eligible to join the American Society of Magazine Editors, American Society of Journalists and Authors, Inc., and other writers' trade groups. Men and women journalists may join the Association for Women in Communications. The Newspaper Guild represents employees on some major news and feature magazines.

COPY EDITOR

CAREER PROFILE

Duties: Oversee all editorial copy for grammar and style; prepare copy for production; check facts

Alternate Title(s): Copy Chief; Assistant Managing Editor; Production Assistant; Proofreader

Salary Range: $15,000 to $45,000+

Employment Prospects: Fair

Advancement Prospects: Fair

Prerequisites:

Education—Undergraduate degree in English, communications, liberal arts, or journalism; advanced course work or knowledge of specialized fields necessary for certain technical publications

Experience—Not necessary for entry-level jobs; otherwise, work as editorial assistant or professor's assistant beneficial

Special Skills—Good command of English punctuation, grammar, and spelling; organizational skills; patience; attention to detail

CAREER LADDER

```
┌─────────────────────────────────────┐
│  Associate Editor; Assistant Editor; │
│       Reporter; Researcher           │
└─────────────────────────────────────┘

┌─────────────────────────────────────┐
│             Copy Editor              │
└─────────────────────────────────────┘

┌─────────────────────────────────────┐
│   Editorial Assistant; College       │
└─────────────────────────────────────┘
```

Position Description

The copy editor takes each article through the successive steps of accuracy and fit, readying it for typesetting and, finally, print. He or she checks each story for grammar and magazine style, and may be responsible for fact-checking as well. On smaller publications without separate researchers, the copy editor handles fact research, working directly with the writers and editors.

Copy editors must have a good working knowledge of magazine production. If a story is too long or too short, the copy editor is usually the person responsible for cutting or lengthening it. If the piece is too short, the copy editor will prefer to go back to the original writer, but he or she may have to act alone if pressured by production deadlines. Copy editors often write headlines, captions, and "decks" (the large quotes which highlight a page of copy). They check relentlessly for typographical errors, misspelled words, and incorrect usage in the original manuscript, and proofread various stages of proofs for errors that may have slipped by earlier or have been incorrectly set by the typesetter. Other production duties may include working with the layout or managing editor to decide article placement, determining use of photos and other artwork, and giving final approval of page layouts. In addition, copy editors may spend time with managing editors at typesetters' or printers' shops, and substitute for the managing editors when necessary.

Large publications usually employ several copy editors for individual sections, but one copy editor may serve for an entire small magazine. Copy editors are valued for their unruffled personalities and meticulous attention to the smallest details.

Salaries

Most small trade magazines start copy editors at about $15,000, while large consumer publications start copy editors at about $23,000. A good copy editor with experience can generally earn about $45,000.

Employment Prospects

Competition is stiff and is characterized by high turnover. Many copy editors work on a part-time basis for more than one publication, or work as freelancers (for free-lance rates, see Section 8).

Advancement Prospects

Advancement potential for copy editors is fair. A beginning copy editor can move on to associate or assistant editor, perhaps eventually to senior editor. Knowledge of magazine production is always helpful at higher editorial positions, and the copy editor is in a perfect position to acquire such information.

Education

As with all magazine-writing jobs, an undergraduate degree in English, journalism, communications, or liberal arts is a must. After that, a copy editor would do well to brush up on grammar and writing skills through course work and/or seminars and internships. Advanced course work for specialized publications gives the copy editor familiarity with technical concepts and jargon connected to a particular field.

Experience/Skills

Although a background in writing or journalism is helpful, the copy editor's most important skill is a thorough command of English grammar, punctuation, and style. Copyediting work for any general-interest publication stands as a good recommendation for any other general-interest magazine. Secretarial skills acquired along the way, for organizational purposes, are also helpful.

Finally, a copy editor would do well to learn how to communicate easily and courteously with people, since some writers are not predisposed to hear about their sloppy grammar, incorrect information, and terrible spelling.

Unions/Associations

There are no unions for magazine editorial personnel. Professional organizations available include the American Society of Magazine Editors, as well as writers' trade groups.

ASSOCIATE EDITOR

CAREER PROFILE

Duties: Assign, read, and edit articles; write articles, columns, and copy; handle production

Alternate Title(s): Assistant Editor

Salary Range: $20,000 to $50,000+

Employment Prospects: Fair

Advancement Prospects: Fair

Prerequisites:

Education—Undergraduate degree in journalism, communications, or liberal arts; advanced or specialized degrees for technical, scientific, or business publications

Experience—None for entry level; otherwise, background as journalist, editorial assistant, or as associate editor on a smaller publication is needed

Special Skills—Editing; organization; production skill; graphics sense

CAREER LADDER

```
┌─────────────────────────────────┐
│      Editor; Senior Editor      │
└─────────────────────────────────┘

┌─────────────────────────────────┐
│        Associate Editor         │
└─────────────────────────────────┘

┌─────────────────────────────────┐
│ Editorial Assistant; Journalist;│
│        Writer; College          │
└─────────────────────────────────┘
```

Position Description

Associate editors have varying degrees of responsibility, depending on the size of the magazine. On a small trade magazine, for example, an associate editor can be second in command, reporting to an editor. On a larger publication, an associate editor may work under a senior editor and be assigned to a particular department.

Associate editors screen the unsolicited manuscripts that are initially screened and routed to them by editorial assistants; in some cases, they may do all the screening themselves. They assign articles to freelance writers, edit manuscripts, plus write headlines, cutlines, and other copy as needed. They are responsible for assigning photographic coverage or art illustrations to accompany articles. They either direct editorial assistants in research and fact-checking or are responsible for those duties themselves.

Associate editors participate in regular editorial meetings at which ideas are suggested and content for future issues planned. They may be assigned responsibility to generate articles on certain topics, which they in turn assign to writers.

In addition, associate editors may:

- handle production tasks, such as proofreading galleys;
- represent the magazine at professional functions; attend workshops, seminars, and trade conventions to stay abreast of industry trends and techniques.

Salaries

The Newspaper Guild, which negotiates the salaries for unionized magazines, reported that the top minimum for an associate editor at the *Nation* magazine in 1999 was about $47,808 after six years. Associate editors generally earn less than this, somewhere between $20,000 and $35,000.

Employment Prospects

The best job opportunities are on small and special-interest magazines, though job security is low. Many trade publications do not require experience or education in the industry they serve; background information is learned on the job.

Advancement Prospects

Work as an associate editor provides the necessary skill and background for higher editorial positions. There is a great deal of movement from one publication to another, especially in cities such as New York, which have a high concentration of publications. It is also possible to move into book-publishing editorial jobs.

Education

Associate editors are expected to have undergraduate degrees in communications, journalism, or liberal arts. Courses in publishing and advanced degrees in communications provide one with a competitive edge. Degrees in specialized fields are required by many technical, law, economics, scientific, and medical publications.

Experience/Skills

Prior experience as an editorial assistant, writer, or journalist is necessary for most associate-editor positions, though some jobs are at entry level. Also, work as an associate editor on a small magazine may be necessary to advance to associate editor on a large magazine.

Associate editors should be organized and deadline conscious. They should write and edit well, and understand the production process. They must be able to manage and direct others.

Unions/Associations

The Newspaper Guild represents employees of some major news and feature magazines, but by and large magazine editors are non-union. The principal professional association is the American Society of Magazine Editors. Many editors join trade associations and are auxiliary members of writers' groups. The Association for Women in Communications is open to women and men in all media.

SENIOR EDITOR

CAREER PROFILE

Duties: Supervise major editorial department; manage lower-level editors, freelancers, and/or photographers; write some articles and columns

Alternate Title(s): Executive Editor; Associate Editor

Salary Range: $22,000 to $115,000+

Employment Prospects: Fair

Advancement Prospects: Poor

Prerequisites:

Education—Undergraduate degree in journalism, English, communications, or liberal arts; advanced degree in journalism or specialized degrees for technical, scientific, or business publications

Experience—Background as journalist, writer, or editor essential; academic career sometimes beneficial

Special Skills—Editing; organization; managerial skills; knowledge of a particular field or specialty; production and graphics knowledge

CAREER LADDER

```
┌─────────────────────────────────┐
│    Editor; Executive Editor     │
└─────────────────────────────────┘

┌─────────────────────────────────┐
│         Senior Editor           │
└─────────────────────────────────┘

┌─────────────────────────────────┐
│        Associate Editor         │
└─────────────────────────────────┘
```

Position Description

Senior editors may have almost as much responsibility for a magazine's content as the editor. On small trade magazines, senior editors usually write the longest, most comprehensive articles as well as news. They offer story ideas and may even pass these ideas on to other writers. On larger publications, especially consumer magazines, senior editors manage a single major editorial department. In fact, the senior editor's title may reflect his or her area of responsibility, such as sports editor or fashion editor.

Although associate editors under the senior editor's supervision may handle all of the day-to-day tasks—reading unsolicited manuscripts, working with freelancers—the senior editor has ultimate responsibility for this work. Senior editors may deal directly with freelancers and occasionally assign photographs and illustrations for particular stories. If there are any changes in an assigned article's composition, or if the writer is having problems, the senior editor should—and must—know about them.

Senior editors participate regularly in editorial meetings, keeping the editor informed of the department's progress and suggesting story ideas. On a large publication, the senior editor may have the freedom to assign stories or columns without first getting the editor's approval. Such assignments may be the senior editor's ideas, but it is usually the associate editor's responsibility to write the stories or hire freelancers for the task.

Particularly on smaller magazines, the senior editor also writes. He or she may have a regular column or may produce articles or features as assigned. Senior editors for larger magazines rarely write; their supervisory and editorial duties take up a great deal of time.

In addition, senior editors may:

- handle production tasks, such as editing manuscripts and proofreading galleys;
- attend workshops, seminars, and trade shows to keep abreast of trends in the industry;
- represent the magazine at professional meetings and functions;
- handle day-to-day dealings with the printer.

Salaries

Senior editors of consumer magazines are typically paid more than those at business-to-business (trade) magazines. However, in 1999 the gap narrowed, according to *Folio*'s 1999 editorial salary survey. Consumer senior editors got 5.3 percent raises, while business-to-business editors got raises of 6.2 percent.

Senior editors' average salaries varied from the high $30,000s to the high $60,000s according to their age, how many magazines and employees they supervised, how frequently their magazine(s) were published, how many total pages they produced annually, and the circulation of the magazine(s). In 1999 senior magazine editors received bonuses averaging $4,871.

Employment Prospects

The best job opportunities for senior editors are on small and special-interest publications, especially trade magazines. Such publications have smaller staffs and often need people who are experienced writers and editors. Background information may be learned on the job, but familiarity with a given industry is preferable.

Advancement Prospects

Opportunity to move up the ladder to executive editor and/or editor depends on the publication. Although senior editors at smaller magazines have more visibility and perhaps perform more duties—both writing and editing—advancement may be stymied if the longtime editor has no plans to step down. At a larger magazine, senior editors have more chance to change departments (often with more responsibility) or to be promoted to executive editor. This is because editors at large publications tend to move more frequently to other magazines or even decide to start their own publications.

Education

Senior editors should have degrees in journalism or English; communications or other liberal-arts fields are also acceptable. An advanced degree can give the senior editor an edge. For specialized fields, such as law, economics, medicine, science, or technology, course work or degrees in that specialty are essential.

Experience/Skills

Prior experience as a journalist or lower level editor is often required to become senior editor. Academic experience as a professor or researcher is often acceptable as one's only qualification for becoming a senior editor in a specialized field, such as medicine or science—particularly if he or she will be writing a regular column.

Since so much of the senior editor's duties are supervisory, he or she must be well organized and able to manage people well. Senior editors have to have excellent editing skills and should write well also.

Unions/Associations

The American Society of Magazine Editors is the principal professional organization for editors. Writers and editors also often join writers' groups, such as the American Society of Journalists and Authors, Inc. All writers and editors are eligible to join the Association for Women in Communications. Editors of large news and feature magazines may belong to the Newspaper Guild.

EDITOR

CAREER PROFILE

Duties: Supervise magazine preparation; manage staff; rewrite and edit

Alternate Title(s): Editor-in-Chief; Editorial Director

Salary Range: $40,000 to $108,000+

Employment Prospects: Poor

Advancement Prospects: Poor

Prerequisites:
Education—Undergraduate degree in communications, journalism, or liberal arts; specialized degrees for scientific and technical publications
Experience—Background as editor and journalist or writer essential
Special Skills—Grammar and editing knowledge; self-motivation; intellectual curiosity; administrative ability

CAREER LADDER

```
┌─────────────────────────────────┐
│           Publisher             │
└─────────────────────────────────┘

┌─────────────────────────────────┐
│            Editor               │
└─────────────────────────────────┘

┌─────────────────────────────────┐
│  Senior Editor; Associate Editor;│
│        Assistant Editor         │
└─────────────────────────────────┘
```

Position Description

The editor has complete responsibility for the editorial content and production of a magazine. He or she reports to the publisher; in some cases, the editor may be the publisher as well.

Responsibilities depend on the size of publication. On a small magazine, the editor may perform many of the day-to-day editing and production tasks. On a larger publication, those tasks are all delegated, and the editor concentrates on broad administrative duties. Some editors may be in charge of groups of publications under a common ownership.

The typical magazine editor divides working time between editorial, production, and administrative duties. Editorial duties include planning future issues, making assignments to the staff and freelance writers, editing and rewriting manuscripts, and assigning photo coverage. Editors supervise the activities of subordinate editors, as well as monitor work-in-progress against deadlines. They have ultimate approval of all articles and copy.

Production duties include working with a layout editor to decide placement of articles, use of photos, and other artwork, plus final approval of page layouts. On small publications, the editor may have sole responsibility for production;

this may entail proofreading galleys and spending time at the typesetter's shop.

Administrative duties include hiring and firing staff members, planning and managing budgets, negotiating freelance contracts, writing reports, answering letters from readers, and other managerial tasks.

In addition, editors may:

- attend trade conventions;
- participate in promotional and publicity activities for the publication;
- write signed or bylined columns or editorials.

Salaries

Editors of consumer magazines are typically paid more than those at business-to-business (trade) magazines. However, in 1999 the gap narrowed, according to *Folio*'s 1999 editorial salary survey. Editors' average salaries varied from the low $40,000s to $108,000 according to their age, how many magazines and employees they supervised, how frequently their magazine(s) were published, how many total pages they produced annually, and the circulation of the magazine(s). Salaries for editors increase dramatically as they age, jumping in some cases by as much as $20,000 per decade. In 1999 magazine editors received bonuses averaging $7,034.

Employment Prospects

The market is competitive and characterized by high turnover. The best opportunities will be in business and trade publications, especially those serving growth industries such as executive management, computers, and health. The consumer field is unstable.

Advancement Prospects

Editor is the top position of many magazines, directly under the publisher (who almost always comes from the advertising and marketing side of the business). Since editor usually is the top position, advancement can only be made by moving on to bigger, more prestigious publications. Such advancement opportunities can be slow in coming—turnover is less frequent at higher editorial positions.

Education

As with many writing and editing jobs, there is little agreement as to the preferred major. Many editors have undergraduate degrees in communications or journalism, while others have degrees in liberal arts, history, philosophy, or the social sciences. Some editing jobs require business, economics, science, or engineering degrees.

Experience/Skills

The amount of experience required to be editor depends on the publication. Three to five years may be necessary for some jobs; ten years or more for others. Experience can include work as a journalist, assistant news editor, copy editor, or section editor; work in book publishing as a junior editor or editor; or work on a magazine staff in lower editorial positions.

Editors should have good judgment about what to publish and what to reject; they should have tact and the ability to direct and motivate staff members and freelance writers. They should be creative, highly self-motivated, and have a strong sense of curiosity. They should be able to meet deadlines and manage budgets. Production knowledge is also important.

Unions/Associations

Major professional associations include the American Society of Journalists and Authors, Inc.; American Society of Magazine Editors; and Association for Women in Communications. Other writer associations as well as trade and industry groups are open to magazine editors. The Newspaper Guild represents some employees on major news and feature magazines.

EXECUTIVE EDITOR

CAREER PROFILE

Duties: Supervise magazine preparation; manage staff; assign stories; rewrite and edit

Alternate Title(s): Editor; Senior Editor; Managing Editor; Editorial Director

Salary Range: $30,000 to $107,000+

Employment Prospects: Fair

Advancement Prospects: Fair

Prerequisites:
  Education—Undergraduate degree in journalism, English, communications, or other liberal arts; advanced or specialized degrees for scientific, technical, or specialty publications
  Experience—Several years' background as journalist, writer, or editor is essential
  Special Skills—Knowledge of editing and grammar; good organization; knowledge of a particular field or specialty; ability to manage and direct people

CAREER LADDER

```
┌─────────────────────────────────────┐
│              Editor                 │
└─────────────────────────────────────┘

┌─────────────────────────────────────┐
│          Executive Editor           │
└─────────────────────────────────────┘

┌─────────────────────────────────────┐
│   Senior Editor; Associate Editor;  │
│           Assistant Editor          │
└─────────────────────────────────────┘
```

Position Description

The executive editor is a title more closely associated with larger publications, since smaller magazines allocate the executive editor's duties to senior editors and the top editor. The executive editor may have total responsibility for a particular magazine, reporting to the editor in chief in charge of a magazine group under common ownership. The structure of magazine staffs varies greatly from one publication to another.

Like senior editors, executive editors supervise lower-level editors and may take responsibility for freelancers, photographers, and illustrators. Executive editors assign stories, monitor the department or entire magazine's work, and have ultimate responsibility for final editing. They may also write features or articles, but usually they confine their responsibilities to editing. They are responsible for meeting deadlines.

Usually second in command to the editor, executive editors delegate authority and story assignments often without prior approval. Should the editor be out of town or ill, the executive editor takes over complete control of the magazine.

In addition, the executive editor may:

- represent the magazine at professional meetings or functions;
- attend workshops, annual meetings, seminars, and trade shows to stay abreast of industry trends;
- work with the editor on budget and give approval for editorial expenses;
- handle production duties, such as page-checking and proofreading.

Salaries

Executive editors of consumer magazines are typically paid more than those at business-to-business (trade) magazines. However, in 1999 the gap narrowed, according to *Folio*'s 1999 editorial salary survey—except for the top editorial spot. Consumer executive editors got raises averaging $8,000, bringing their average pay to $88,100, while business-to-business editors got raises of $5,400, bringing their average pay to $84,300.

Executive editors' average salaries varied from the mid $30,000s to $107,000 according to their age, how many magazines and employees they supervised, how frequently magazine(s) were published, how many total pages they produced annually, and the circulation of the magazine(s).

Employment Prospects

The best opportunities for an executive editor are with large publications, since smaller magazines often have no executive editorial position. Competition is strong, however. It is less likely that an executive editor will be hired from outside than promoted from within the organization.

Advancement Prospects

Since the executive editor is directly under the editor or editor in chief, advancement prospects are less promising than for senior editor. If the editor has been with a publication for many years and has no intention of leaving, an executive editor may have to move to another publication to advance to the editor's slot. Editors do move though, often to start their own magazines.

Education

Any executive editor worth his salt will have an undergraduate degree in journalism, English, communications, or liberal arts. Most have probably acquired advanced degrees in journalism or technical fields along the way as well or, at least, have taken advanced course work. Specialized publications, such as those for medicine, science, law, or high technology require advanced education.

Experience/Skills

Prior experience as a senior editor or editor of a smaller publication is usually necessary for most executive-editor positions. Work as a professor or academic researcher may be sufficient for certain spots, especially if there is more writing and less editing involved. In these cases, the executive editor's title reflects background and expertise more than editing and managerial functions.

Good writing and editing skills, as well as the ability to manage people effectively, are vital to an executive editor. Depending upon the executive editor's level of responsibility, he or she must also deal with the publisher, the advertising department, and the readers.

Unions/Associations

Executive editors, like their counterparts in magazine publishing, may belong to the American Society of Magazine Editors or various writers' trade organizations.

NEWS LIBRARIAN

CAREER PROFILE

Duties: Organize a library containing books, clippings, and databases to support research of magazine articles; assist writers and researchers; share information with other libraries

Alternate Title(s): Information Manager; Library Director; Director of Information Services; Information Specialist, Supervisor of Information Services

Salary Range: $18,000 to $60,000+

Employment Prospects: Fair

Advancement Prospects: Poor

Prerequisites:

Education—For higher-level jobs, a master's degree in library science; a second advanced degree in another field is also helpful, such as a degree in English or political science

Experience—A part-time or summer job in a newsmagazine library or other library; familiarity with computer databases and database research; or familiarity with the news magazine business

Special Skills—Ability to work with journalists on deadline; good organizational skills; good research skills

CAREER LADDER

```
┌─────────────────────────────────┐
│      News Library Director      │
└─────────────────────────────────┘

┌─────────────────────────────────┐
│          News Librarian         │
└─────────────────────────────────┘

┌─────────────────────────────────┐
│    Library Clerk; Researcher    │
└─────────────────────────────────┘
```

Position Description

The most extensive libraries maintained by magazines can be found at news magazines, where a given week's editorial content can be extremely diverse. Although automation through computers has eliminated some library jobs, the use of computer databases and information networks with other librarians has made computer skills increasingly important. In fact, the field is evolving from traditional librarianship into information management.

Within a news magazine library, staffers are divided into different areas of expertise, where they field requests for information from the magazine's researchers and writers. Writers for overseas editions of the magazine may deal with a librarian assigned to that edition.

Lower-level jobs, such as filer, may be part-time or summer jobs with no experience needed. Higher-level jobs, however, invariably require library training, unlike the old days of the "morgue," when library staffers were generally magazine staffers who were near retirement, with no special training.

Librarians oversee collections of print material, still very important since most pre-1975 material is not available in computer databases. They are also responsible for collections of pictures and photographs. Librarians also may field requests from the public for specific stories that appeared in the magazine, finding the edition they appeared in and mailing them out.

Because news is continuously evolving, research often has to be done on a moment's notice to meet deadlines.

Salaries

A filer at one of the major news magazines may start at $18,000. A clerk may start at slightly more, around $20,000.

Librarians start around $23,000, and senior librarians at $26,300.

Unionized librarians, represented by the Newspaper Guild, have their raises negotiated, usually about $15 or more per week per year.

Employment Prospects

While the use of computer technology may have initially reduced the number of library staffers needed at news magazine libraries, as magazines go on-line and the use of computer-aided research increases, there may be more call for people skilled at finding information fast.

Employment in special libraries, such as news magazine libraries, in-house private libraries for businesses or law libraries, is expected to be more promising than employment in traditional public libraries.

Advancement Prospects

Staffers may have to wait a long time to advance. At some news magazines, employees stay within the library for 10 years or more. However, many of these employees began as filers or summer interns and rose within the library as they obtained more training. Many hold dual degrees—one in library science, one in an area of expertise.

Library employees can also move on to become researchers or writers, or go on to work in other "specialty" libraries, such as an in-house library at a business or a law firm.

Education

To rise within a news magazine library, a master's of library science is essential. A second degree in a specialty area, such as political science, is also very helpful. Computer research experience is also increasingly important.

Experience/Skills

Library jobs require specific combinations of skills. Librarians need to know the news magazine business and what journalists require to satisfy their deadlines. They also must be versed in the techniques of research and library management. Many news librarians also are experts in a specific field. They must be well-organized, respond well to pressure, and have good communications skills.

Unions/Associations

The Special Libraries Association has a division for news libraries. News librarians are also represented by the Newspaper Guild at unionized magazines. Other organizations include the American Library Association and the American Society for Information Science.

TELEVISION

DESK ASSISTANT

CAREER PROFILE

Duties: Provide clerical and general assistance to television newsroom personnel

Alternate Title(s): News Desk Assistant

Salary Range: $14,000 to $22,000

Employment Prospects: Good

Advancement Prospects: Good

Prerequisites:

　　Education—High school diploma; some college preferred

　　Experience—None necessary, but news-related work is helpful

　　Special Skills—Clerical skills; writing ability; organization skills

CAREER LADDER

```
┌──────────────────────────────┐
│    News Writer; Reporter;     │
│     Production Assistant      │
└──────────────────────────────┘

┌──────────────────────────────┐
│        Desk Assistant         │
└──────────────────────────────┘

┌──────────────────────────────┐
│     High School; College      │
└──────────────────────────────┘
```

Position Description

Persons who are interested in careers in television news often begin as desk assistants, general apprentices who perform routine office and clerical tasks while learning the trade.

Generally this job is found only at medium and large stations and networks, where staffs are large enough to need desk assistants. Desk assistants may work part or full time, any hours of the day or night, any days of the week.

Duties include fielding telephone calls, distributing messages and mail, running errands, typing letters, reports, and scripts, and filing them. Desk assistants may be responsible for maintaining office supplies and seeing that equipment such as typewriters and copiers are serviced and repaired.

Duties relating directly to news operations include monitoring and ripping the copy from wire service printer terminals, and disseminating it among reporters and editors, as well as filling requests for information and tapes from the library or videotape storage room. Tapes must be logged in and out. Desk assistants may also handle the sending and receiving of tapes to and from sister stations and affiliates; they themselves may be required to act as couriers.

Desk or production assistants help with script preparation. "Breaking script," as it is called, is done for every news broadcast; this includes typing, updating, and delivering scripts to all appropriate persons. It's not unusual for multiple updates to be done for each broadcast, especially when major stories happen.

In addition, desk assistants may:

- do research work for reporters, such as collecting background information and updating facts, sports scores, and weather reports;
- learn production work by assisting in the control room;
- learn reporting by accompanying reporters on assignments.

Salaries

Entry-level jobs in television pay low salaries. Most desk assistants earn between $14,000 and $22,000, even at large stations and networks. Earnings over $22,000 are rare. Desk assistants are paid either a weekly rate or, if part time, an hourly rate.

Employment Prospects

Most desk-assistant jobs are concentrated in medium to large market cities, including network headquarters and bureaus. Cable is opening more opportunities for desk assistants. Relatively rapid turnover in the job as individuals are promoted or leave the field keeps demand steady. Once in the field, prospects are good for advancement because of high turnover.

Advancement Prospects

The desk assistant is in an excellent position for internal promotion to production, newswriting, or reporting work. The successful candidate for advancement must demonstrate a knowledge of broadcasting operations, good writing and speaking skills, and good news judgment. He or she should be highly motivated, seeking assignments beyond the normal range of the desk assistant's duties.

Education

A college degree is not necessary for desk-assistant jobs, but it is preferred for higher positions. Some desk assistants work part time while they attend college. Studies should include communications, liberal arts, history, social sciences, and courses in broadcasting.

Experience/Skills

Any kind of experience in a news-related job is helpful, such as working on a community newspaper, or school publication, radio, or TV station. Clerical and office skills are paramount for desk assistants, who must type and file reports, correspondence, and scripts. Good organization also is important; desk assistants may have to quickly locate or handle information for someone under deadline pressure. Those who aspire to newswriting or reporting jobs should have good journalistic research and writing skills, as well as strong self-motivation.

Unions/Associations

At many major stations and the networks, desk assistants belong to such unions as the National Association of Broadcast Employees and Technicians, American Federation of Television and Radio Artists, or Writers Guild of America.

RESEARCHER

CAREER PROFILE

Duties: Assist television staff with background research for news and other programs

Alternate Title(s): None

Salary Range: $14,300 to $35,000

Employment Prospects: Fair

Advancement Prospects: Good

Prerequisites:

Education—Undergraduate degree in communications or liberal arts

Experience—Any background in the media helpful

Special Skills—Accuracy; good organizational skills; attention to details; good writing ability; curiosity

CAREER LADDER

```
┌─────────────────────────────┐
│   Reporter; News Writer;     │
│     Associate Producer       │
└─────────────────────────────┘

┌─────────────────────────────┐
│         Researcher           │
└─────────────────────────────┘

┌─────────────────────────────┐
│   College; Desk Assistant;   │
│    Production Assistant       │
└─────────────────────────────┘
```

Position Description

Most researchers employed at television stations work in the news department. The job is an entry-level position, though there may be levels of junior and senior researchers at large stations and networks.

Researchers assist reporters, news writers, and news directors or editors with gathering background information for stories. A half-hour broadcast can contain anywhere from 14 to 30 stories, and a single researcher may be assigned to work on several stories for each broadcast.

They do most of their work by telephone, pre-interviewing sources to find the best ones for the reporter to then interview on tape. They also interview sources in order to gather and check information pertaining to stories, then write summary reports of their findings for reporters or news writers to use. The job is often demanding and pressured, and researchers must be able to absorb a wide range of information quickly, sorting out the most important material.

Researchers also generate ideas for stories. They maintain contact with news sources, and they scan magazines and newspapers. They may be assigned a geographic area of responsibility or to certain topics, such as education, business, or government.

Researchers help reporters assemble audio and visual materials for stories, searching library files or contacting other stations to acquire film or videotape footage.

In addition, researchers may:

- do follow-up work on stories to check for new developments;
- work on other programs or documentaries;
- work in the marketing department, tracking ratings.

Salaries

Researchers are likely to be paid on a weekly or hourly rate, with extra compensation for overtime. Some may work only part time. Junior researchers earn roughly $14,300 to $16,000 a year, while senior researchers with more than three years of experience can earn up to $35,000, including overtime. The best-paying jobs are at large stations and the networks.

Employment Prospects

Researcher usually is considered an entry-level position in the news department, though large stations and networks may require some experience. Part-time openings, if offered, should be seriously considered; they may lead to full-time work.

Advancement Prospects

It may be difficult to find a job as a researcher but, once established, advancement opportunities are good. Researchers have several avenues open to them: reporting the news; writing scripts for the news; or assisting in the production of news and other programs.

Education

Undergraduate degrees in communications, history, social sciences, or liberal arts are preferred for jobs in the news media. Also acceptable are degrees in political science or business. Courses in broadcasting are helpful.

Experience/Skills

Any experience in the news media is helpful for competing for researcher positions, including school or community publications. Researchers may have previously worked as desk or production assistants, reporters, or news writers for newspapers or radio stations.

Researchers should be adept at quickly gathering information. They should be well organized, detail-oriented, and comfortable with interviewing over the phone. They should be able to handle pressure well, and provide clearly written reports and summaries of their findings. News judgment also is important.

Unions/Associations

Researchers may belong to such unions as the American Federation of Television and Radio Artists, Writers Guild of America, or National Association of Broadcast Employees and Technicians. Some researchers may join professional associations as well, such as the National Academy of Television Arts and Sciences or the Academy of Television Arts and Sciences.

REPORTER

CAREER PROFILE

Duties: Prepare news and feature stories; report on air

Alternate Title(s): Newscaster; Correspondent

Salary Range: $14,000 to $130,000

Employment Prospects: Poor to fair

Advancement Prospects: Poor to fair

Prerequisites:
   Education—Undergraduate degree in communications, liberal arts, history, social sciences, or political science
   Experience—Work as news writer or researcher helpful
   Special Skills—Good reporting, writing, and speaking ability; self-motivation; astute news judgment; being comfortable on camera

CAREER LADDER

```
┌─────────────────────────────┐
│   Anchorperson; Assistant    │
│       News Director          │
└─────────────────────────────┘

┌─────────────────────────────┐
│          Reporter            │
└─────────────────────────────┘

┌─────────────────────────────┐
│  News Writer; Researcher;    │
│     Assistant; College       │
└─────────────────────────────┘
```

Position Description

The prime responsibility of a television reporter is to gather news and prepare stories for broadcast. The work involves interviewing sources, researching facts, directing a film crew, writing a script, delivering news on the air, and working with film editors.

Time pressures are enormous. Not only do reporters work against the clock for scheduled news programs—they are limited severely in the amount of time they have to present a news story. A major story typically runs about two minutes; many stories run 90 seconds or less. Reporters must strive to summarize highlights, give important information, and make the story visually interesting as well.

Reporters are assigned stories and estimated time allotments by an assigment editor or news director. Editors often rely on a reporter's news judgment to determine the slant and length of a story. Some reporters, especially those at large stations, may specialize in certain areas, such as business or politics, and have more control over the stories they generate.

Gathering information involves interviewing people by phone and in person. Some stations employ researchers and assistants to do background legwork and news writers to write scripts. Otherwise, reporters do those tasks themselves.

Reporters then go on location with a camera crew and direct the shooting. Their on-air report may include portions of a taped interview, a voice-over of the visuals, and a stand-up summary. Live reports have gained increasing popularity as new technology has made smaller, more portable cameras available.

Reporters are usually assigned a day or evening shift. Stories can run the gamut from city council meetings to major disasters. Covering stories such as wars, political uprisings, and natural disasters is often dangerous work, but some reporters find it exciting. Stories can also be features or investigative pieces. Some reporters occasionally prepare special series.

Salaries

Entry-level pay for television reporters is less than for newspaper reporters. A 1999 study by Kosicki and Becker found that median annual first-year pay was $18,200 for television reporters and $22,600 for daily newspapers. In fact, the same study found, the gap had doubled between 1989 and 1999. This is partly because the demand for television jobs is higher: ten applicants for each television job versus only four for each newspaper job. Also, competition for advertising revenues is greater when three or more television stations exist in the same area, whereas most daily newspapers enjoy a monopoly.

Another survey conducted by the Radio-Television News Directors Association and Ball State University showed that median salaries for television reporters have increased 26.3 percent between 1995 and 1998. Their median 1998 salary in this study was $24,000. The overall salary range was from $14,000 to $130,000.

Market size has a great deal of influence over television salaries, and more so for reporters than for producers. Some reporters may advance by moving to larger stations. The best salaries are offered in the East, and lowest in the Midwest and South. Those who specialize in such areas as business, consumer, and health news may have an advantage in the job market.

Advancement Prospects

The Bureau of Labor Statistics projects a decline in the number of jobs available for reporters through 2006. Most job openings will arise from the need to replace reporters and correspondents who leave the occupation. Turnover is relatively high, perhaps because of the stressful nature of the occupation and irregular hours.

Reporters generally begin at a station in a small community and then try to move to a job in a large city. Many reporters also aspire to anchor positions, jobs with semi-celebrity status, high salaries, and glamour. Prospects for obtaining these jobs are poor, with intense competition for limited openings.

Off-camera jobs that might interest ambitious reporters include assistant news director or news director.

Education

Most employers prefer individuals with a degree in journalism, communications, or liberal arts, but some hire graduates with other majors. Taped auditions also weigh heavily. Specialized degrees in business, health, or law may be advantageous. Communications courses should include study in broadcasting. A knowledge of news photography is useful for entry-level positions for combination reporter/camera operator or reporter/photographer.

Internships with news organizations provide excellent experience for those who hope to enter this field. High school or college courses in English, public speaking, drama, foreign languages, and electronics may also prove valuable.

Experience/Skills

At very small stations and cable operations, it may be possible to get a reporting job right out of college. At such small stations, a reporter may be required to shoot his or her own film, edit it, and deliver it on air.

However, most reporters have had some kind of experience before they go on the air. Good entry-level jobs include production assistant, researcher, production secretary, or news writer. Some newspaper reporters are also able to switch to television.

Experience on college publications or radio and television stations is also an asset. A reporter should have a pleasant and well-controlled voice, good timing, good pronunciation, use correct English, and appear neat and well-groomed. Knowledge of a wide variety of subjects also helps, as reporters are often required to ad-lib on the air.

Television reporters also need the same skills as all journalists—accuracy, astute news judgment, ability to work under pressure, and strong self-motivation.

Unions/Associations

The Writers Guild of America, National Association of Broadcast Employees and Technicians, and American Federation of Television and Radio Artists are major unions representing many TV reporters. Small stations may not be unionized. Professional associations include Radio-Television News Directors Association; International Radio and Television Society; Radio-Television Correspondents' Gallery (for Congressional reporters); National Academy of Television Arts and Sciences; Association for Women in Communications; Academy of Television Arts and Sciences; and Society of Professional Journalists, Sigma Delta Chi.

ANCHOR

CAREER PROFILE

Duties: Host news or other shows; read the news or other copy on air; interview guests; may also go on location for coverage of major events

Alternate Title(s): Anchorperson

Salary Range: Under $15,000 to $800,000+

Employment Prospects: Poor

Advancement Prospects: Poor

Prerequisites:

Education—Undergraduate degree in communications or political science with emphasis on liberal arts; graduate degree may be preferred

Experience—Many years as reporter, correspondent, or other television positions

Special Skills/Attributes—Pleasing appearance on camera; good voice; competitiveness; ability to work under pressure; ability to be spontaneous

CAREER LADDER

```
┌─────────────────────────────┐
│    Major Market Anchor      │
└─────────────────────────────┘

┌─────────────────────────────┐
│           Anchor            │
└─────────────────────────────┘

┌─────────────────────────────┐
│   Reporter or Correspondent │
└─────────────────────────────┘
```

Position Description

The anchor job is the brass ring sought by many who start careers in television reporting. Competition for these coveted jobs is fierce. Anchors earn their jobs by putting in years of hard work as reporters or correspondents, and by becoming well-versed in politics and other issues of great public concern.

The anchor serves as host to a news or entertainment show and reads the news, introduces the stories, and interviews the guests who appear on the show. Essentially, the entire show revolves around the anchor or anchors. These individuals become public personalities and celebrities.

In small markets, anchors do their own research and writing and work with production on editing videotape for broadcast. In larger markets, these functions are performed by supporting staff, and the anchor's primary job is to read the copy and perhaps interview guests. Prior to broadcast time, all anchors review the contents of the broadcast with staff. The anchor has a say in determining the content and in giving time priority to various stories. Increasingly, news and entertainment shows provide time for anchors to question reporters and exchange conversation and banter. Some of this is orchestrated and some is spontaneous.

In addition to the regular show, anchors may go on location for major events, such as conferences and conventions, and may work on documentaries or specials to be broadcast at different times.

Salaries

As with other television news jobs, salaries of anchors largely depend on the size of the market in which they work. According to a study by the Radio-Television News Directors Association, in 1998 TV news anchors' salaries ranged from $9,000 all the way to $800,000, with a median of $44,000. Sports anchors' salaries ranged from $15,000 to $260,000, with a median of $33,000.

Anchors in major markets have the only jobs in television news that pay better than comparable print positions, according to the Radio-Television News Directors Association.

Employment Prospects

Only a small percentage of television reporters ever become anchors. The typical station hires two or more anchors, while major stations and networks have numerous anchors. The constant emphasis on ratings creates high turnover as anchors don't make the grade or are picked off by competing stations or higher-paying stations in larger markets. The expansion of cable television news programs is likely to increase employment opportunities in the future. Job openings are somewhat better for women and minorities, as stations seek to provide a balance in highly visible positions.

Advancement Prospects

The anchor job is the highest position for a reporter or correspondent, and the only advancement then can be achieved by moving up to larger markets or the networks.

Education

Virtually all jobs in television news require an undergraduate degree in communications or one of the liberal arts; some posts may require a graduate degree. Other fields of study can include political science.

Experience/Skills

Reporters typically spend many years in the field before becoming eligible for promotion to anchor. Grooming is of paramount importance. Anchors must have a pleasing on-camera appearance and personality and a good, clear voice. They must convey authority to the viewer. They also must be able to ad-lib and think on their feet in the event something unexpected happens live on the air. When major stories break, they must be able to react quickly. Because competition for these jobs is keen, anchors must be tough and stay on their toes.

Unions/Associations

Anchors may belong to the Writers Guild of America, the American Federation of Television and Radio Artists, the Radio-Television News Directors Association, and the Society of Professional Journalists.

NEWS WRITER

CAREER PROFILE

Duties: Write scripts for news programs

Alternate Title(s): Senior Editor

Salary Range: $20,000 to $76,000+

Employment Prospects: Fair to good

Advancement Prospects: Fair to good

Prerequisites:

Education—Undergraduate degree in liberal arts, history, social sciences, or communications

Experience—None to several years in similar or related position

Special Skills—Good news judgment; script-writing ability; speed

CAREER LADDER

```
┌─────────────────────────────────────┐
│   News Editor; Reporter; Producer    │
└─────────────────────────────────────┘

┌─────────────────────────────────────┐
│            News Writer               │
└─────────────────────────────────────┘

┌─────────────────────────────────────┐
│  College; Desk Assistant; Researcher │
└─────────────────────────────────────┘
```

Position Description

News writer is a fast-pace, high-pressure job in television news departments. It requires quick, sound news judgment, good reportorial skills, and the ability to write for the ear rather than the eye.

News writers may be assigned any shift around the clock, any day of the week, depending on the station's needs. They usually begin their work day by reviewing wire copy, newspapers, and stories aired on previous newscasts. They attend one or more editorial meetings each day; decisions at these meetings are made on what stories to cover and who will be responsible for tracking and updating breaking stories.

A single news writer may be responsible for writing copy for a major newscast and one or more regularly scheduled news breaks or digests (which typically include about 30 seconds of news). News writers often do their own research, corroborating other news sources and checking out conflicting reports, such as differences in the number of fatalities in a disaster or accident. They interview sources by phone and research information in the station's library. Often they are aided by researchers and desk assistants. They also coordinate graphics and tapes to be used during newscasts, working with artists, producers, and representatives of other television stations.

News writers must be able to write tight scripts that are easy to read and easy for listeners to understand—and also fit a teleprompter screen. They are restricted by time—news stories seldom run over 90 seconds and may be as short as 10 seconds for news breaks—and their scripts must match what viewers see on their sets. News writers either preview tapes or receive "shot sheets" that describe visuals and time lengths. Scripts are written down to the second, a skill that can only be developed over time, with experience.

The daily workload for news writers often varies. Reporters write their own scripts, and anchors often write scripts for the lead stories. The workload also depends on the day's news—a news writer may work on a few big stories or on many small ones.

News writers work under the supervision of an editor, assistant news director, or news director. Overtime is often required, and shifts of 10 to 11 hours are not uncommon.

In addition, news writers may:

- produce news digests, documentaries, or other programs;
- supervise tape editing for news reports;
- write promotional scripts to publicize upcoming broadcasts.

Salaries

The median annual earning for news writers in 1997 was $26,300. The lowest 10 percent earned less than

$20,920 and the highest 10 percent earned more than $76,660.

Employment Prospects

Job prospects for news writers are fair to good, though beginners usually will have to go to small stations. Networks and large stations hire only seasoned news writers who have worked their way up the markets. Cable and independent stations may offer the best prospects for beginners.

Advancement Prospects

News writers have fair to good chances for advancement, either as news editors, news directors, or as producers. Some experienced news writers take on production assignments as part of their development.

Education

News writers must be able to handle wide ranges of topics and need some historical perspective of news events. A broad education in liberal arts, social sciences, history, or political science can be better preparation than a degree in communications or broadcasting. Broadcasting courses are helpful for learning the technical end of the business.

Experience/Skills

At small stations, news writer is often an entry-level position. Large stations and networks require experience and proven skills. Candidates typically work as desk assistants or researchers before becoming news writers.

News writers must be able to condense important information into scripts written for the ear. They seldom have time to revise. They must be good, accurate, detail-oriented researchers. News writers also must be adaptable and versatile, able to understand many different topics and issues.

Unions/Associations

News writers in large markets usually are members of a union, such as Writers Guild of America, National Association of Broadcast Employees and Technicians, or American Federation of Television and Radio Artists. Major professional associations are the National Academy of Television Arts and Sciences; Academy of Television Arts and Sciences; Radio-Television News Directors Association; and Society of Professional Journalists, Sigma Delta Chi.

ASSISTANT NEWS DIRECTOR

CAREER PROFILE

Duties: Assign news coverage; manage news operations

Alternate Title(s): Assistant News Editor; Assignment Editor; Managing Editor; City Editor

Salary Range: $18,000 to $110,000+

Employment Prospects: Poor

Advancement Prospects: Good

Prerequisites:
    Education—Undergraduate degree in communications, liberal arts, history, social sciences, or political science
    Experience—Several years' experience as reporter
    Special Skills—Good news judgment; managerial ability; organizational skills

CAREER LADDER

```
┌─────────────────────────────────┐
│         News Director           │
└─────────────────────────────────┘

┌─────────────────────────────────┐
│     Assistant News Director     │
└─────────────────────────────────┘

┌─────────────────────────────────┐
│            Reporter             │
└─────────────────────────────────┘
```

Position Description

Assistant news directors are middle managers responsible for the day-to-day supervision of television station newsrooms. They work under the supervision of a news director, executing the director's decisions. Depending on the size of staff, they have a certain amount of their own decision-making authority for assigning reporters and crews to stories. They evaluate suggestions for stories and monitor the reports made by reporters.

Assistant news directors are responsible for many of the nuts and bolts of daily operations. They may make up work schedules so that the newsroom has adequate personnel at all times and complies with any union regulations concerning varying shifts in a given period of time. They also monitor assignments and work-in-progress. They may assume complete responsibility for fast-breaking stories.

Managerial responsibilities include coordinating the work of various departments, solving problems, and handling complaints. Assistant news directors are in complete charge of the newsroom in the absence of the news directors.

At some small stations, assistant news directors may do some of the writing, editing, and reporting for newscasts.

Salaries

A study by the Radio-Television News Directors Association found that the salary range for assistant news directors ranged from $18,000 to $110,000 in 1998. The average salary was $51,600; the median was $50,000. Assistant news directors received an average raise of 7.3 percent or more between 1997 and 1998. Salaries are highest at the stations with the largest markets.

Employment Prospects

Job turnover is high, but candidates for assistant news director have poor employment prospects due to keen competition. Small stations may not have this middle-management position, but large stations or networks may have several. Assistant news directors usually are promoted from within, from the ranks of reporters. More opportunities are becoming available in the rapidly growing cable industry.

Advancement Prospects

Assistant news directors are directly in line for news-director positions, which undergo high turnover. The best opportunities are in commercial and cable television; public television staffs are shrinking due to cutbacks in federal support. Assistant news directors may also advance their careers by switching to a related field, such as newspapers, wire services, or government.

Education

An undergraduate degree in communications, English, liberal arts, history, or social sciences is considered the minimum educational requirement. Other degrees include political science, economics, or business.

Experience/Skills

Assistant news directors typically have worked for several years as reporters, researchers, or news desk assistants. They may also have had experience in radio or print journalism. They should be familiar with video and studio operations.

Sound news judgment and leadership qualities are important for this job. Decisions must be made quickly and often under pressure. Assistant news directors need to be able to edit, write, and even report, as needed. They should have managerial and leadership qualities. In addition, they should understand Federal Communications Commission regulations governing fairness and equal-use time, as well as laws concerning copyright and libel.

Unions/Associations

The major professional associations are the Radio-Television News Directors Association, National Academy of Television Arts and Sciences and Academy of Television Arts and Sciences. Both women and men may join the Association for Women in Communications. Assistant news directors who write or report on air may belong to such unions as the American Federation of Television and Radio Artists; Writers Guild of America; or National Association of Broadcast Employees and Technicians. In addition, some assistant news directors may belong to the Society of Professional Journalists, Sigma Delta Chi.

NEWS DIRECTOR

CAREER PROFILE

Duties: Assign news coverage; manage entire news operations of a TV station; determine policy

Alternate Title(s): News Editor

Salary Range: Under $28,895 to $250,000+

Employment Prospects: Poor

Advancement Prospects: Poor

Prerequisites:
  Education—Undergraduate or graduate degree in communications, liberal arts, history, social sciences, or political science
  Experience—Several years in TV or radio news work
  Special Skills—Good news judgment; managerial and administrative ability

CAREER LADDER

```
┌─────────────────────────────┐
│      General Manager;        │
│     News Vice President      │
└─────────────────────────────┘

┌─────────────────────────────┐
│        News Director         │
└─────────────────────────────┘

┌─────────────────────────────┐
│ Assistant News Director; Reporter │
└─────────────────────────────┘
```

Position Description

Television news directors have overall responsibility for stations' news operations. They decide and coordinate the content of news programs, including what will be covered, how the stories will be presented, and which reporters will be assigned to them. They edit and review scripts and file reports. Ultimate responsibility for and authority over what appears on the air is theirs.

An average station has a news staff of about 10; larger stations typically have 40 or more. In addition, news directors coordinate the technical operations of news production. This involves assigning camera crews to stories and camera operators to work in the studio.

News directors report to station general managers or, in the case of large stations, to vice president of news. They often work long hours under great pressure, and their jobs are heavily dependent on ratings. In breaking major stories, they must make quick decisions.

News directors hire and promote news staffs. They are involved in determining budgets, and they handle many administrative responsibilities. At small stations, news directors may also take part in news gathering and reporting, or they may act as talk show hosts.

In addition, news directors may supervise public-affairs programs; they may also coordinate news activities with programming and other departments.

Salaries

Television news directors' salaries ranged from $20,000 to $250,000 in 1998, according to a study by the Radio-Television News Directors Association. The average salary was $66,000; the median was $56,000.

The same study found that salaries are highest at the stations with the largest markets, and at stations where the news director supervises the largest staff. At stations with a news staff of 10 or fewer, the news directors' average salary was $30,500. At stations with more than 51 employees, their average salary was $100,000.

Employment Prospects

Though the federal government projects moderate overall growth in TV jobs during the next decade, competition will remain strong for news-director positions, particularly in major cities. Turnover is high, especially at large stations where news directors seldom stay more than two to three years. Aggressive job candidates, however, are many. More opportunities are available in the rapidly growing cable industry.

According to a study by Vernon Stone of the Missouri School of Journalism, the glass ceiling for women in TV news was shattered during the 1990s. In 1972 only 0.5 percent of news director positions were held by women; in 1996 it was 14.1 percent, and indicators suggest that by the year 2001, a third of all TV news directors will be women.

There is less change for minorities. As women gained a larger share of the news director jobs, minorities lost slightly—but white men lost even more.

Advancement Prospects

News directors face limited opportunities for advancement; at many stations their job is the highest on the news side. Some may be promoted to general managers, though sales managers are the most likely candidates for that position. Large stations and networks offer vice president and assistant vice president positions in news.

Education

An undergraduate degree in communications, liberal arts, history, English, or social sciences is considered the minimum educational requirement. Many news directors have degrees in political science. A master's degree may be helpful for employment and advancement.

Experience/Skills

Television news directors generally have had at least several years' seasoning as reporters or assistant news directors in TV or radio. Large stations require more experience than small stations. News directors need sound news judgment and the ability to make quick decisions. They should understand Federal Communications Commission regulations governing fairness and equal-use time, as well as laws concerning copyright and libel.

Unions/Associations

The major professional associations are the Radio-Television News Directors Association, National Academy of Television Arts and Sciences, and Academy of Television Arts and Sciences. Both women and men may join the Association for Women in Communications. Since news directors are managers, they generally do not belong to unions.

NEWS LIBRARIAN

CAREER PROFILE

Duties: Catalog and maintain a library of reference materials and an archive of videotape; provide background information and previously shot videotape for news segments; license archival material for sale to viewers who request a taped copy of a story or to production companies who need footage for films, documentaries, or other media productions

Alternate Title(s): News Information Resource Manager; News Library Director; Information Manager

Salary Range: $24,000 to $60,000

Employment Prospects: Fair

Advancement Prospects: Fair

Prerequisites:

    Education—A master's degree in library science is necessary for top positions

    Experience—Familiarity with television and video helpful; computer-aided research experience another plus

    Special Skills—Ability to work quickly on deadline; good organizational skills; knowledge of television news production needs and news journalism; good oral and written communication skills

CAREER LADDER

```
┌─────────────────────────────┐
│   News Library Manager      │
└─────────────────────────────┘

┌─────────────────────────────┐
│      News Librarian         │
└─────────────────────────────┘

┌─────────────────────────────┐
│  Library Clerk; Researcher  │
└─────────────────────────────┘
```

Position Description

A good library with professionally cataloged videotape is a vital component of larger television news operations. Although some television libraries rely on staffers with backgrounds in video, larger libraries now hire professional librarians with degrees in library science, and train them in television.

Television news librarians function as broadcast journalists, part of a production team that includes writers, editors, technicians, producers, graphic artists, and reporters.

They must ensure that every news video cataloged includes the necessary journalistic elements of who, what, where, and when. Much of the video included in the library contains "raw" or unedited footage, which is more valuable than polished, edited footage for future production and historical purposes.

News librarians also provide background information for news segments, researching the lives of key figures in a news event and happenings leading up to the story. Often the reference librarians have two hours or more to answer questions, but sometimes they are left with just a minute or two.

Computer databases are used for research, as are books, newspapers, magazines, and clipping files.

The library also coordinates sales of videotape, a money-maker for news organizations. The tapes are sought by people who want copies of a specific news segment and those seeking tape of a historic nature for documentaries, films, and other media productions.

The library staff must decide which tape to save and document and which to discard. Videotape not properly documented can be lost to history.

Salaries

Salaries can range from $24,000 to $60,000. Pay at network news stations can be higher.

Job Prospects

Job prospects can be good for those with the right combination of education and skills. News librarians need both a knowledge of library management techniques and a good understanding of television journalism. Libraries provide a range of job opportunities, starting with tape sales and library assistant jobs that may not require much training or experience, to reference librarian jobs and, at the top, the library manager and director positions. Smaller television stations may not hire any professional library staff.

Employment prospects for news librarians are better in newspapers than in television.

While news libraries employ relatively small numbers of people, the need for information and the importance of good library systems to news organizations is likely to grow. Because libraries can also sell videotape at a profit, staff will be needed to provide this service as well.

Advancement Prospects

Advancement can be slow as those in the limited number of high-level jobs hang on to them for some time. With the proper education, employees who start in entry-level jobs can hope to advance, move to other types of television jobs, or move to other types of special libraries.

Education

A master's degree in library science is increasingly required for higher-level library jobs. In the past, experience with video might have been good enough. Smaller stations also might not require professional library training.

Experience/Skills

Computer research skills, good organizational skills, and knowledge of the basics of journalism are needed for this position in addition to training in basic information storage and retrieval.

Unions/Associations

The Special Libraries Association has a division for news libraries. News librarians may also belong to the National Academy of Television Arts and Sciences.

COMMUNITY-AFFAIRS DIRECTOR

CAREER PROFILE

Duties: Write and produce public-service announcements and programs; meet with community groups

Alternate Title(s): Community-Relations Director; Public-Service Director

Salary Range: $19,000 to $69,000+

Employment Prospects: Poor

Advancement Prospects: Fair

Prerequisites:
   Education—Undergraduate degree in social sciences, liberal arts, or communications
   Experience—Background in nonprofit or service organizations
   Special Skills—Good writing ability; interpersonal skills

CAREER LADDER

```
┌─────────────────────────────────┐
│   Program Director; Producer     │
└─────────────────────────────────┘

┌─────────────────────────────────┐
│   Community-Affairs Director     │
└─────────────────────────────────┘

┌─────────────────────────────────┐
│  Nonprofit-Organization Director │
└─────────────────────────────────┘
```

Position Description

The Federal Communications Commission (FCC) requires all licensed commercial and public television stations to devote a certain amount of air time to community affairs and public-service announcements (PSAs). At many stations, the responsibility for managing and coordinating these operations is given to community-affairs directors.

Community-affairs directors plan—and in many cases write and produce—public-affairs programs on local news and issues. These may include talk and panel shows or documentaries. Sometimes the community-affairs directors work on-air as hosts, moderators, or narrators of programs. In addition, they develop, prepare, and supervise the production of public-service announcements—short spots that feature upcoming community events or highlight the services of particular groups. The station's public-service activities and feedback from the community are documented for the FCC.

Community-affairs directors spend much of their time meeting with local nonprofit and service groups to discuss proposals and concerns, which they then evaluate for air time. They also represent the station at group meetings, sometimes as featured speakers. They may also plan special public-service events sponsored by their stations.

Community-affairs directors generally work regular business hours, though evening and weekend work is often required for organization meetings. They report either to program directors or general managers.

In addition, community-affairs directors may:

- perform publicity and promotion duties;
- conduct station tours for the public;
- coordinate speaking engagements for other station personnel.

Salaries

Community-affairs directors earn moderate salaries, averaging about $39,856 in 1997, according to the National Association of Broadcasters. Small stations pay considerably less, as low as $19,000, while large stations pay up to $60,000 or more.

Employment Prospects

Job opportunities are poor, due to limited job openings in commercial television and budget cutbacks in public television. Opportunities may be further limited by locale. Stations frequently select candidates who already are familiar with local community groups and concerns. Many small stations do not have designated positions for community affairs.

Advancement Prospects

Prospects are fair for advancement into programming or producing; these jobs, however, require additional skills. Community-affairs directors may also advance by moving to positions in other fields, such as nonprofit organizations or the federal government.

Education

A broad education in liberal arts or social sciences is ideal for service work. The minimum requirement is an undergraduate degree. Other areas of emphasis include urban affairs, government, public relations, and communications.

Experience/Skills

Most community-affairs directors enter television with at least two years of experience in a nonprofit organization, as director or as manager of public information. They are familiar with local businesses and government units. They understand local social issues and concerns.

Community-affairs directors are personable and sensitive in their relationships with the community. They also must be good writers and speakers, and understand television production.

Unions/Associations

Community-affairs directors may belong to a variety of associations, depending on their communities and major interests. They may also belong to the Public Relations Society of America, Inc.; Association for Women in Communications; National Academy of Television Arts and Sciences; or Academy of Television Arts and Sciences.

RADIO

REPORTER

CAREER PROFILE

Duties: News gathering, rewriting, and editing; announcing

Alternate Title(s): Newscaster

Salary Range: Under $16,000 to $40,000+

Employment Prospects: Fair to good

Advancement Prospects: Good

Prerequisites:
    Education—High school diploma sufficient for some entry-level jobs; undergraduate degree in communications, broadcasting, or liberal arts necessary for most positions
    Experience—None to one or more years
    Special Skills—Sound news judgment; concise writing; good speaking ability; tape editing skills

CAREER LADDER

```
┌─────────────────────────────────┐
│  News Director; Air Personality; │
│     Announcer; Anchor            │
└─────────────────────────────────┘

┌─────────────────────────────────┐
│          Reporter                │
└─────────────────────────────────┘

┌─────────────────────────────────┐
│  Continuity Writer; College;     │
│       High School                │
└─────────────────────────────────┘
```

Position Description

Radio reporters generally have two primary responsibilities: to collect and prepare news stories for broadcast, and to read their copy on the air. At large stations, these responsibilities may be divided into two jobs held by different persons—one who collects, writes, and edits; and one who announces.

Reporters do most of their work in the studio, where they monitor incoming wire-service copy and other news sources. They select stories for the newscasts, and they rewrite and edit the copy to fit time limitations and the interests of their audiences. Some reporters may do their own news gathering, by taping interviews over the phone or in person. Some may actually be sent out of the studio to cover disasters or major news events. Covering stories such as wars, political uprisings, and natural disasters is often dangerous work, but some reporters find it exciting. The tapes, called "actualities," are edited for quotes to be aired. It's not uncommon to have to rewrite copy just before airtime.

Most radio stations air news breaks on the hour, giving shorter, periodic updates as well, especially for major, breaking stories. Many AM radio stations are all news/talk, a format that has gained considerable popularity in recent years. The news/talk format allows longer and more in-depth stories, providing more opportunities for feature stories and personality interviews as well.

Reporters work under the direction of a news director who assigns coverage and responsibilities. Working hours can range anywhere around the clock, seven days a week; most beginners usually draw evening, night, and weekend shifts. Overtime is often required.

Most radio stations have small facilities and staffs. At smaller stations, reporters are more likely to either work part-time or share other duties, such as ad copywriting or programming.

In addition, reporters may prepare and read news analyses or editorials, and research stories for major air personalities.

Salaries

A survey by the Radio-Television News Directors Association found that radio salaries rose 3.2 percent between 1997 and 1998. Between 1995 and 1998, median salaries for radio increased from $19,000 to $24,000, a gain of 26.3 percent. In 1998 the salary range was from $16,000 to $38,000. A December 1997 survey by *Advertising Age* found that the employee's level and quality of education, and previous industry experience, such as an internship, influenced starting position and salary considerably.

The larger the radio station's market, the higher the reporters' median pay. According to a survey by the National Association of Broadcasters, annual average salaries of radio reporters was $18,324 more at the largest stations than at the smallest ones in 1996.

Salaries were best in the East and worst in the South. Radio salaries also ran a distant third when compared to television and newspaper salaries.

Employment Prospects

Most of the nation's 4,500 AM radio stations and 4,000 FM stations have at least one full-time newsperson. Most have more than one, and medium to large stations have news staffs of 10 to 40 persons or more. Other broadcast news jobs are available at the major networks and news wire services. Beginners will find their best opportunities at small stations. Competition is keen, and employment is expected to decline through the year 2006.

Advancement Prospects

Turnover in radio jobs in general is high. In addition, according to industry sources, openings occur more frequently in news and clerical positions than in such other areas as programming and ad copywriting. A reporter can advance to news director, or build an audience to become an air personality or announcer.

Education

A high school diploma is the minimum requirement for many entry-level jobs. A college degree in broadcasting or mass communications is strongly recommended to be competitive for more prestigious, higher paying positions.

As a result of the Telecommunications Act of 1996, the Federal Communications Commission (FCC) no longer requires anyone who works for a broadcasting station to have a license. Only the station is required to be licensed.

Experience/Skills

Beginners who have had experience at school newspapers or radio or TV stations have significant advantages for acquiring reporter jobs. Most large radio stations, however, hire experienced newscasters from smaller stations rather than novices fresh from college. Continuity writing, which is writing advertising copy for broadcast, is excellent experience.

Reporters should have good news judgment and be able to work quickly under deadline pressure. They should be able to write "for the ear" and know how to handle studio taping and broadcasting equipment. Good speaking ability is essential—with clear enunciation and using correct grammar.

Unions/Associations

Many broadcast professionals are represented by unions, such as the American Federation of Television and Radio Artists; National Association of Broadcast Employees and Technicians; or Writers Guild of America. Other major professional associations include American Women in Radio and Television, Inc.; Radio-Television News Directors Association; National Association of Broadcasters; and Association for Women in Communications.

NEWS DIRECTOR

CAREER PROFILE

Duties: Supervise content of newscasts; report, write, edit, and deliver news as needed

Alternate Title(s): News Editor

Salary Range: $12,000 to $70,000+

Employment Prospects: Fair to good

Advancement Prospects: Fair

Prerequisites:
Education—Undergraduate degree in communications, English, history, or liberal arts
Experience—Several years in broadcast journalism
Special Skills—Decision-making; managerial ability; sound news judgment

CAREER LADDER

```
┌─────────────────────────────────────┐
│ Program Director; General Manager    │
└─────────────────────────────────────┘

┌─────────────────────────────────────┐
│          News Director               │
└─────────────────────────────────────┘

┌─────────────────────────────────────┐
│        Reporter; College             │
└─────────────────────────────────────┘
```

Position Description

Radio news directors are in charge of their station's news operation. They supervise other newscasters or news writers, assign coverage of stories, and make decisions concerning the content of news broadcasts. They set news-gathering and writing policies. They are often called upon to make quick decisions on breaking news stories. Many news directors have production responsibilities as well, which include tape editing and overall supervision of a program.

At large stations, radio news directors may be in charge of staffs of 30 to 40 persons. Most stations have much smaller staffs; at some stations, the news director is the entire staff—reporter, editor, director, and newscaster all rolled into one.

News directors have hiring and firing responsibility. They report to general managers or station managers. Their responsibilities also include administrative tasks, correspondence, reports, and paperwork.

In addition, radio news directors may also act as working reporters—gathering, editing, and rewriting news stories. Occasionally, they deliver the news on the air.

Salaries

A survey by the Radio-Television News Directors Association found that radio news directors' salaries ranged from $12,000 to $70,000. The average was $26,000; the median was $25,000. Median salaries increased 19 percent from 1995 to 1998. The larger the radio station's market, the higher the news director's median pay.

Employment Prospects

Small and medium markets offer the best job prospects for persons seeking news-director positions. Turnover in radio is high, and news directors average one to two years in a particular job. Competition is tougher for jobs at stations and networks that have large news staffs.

Advancement Prospects

The increasing importance and profitability of news operations in recent years has greatly enhanced opportunities for advancement for radio news directors. Most general managers of stations typically have come from the sales and programming operations, but more and more are coming from the news department. Ambitious news directors should become familiar with all station operations, including sales, programming, engineering, and production.

Education

An undergraduate degree in communications, liberal arts, or other fields is preferred. Some broadcast journalists have graduate degrees in communications.

Experience/Skills

Most radio news directors have had several years' experience as radio newscasters or news writers; some start their careers as directors at very small stations that have one-person news operations. In addition to newswriting, some also have experience in production.

Skills for this job include the ability to supervise others, make decisions and assignments, and have good news judg-ment. News directors should be good writers and editors, with good speaking skills. A familiarity with other station operations is advantageous.

Unions/Associations

Many broadcast professionals are represented by such unions as the American Federation of Television and Radio Artists; National Association of Broadcast Employees and Technicians; or Writers Guild of America. Other major professional associations include American Women in Radio and Television, Inc.; Radio-Television News Directors Association; National Association of Broadcasters; and Association for Women in Communications.

BOOK PUBLISHING

ADMINISTRATIVE ASSISTANT

CAREER PROFILE

Duties: Assist publicity, promotion, production, or advertising managers with routine tasks and minor writing activities

Alternate Title(s): Executive Assistant; Publicity Assistant; Promotion Assistant; Advertising Assistant; Marketing Assistant; Production Assistant

Salary Range: $15,000 to $30,000

Employment Prospects: Fair

Advancement Prospects: Fair

Prerequisites:

Education—Undergraduate degree in communications, liberal arts, advertising, or marketing

Experience—Background in publishing, media, advertising, or public relations helpful

Special Skills—Writing; organization; clerical skills

CAREER LADDER

```
┌─────────────────────────────────────┐
│  Publicity Specialist; Promotion     │
│  Specialist; Advertising Specialist; │
│  Marketing Specialist                │
└─────────────────────────────────────┘

┌─────────────────────────────────────┐
│      Administrative Assistant        │
└─────────────────────────────────────┘

┌─────────────────────────────────────┐
│              College                 │
└─────────────────────────────────────┘
```

Position Description

Administrative assistant is an entry-level position found in almost all publishing departments. Many of the duties usually are low-level, routine clerical and secretarial tasks, although they can involve higher responsibilities. The job does provide one with an excellent background and training in how books are produced, publicized, advertised, and marketed. With experience, one's responsibilities increase; this can lead to more interesting work and, in some cases, direct contact with prominent authors.

Administrative assistants may be assigned to one department and limited to tasks in a particular function, such as production, publicity, advertising, or promotion. Some assistants work in the sales and marketing department. Other assistants may be shared by several departments and have broader, more versatile responsibilities.

Routine tasks common to all departments include word processing on a computer, filing, answering the telephone, placing calls, running errands, and performing general office duties.

Administrative assistants also maintain mailing lists, updating them as necessary; handle correspondence, including routing letters and writing letters for their supervisors to sign; stuff envelopes, press kits and sales kits; and prepare materials for meetings and conferences.

They also maintain records, such as sales figures, price changes, as well as ad and publicity campaign results. They distribute review copies and press releases.

Writing duties may include departmental reports; material for press kits; promotional or advertising copy; and copy for sales catalogs, which describes books, gives the track records and expertise of authors, and the commitment the publisher expects to make for advertising, publicity, and promotion.

In many cases, administrative assistants act as liaisons between departments, helping coordinate various activities that support the marketing of books. Administrative assistants often work long hours and have many deadline pressures. They must be flexible and able to accommodate last-minute changes. Travel is seldom required.

In addition, administrative assistants may:

• help organize sales conferences, publicity, and promotional events;

- work with film and television contacts concerning movie and TV tie-ins;
- assist in the booking of author tours and speaking engagements.

Salaries

Administrative assistant salaries vary from department to department, and also depend on the size of the publishing house and the geographic location. Average salaries are in the $24,000 to $26,000 range in the editorial and art departments, while advertising and publicity departments pay an average of about $26,000. Salaries can start as low as $15,000, even in advertising/publicity.

Employment Prospects

Job candidates have a fair chance of finding entry-level assistant positions. In some publishing houses, the job may be limited to publicity functions, while in others it may cover other departments as well, such as advertising and promotion. The Bureau of Labor Statistics predicts that employment of administrative assistants outside the legal and medical fields will decline through the year 2006 because of office automation.

Advancement Prospects

Administrative assistants have few opportunities to advance in publicity, due to the limited number of managerial positions in the industry. Some may find more opportunities in the sales promotion and advertising departments in publishing. Advancement may also be achieved with lateral moves to other fields, such as magazines, news media, or corporations. Others may move from administrative assistant to editorial assistant, and from there to various editorial jobs, but this is not easy.

Education

An undergraduate degree in communications, especially journalism or liberal arts, provides a good background for publicity work. Publishing courses are not as helpful as media courses. Familiarity with advertising and public relations is advantageous.

Experience/Skills

Most administrative-assistant jobs are entry-level positions and require no experience. Candidates who've had college internships, summer jobs, or experience on school publications have significant competitive advantages. Some assistant jobs—particularly at major publishers—are more advanced, carrying greater responsibilities. One or two years' experience at another publisher is often required for such positions.

Administrative assistants should be able to juggle many projects at the same time, paying close attention to detail and follow-through. They should have good written and oral communications skills, and be self-motivated and disciplined.

Unions/Associations

Some administrative assistants belong to the International Association of Administrative Professionals. Others may belong to the Publishers' Ad Club; Public Relations Society of America, Inc.; Publishers' Publicity Association, Inc.; American Publicists Guild; and Association for Women in Communications. Local 2110 of the United Auto Workers represents some employees at major publishers.

EDITORIAL ASSISTANT

CAREER PROFILE

Duties: Clerical, secretarial, and minor editorial tasks

Alternate Title(s): Editorial Secretary; Editorial Trainee

Salary Range: $20,500 to $25,000

Employment Prospects: Fair

Advancement Prospects: Good

Prerequisites:
  Education—Undergraduate degree in liberal arts, English, history, or communications
  Experience—Secretarial training helpful
  Special Skills—Organizational ability; office and computer skills; knowledge of grammar

CAREER LADDER

```
┌─────────────────────────────┐
│      Assistant Editor       │
└─────────────────────────────┘

┌─────────────────────────────┐
│     Editorial Assistant     │
└─────────────────────────────┘

┌─────────────────────────────┐
│     College; Secretary      │
└─────────────────────────────┘
```

Position Description

Editorial assistant is the entry-level editorial job in a publishing house. It is largely a training position for more advanced editorial posts. Most of the duties revolve around office tasks, such as receptionist duties, filing, word processing, and running errands. Editorial assistants usually work for one or more editors, such as an editorial director and assistant or associate editors, depending on the size of the publishing house.

Publishing houses receive thousands of manuscripts every year. Most are unsolicited and relegated to what is called the "slush pile." In some major publishing houses, the slush pile can fill an entire storage room. Editorial assistants usually are responsible for the initial handling of all incoming manuscripts, directing some to the appropriate editors and assigning the rest to the slush pile.

Reading the slush to search for publishable manuscripts is a job often shared by editorial assistants as well as lower-level editors. In some houses, editorial assistants may not be allowed to read the slush, while in others they may have the entire responsibility for it. First readings of most manuscripts are quick and partial, due to limited time. Rejected manuscripts are returned, usually with form letters. For manuscripts that look promising, editorial assistants write summary reports on the plots, including their opinions and recommendations. They then pass the manuscripts and reports to the appropriate higher editors for evaluation.

Editorial assistants also act as coordinators and liaisons for a variety of functions. For example, they work with copy editors and proofreaders, who may either be on staff or be hired freelancers. They monitor production schedules for editors—researching and relaying information on cost estimates for design work and typesetting, as well as giving the status of production work for various manuscripts. They may also act as liaisons with authors, handling phone calls and correspondence, and typing book contracts.

In addition, editorial assistants may have responsibility for copyright applications and may route requisitions for author advances, editorial expenses, freelancer invoices, and other bills. They may also do easy editorial tasks like checking corrections on second-pass proofs.

Salaries

In 1998, the average salary for editorial assistants was $23,000. Those working for a company with revenues of less than $10 million averaged $20,500; those working for companies with revenues of more than $100 million averaged $25,000.

Employment Prospects

Publishing is a glamour industry and attracts many job applicants. Competition is fierce, however, because jobs are limited, partly because of the many recent mergers and acquisitions in book publishing. Most jobs are in the New York City area, the center of publishing.

Advancement Prospects

Job turnover in publishing is high, especially at the lower editorial levels. Editorial assistants have good chances of moving up to assistant or associate editors.

Education

Persons interested in careers as book editors should have well-rounded undergraduate educations in liberal arts, English, history, or communications, including publishing courses. Some universities have specialized publishing curricula. A number of summer institutes offer intensive publishing programs. For work in educational publishing, a degree in education is desirable but not necessary.

Experience/Skills

Any kind of editing experience, such as working on school publications or taking summer jobs on local magazines or newspapers, is helpful. Working in a bookstore also provides excellent experience and understanding of the marketing end of publishing, as well as a sense of what type of books sell well.

Editorial assistants should have good office skills, and be well organized, and be able to monitor many projects at once. They should possess a thorough understanding of grammar and use of the English language.

Unions/Associations

Local 2110 of the United Auto Workers represents editorial assistants at some of the large book publishers. Editorial assistants may also belong to the Association for Women in Communications and a variety of groups related to writing or book publishing.

COPY EDITOR

CAREER PROFILE

Duties: Edit manuscripts for grammar, style, and consistency; proofread

Alternate Title(s): None

Salary Range: $23,000 to $48,000+

Employment Prospects: Fair

Advancement Prospects: Fair

Prerequisites:
   Education—Undergraduate degree in liberal arts or communications preferred
   Experience—Background as editorial or production assistant preferred
   Special Skills—Thorough knowledge of grammar and style; attention to detail; production knowledge

CAREER LADDER

```
┌─────────────────────────────────────┐
│  Production Editor; Managing Editor  │
└─────────────────────────────────────┘

┌─────────────────────────────────────┐
│             Copy Editor             │
└─────────────────────────────────────┘

┌─────────────────────────────────────┐
│   Editorial Assistant; Production   │
│        Assistant; College           │
└─────────────────────────────────────┘
```

Position Description

Once book manuscripts have been accepted, edited, and revised to the satisfaction of authors and editors, they are turned over to copy editors for final editing and checking. This vital part of the editing process protects both authors and publishers by ensuring the accuracy and quality of the final end product.

Much of the copy editors' work is meticulous and detail-oriented. They carefully go over each manuscript (including indexes, glossaries, and bibliographies), correcting spelling, punctuation, and other points of grammatical style. Each publishing house has its own internal style for such things as abbreviations, titles, capitalizations, use of italics, etc., and copy editors must make certain all manuscripts conform to that style.

Copy editors may also check for inconsistencies in fact and logic, a time-consuming process that is not always possible at many publishing houses. Copy editors consult reference sources and may even contact authors to verify information in question. They may also consult with other editors over questions about the manuscript.

Copy editors do not change the substance of a manuscript or alter an author's style or "voice." Revisions or rewrites are the prerogative of the authors and their "line" editors—assistant, associate, or senior editors.

While copy editors must be thorough in their editing, they also must adhere to production schedules, delivering manuscripts on time for typesetting. In other stages of production, copy editors usually proofread typeset page proofs for typographical errors and check to see that typesetting instructions have been followed. They also proofread mechanicals and check any layouts, such as artwork and captions.

Copy editors work under the direction of a production editor or managing editor, and may themselves supervise production assistants and freelance copy editors and proofreaders. They are a liaison between editorial and production functions. Their work can be tedious, requiring patience and great attention to detail. Errors should be caught early in the production process to avoid delays and costly corrections.

Most publishers now edit manuscripts on computer terminals and transmit them electronically from one department to another, and outside—to author and typesetter—as well. Copy editors must understand how to use computer technology.

Salaries

The average salary for copy editors in 1999 was about $40,000, with those working at smaller publishers making less and men making considerably more than women. (In many smaller publishing houses, higher-level employees are also taking on copyediting duties.)

Those working for companies with higher revenues made more than those working for companies with lower revenues.

Employment Prospects

Most publishers employ copy editors. Many copy editors start as production assistants. The greatest job opportunities are in New York City, the center of the publishing industry, although the rise of small and moderate-sized publishers throughout the country offers prospects elsewhere, albeit usually at lower pay.

During the 1990s, more and more book publishers have downsized, partially because of mergers and acquisitions. Some jobs that used to be done in-house are now being done by freelancers to save overhead and benefits costs. Many copy editors now work as freelancers.

Advancement Prospects

The most likely advancement opportunities for copy editors are on the production side of publishing—to production or managing editors. Computer technology is creating new growth in production-oriented jobs, and copy editors who have experience in using computer systems will have an advantage for advancement. It is possible, but difficult, to switch to the editorial side and become an assistant editor.

Education

Copy editors should have a minimum of three years of college, though preference is given to those who have earned undergraduate degrees. Areas of study include liberal arts, communications, and publishing. Additional training in editing and production is valuable.

Experience/Skills

A production background is preferred for copyediting positions. Work as a production assistant, or any editing and production work done in college, is helpful for getting a job.

Copy editors must be familiar with production stages and with typesetting symbols and terminology. They should be excellent spellers and know rules of grammar and style. Also, they should have a high tolerance for detail work. Copy editors who can work with computer systems will be more in demand as publishers increasingly computerize their operations.

Unions/Associations

Industry associations include the Women's National Book Association and Association for Women in Communications. Copy editors who freelance on the side may belong to the Editorial Freelancers Association. Some at large publishing houses may be represented by a union, Local 2110 of the United Auto Workers. They may also belong to a variety of groups related to writing and book publishing.

ASSISTANT EDITOR

CAREER PROFILE

Duties: Screen, edit, and occasionally acquire manuscripts; monitor production

Alternate Title(s): Editorial Assistant

Salary Range: $18,000 to $25,000+

Employment Prospects: Fair

Advancement Prospects: Good

Prerequisites:
    Education—Undergraduate degree in liberal arts, English, history, or communications; publishing courses
    Experience—Work as editorial assistant or trainee
    Special Skills—Editing; organization

CAREER LADDER

```
┌─────────────────────────────────────┐
│          Associate Editor           │
└─────────────────────────────────────┘

┌─────────────────────────────────────┐
│          Assistant Editor           │
└─────────────────────────────────────┘

┌─────────────────────────────────────┐
│   Editorial Assistant; Editorial    │
│        Trainee; College             │
└─────────────────────────────────────┘
```

Position Description

The assistant editor position usually is one step above editorial assistant, who is essentially a clerk and secretary. In large publishing houses with big and highly structured staffs, assistant editor may be the equivalent of editorial assistant.

Most assistant editors have learned the editorial process, know how to screen manuscripts, and can edit them according to the in-house style of the publisher. They assume more responsibilities than editorial assistants.

Typical duties include reading queries and proposals submitted by authors through agents, and screening unsolicited manuscripts for publishable material. Assistant editors are responsible for helping publish a specified number of books a month or year; this means shepherding the product from manuscript to finished book. The work involves editing and coordinating proofreading and production. Much of the work is routine. Editing is done under the supervision of a higher-level editor. Assistant editors may or may not have direct contact with authors concerning revisions and rewrites. If a staff is small, job duties may be broad enough to include writing jacket copy, as well as proposing publicity and promotion ideas.

Assistant editors report to associate editors, senior editors, managing editors, or editorial directors, depending on the size of the house. They help plan deadlines and production schedules, and they may delegate work to editorial assistants.

In many cases, assistant editors recommend manuscripts for acquisition, and they may even make the initial offer to the author. Actual contract negotiation usually is done by more experienced editors. Assistant editors generally do not work on the most important books.

In addition, assistant editors may write reports and make presentations to recommend manuscripts for purchase, and attend trade and professional meetings.

Salaries

Salaries for assistant editors range from $18,000 to $25,000 and up, depending on their experience, responsibilities, and employer. In general, the higher the revenues of the employer, the higher the pay.

Employment Prospects

Job applicants have a fair chance of getting low-level editing jobs. The best opportunities are at small publishing houses. Employment agencies which specialize in publishing can be helpful in a job search. Employment prospects in educational publishing are decreasing due to school budget cutbacks.

Advancement Prospects

Assistant editors have a good chance of being promoted in-house, due to the high turnover typical of the publishing industry.

Education

An undergraduate degree in liberal arts, history, English, or communications is preferred, though virtually any degree is acceptable. Job candidates benefit from courses in book publishing.

Experience/Skills

Prior experience as an editorial assistant, trainee, editor, or writer in another field is necessary for many assistant-editor jobs. Some positions, however, are entry-level for persons right out of college.

Assistant editors should have good editorial and grammatical skills, and understand the entire editorial process. They should have a good sense of the book marketplace and know what has sales potential. Oral presentation skills are advantageous for editorial and sales meetings.

Unions/Associations

Major professional associations include the Women's National Book Association, Inc., and the Association for Women in Communications. Editorial employees at some large publishers are members of Local 2110 of the United Auto Workers. They may also belong to a variety of groups related to writing and book publishing.

ASSOCIATE EDITOR

CAREER PROFILE

Duties: Screen, edit, and rewrite manuscripts; manage projects; recommend acquisitions

Alternate Title(s): Editor; Project Editor

Salary Range: $20,000 to $55,000+

Employment Prospects: Fair

Advancement Prospects: Poor

Prerequisites:
   Education—Undergraduate degree in communications, liberal arts, English, or history
   Experience—One to two years in editorial work
   Special Skills—Good editing and organization; supervisory ability; business knowledge; presentation skills

CAREER LADDER

```
┌─────────────────────────────────────┐
│              Editor                  │
└─────────────────────────────────────┘

┌─────────────────────────────────────┐
│          Associate Editor            │
└─────────────────────────────────────┘

┌─────────────────────────────────────┐
│  Assistant Editor; Editorial Assistant │
└─────────────────────────────────────┘
```

Position Description

Associate editors may delegate much of the routine work in a publishing house to subordinates, concentrating more on the screening, acquisition, and editing of manuscripts. Their responsibilities are likely to include screening the slush pile of unsolicited manuscripts and evaluating manuscripts that have passed a first screening by a lower level editor or assistant. Associate editors are not likely to do the actual acquiring and contract negotiating, but they do make acquisition recommendations to the editorial board. They must have a clear sense of the needs of the publisher as well as the conditions in the book marketplace. If a publisher is seeking an author to write a book, they may recommend or search for candidates.

Associate editors usually work under the direction of senior editors or editorial directors. They may help plan long-range projects for series of books; this involves scheduling deadlines for acquisitions, editing, production, and promotion, and working within a budget.

They also edit manuscripts and work directly with authors concerning revisions and rewrites (subject to the approval of a superior editor). This sometimes involves a great deal of diplomacy. They may oversee the work done by copy editors and proofreaders.

Associate editors attend regular in-house editorial meetings, during which potential books are discussed and decisions made. They may be asked to make informal or formal presentations explaining why particular manuscripts should be purchased. They make periodical progress reports.

On large staffs, associate editors are likely to have one or more subordinates who help with routine work and correspondence.

In addition, associate editors may maintain contact with literary agents, supervise special editorial projects, write jacket copy, and help plan publicity and promotion.

Salaries

Salaries for associate editors are traditionally modest, for jobs that often involve long hours. The size and revenues of the publisher are also important. A survey of 1998 salaries conducted by *Publishers Weekly* found that associate editors earned an average of $28,613 in companies with revenues from $1 million to $9.9 million; $32,317 in companies with revenues from $10 million to $99.9 million, and $32,000 in companies with revenues of $100 million and up.

Employment Prospects

Turnover is high in publishing. Most low and middle positions, including associate editor, are filled from within. Though much smaller publishing "centers" exist in the areas around Chicago, Boston, San Francisco, Los Angeles, the Pacific Northwest, and Florida, most publishers are located in the New York City area.

Advancement Prospects

Competition is very keen for editorial positions above associate editor. At higher levels, many jobs are filled by outside candidates rather than those promoted within.

Education

Most associate editors have undergraduate degrees in communications, liberal arts, English, or history. Additional courses in publishing are desirable.

Experience/Skills

Most associate editors have had at least one or two years of experience in lower editorial positions; some have worked as editors of magazines and newspapers. Associate editors should have strong editing skills and a good business sense of a book's potential commercial appeal. They should be able to work within budgets and supervise others. Oral presentation skills and the ability to be persuasive are invaluable.

Unions/Associations

Major professional associations include the Association for Women in Communications; Women's National Book Association, Inc.; and authors' groups. Local 2110 of the United Auto Workers represents employees of some large publishers.

EDITOR

Duties: Develop ideas for books, recommend books for acquisition, negotiate deals, work with authors, supervise staff

Alternate Title(s): Developmental Editor

Salary Range: $30,000 to $85,000+

Employment Prospects: Poor to Fair

Advancement Prospects: Poor to Fair

Prerequisites:
    Education—Undergraduate degree in communications, publishing, English, liberal arts, humanities; special publishing courses advantageous
    Experience—Work as editorial assistant, assistant editor or associate editor
    Special Skills—Creativity; organization; knowledge of all phases of publishing process; ability to work well with others and to work under pressure

```
┌─────────────────────────────┐
│        Senior Editor        │
└─────────────────────────────┘

┌─────────────────────────────┐
│           Editor            │
└─────────────────────────────┘

┌─────────────────────────────┐
│      Associate Editor       │
└─────────────────────────────┘
```

Position Description

Editors perform many of the same duties as associate editors, but have more responsibility and work on more important books. Editors read manuscripts and proposals submitted by authors and agents, and make presentations to the editorial board to recommend acquisitions. When they receive the green light to proceed, editors negotiate the terms. Editors also generate book ideas, and then work with agents and authors to develop them into acceptable proposals.

Once a proposal or manuscript is acquired, editors shepherd it through the editing and production process. Editing responsibilities vary considerably according to publishing house. At a large house, an editor does a general edit and asks for revisions if they are necessary. Once the manuscript is acceptable, it is turned over to line and copy editors who read for consistency, grammar, and style. At a small house, the editor may do all of those functions.

The editor coordinates with art, production, marketing, and publicity departments to help meet their needs and deadlines, and contributes information and ideas that will help the success of the book.

Editors talk and meet with agents frequently to discuss ideas and potential book projects. They work closely with authors. They supervise other editors and delegate tasks, and report to a senior editor, editorial director, or executive editor. They attend staff meetings, and spend a certain amount of time reading the "slush," or unsolicited manuscripts and proposals. At a large house, an editor may be responsible for dozens of books a year, requiring constant juggling and attention to detail. Publishing is fraught with delays—especially from authors—and editors must work under pressure.

Salaries

According to a survey done by *Publishers Weekly,* editors at larger houses earned more than those at smaller ones in 1998. The average salary in companies with revenues from $1 million to $9.9 million was $32,750, while in houses with revenues of $100 million and higher, the average editor's salary was $83,333.

Employment Prospects

Major publishing houses, most of which are concentrated in Middle Atlantic and Northeastern United States, are expected to remain under financial pressure, thus limiting job opportunities. Many jobs have been lost due to mergers, acquisitions, and consolidations, and also to ill-conceived spending that has left some houses with piles of debt. The best opportunities may be in the lower end of the market, the small presses and moderately sized independent presses. Although the pay is lower, the opportunities may be greater.

Advancement Prospects

Promotion opportunities are limited for the same reasons.

Education

Most editors have an undergraduate degree in communications, publishing, liberal arts, English, or humanities. Many have taken additional courses in publishing and marketing.

Experience/Skills

The editor's job requires prior experience as an editorial assistant, assistant editor, or associate editor—or two of those positions, depending on the house and the nature of the editor's job.

Editors must be able to work well with a wide variety of people and temperaments. They must be able to supervise, delegate, and work under pressure. They are creative and intuitive when it comes to anticipating trends and interests in the marketplace. They are well organized and able to work with budgets and deadlines.

Unions/Associations

Editors may belong to the Women's National Book Association, the Association for Women in Communications, Inc., or other groups related to writing or book publishing. Some may belong to a labor union, such as Local 2110 of the United Auto Workers.

SENIOR EDITOR

CAREER PROFILE

Duties: Acquire and develop major books and authors; supervise other editors; plan and execute editorial policies

Alternate Title(s): Acquisitions Editor; Project Editor

Salary Range: $40,000 to $90,000+

Employment Prospects: Poor

Advancement Prospects: Poor

Prerequisites:

Education—Undergraduate degree in liberal arts, communications, English, or history
Experience—Three to five years or more in editing
Special Skills—Negotiation and supervisory ability; business and decision-making skills

CAREER LADDER

Editorial Director; Executive Editor

Senior Editor

Associate Editor

Position Description

Senior editors play influential roles in the editorial policies, directions, and products of publishing houses. They are heavily involved in the marketing and business aspects of publishing, and they usually handle the most prestigious books.

Senior editors work under the direction of editorial directors or publishers. They help develop comprehensive, long-range publishing plans, which include acquisition and publishing schedules, budgetary analyses, and sales projections. They have overall responsibility for the completion of book projects, including supervision of editing done by other editors, production work, adherence to schedules and deadlines, and use of freelance and consultant help.

Most senior editors are also responsible for acquisitions, though some large houses may delegate this task to specialized acquisitions editors. Acquisition involves deciding which manuscripts should be purchased, then negotiating the contracts with authors and agents. Each publisher has a standard contract, and senior editors must know the limits of negotiable points. Senior editors often work closely with in-house legal staff and subsidiary-rights editors in contract negotiations. The actual sale of a book's subsidiary rights to foreign publishers, magazines, or paperback publishers may be handled by a senior editor.

Senior editors also work with marketing and publicity/promotion staff to persuade them which titles deserve the most sales, advertising, and publicity support. They make many presentations, some informal at weekly editorial and sales meetings, and others formal, at major sales conferences.

In addition, senior editors may accompany sales representatives on sales calls, and represent their publisher at major industry conventions.

Salaries

The average salary for senior editors ranged from $44,330 to $91,494 in 1998, according to a survey done by *Publishers Weekly*. Those at larger companies earned more than those at smaller ones.

Employment Prospects

Senior-editor positions are highly competitive and require years of experience in the publishing industry. It is often necessary to change employers in order to get a job at this level.

Advancement Prospects

A tight job market in publishing makes advancement to editorial director or executive editor very difficult. There is much less turnover at this level than at lower editorial levels. Advancement usually is made by changing employers.

Education

Senior editors are expected to have undergraduate degrees, most preferably in liberal arts, English, history, or communications. Education ideally should include publishing courses. Additional study at a publishing summer institute is advantageous.

Experience/Skills

Three to five years' experience in editing is required for most senior-editor posts; large publishers may require more experience. A background at one or more publishers is advantageous. Most publishers do not fill senior editor positions from within but instead hire from the outside.

Senior editors should understand publishing contracts and be able to negotiate them. They should have a good grasp of the business and financial side of publishing, be able to develop budget plans, and know how to supervise other employees.

Unions/Associations

The Association for Women in Communications and Women's National Book Association are among the principal professional groups for book editors. In addition, senior editors may belong to authors' organizations, or, at some major publishers, to Local 2110 of the United Auto Workers.

COPYWRITER

CAREER PROFILE	CAREER LADDER

Duties: Write copy for advertising, promotion, and direct-mail campaigns; create flap copy and press releases

Alternate Title(s): None

Salary Range: $18,000 to $40,000

Employment Prospects: Fair

Advancement Prospects: Fair

Prerequisites:
　　Education—Undergraduate degree in communications, advertising, or liberal arts
　　Experience—Background in advertising or marketing
　　Special Skills—Sales orientation; graphic-arts knowledge

```
┌─────────────────────────────────┐
│   Promotion Manager; Advertising │
│     Manager; Sales Manager       │
└─────────────────────────────────┘

┌─────────────────────────────────┐
│            Copywriter            │
└─────────────────────────────────┘

┌─────────────────────────────────┐
│     Administrative Assistant     │
└─────────────────────────────────┘
```

Position Description

Copywriters create many of the materials that help sell books, not only to the public but to booksellers, wholesalers, and the media as well. They usually work under the direction of managers of advertising, sales, or promotion. They write copy for print ads and book catalogs, and scripts for radio commercials. Television ads are uncommon for books but may be required for special, major campaigns or for lines of books. Some romance publishers, for example, advertise their lines in TV commercials. Other sales-oriented material includes literature for the sales force (such as information on discounts to booksellers, sales records of authors' previous books, special displays available, and advertising and publicity plans) plus posters, flyers, and displays for use in bookstores.

In some highly structured publishing houses, copywriters also handle certain editorial copy tasks that might otherwise be done by junior editors. These include creating press releases for the media and book reviewers, material for press kits, and jacket copy. Jacket copy consists of a synopsis of a book's plot, and it is intended to entice customers into a purchase. Sometimes information on the author and his or her previous books is included as well.

Copywriters coordinate their work with others, such as advertising and promotion representatives as well as editors.

They may do their own research for projects or may delegate the work to assistants. They often work with graphic artists in designing and laying out ads, brochures, and catalogs. They must be able to work with space limitations. For example, jacket copy for paperback books must fit the space allowed by the illustration, type, and universal price code. Some copywriters may specialize in certain areas, such as direct mail.

Salaries

Most copywriters earn in the low to mid-twenties, though salaries can range from $18,000 to $40,000, depending on experience, responsibilities, and employer. On the average, copywriting jobs at publishing houses do not pay as well as those at ad agencies or businesses.

Employment Prospects

Copywriting jobs aren't as glamorous as editorial jobs in publishing. However, they may be easier to get, due to the increasing importance of effective book marketing.

Advancement Prospects

Skilled copywriters can advance to managerial positions in sales, advertising, or promotion. Some publishers have direct-mail specialists as well. These business-oriented jobs also lead to higher executive positions overall in publishing houses.

Education

An undergraduate degree in communications or advertising is preferred for copywriting jobs. A degree in liberal arts also is acceptable.

Experience/Skills

A background in advertising or sales-promotion work is usually required for this type of job. Some copywriters come from jobs in advertising agencies, while others start as entry-level assistants.

Copywriters should be able to write crisp, persuasive sales copy. They should also have some knowledge of graphic arts—layout and production.

Unions/Associations

Major professional organizations include the American Advertising Federation; the Direct Marketing Association, and Association for Women in Communications. Employees of some major publishers belong to Local 2110 of the United Auto Workers.

PUBLICITY MANAGER

Duties: Generate publicity for books and authors; arrange for book reviews and author tours

Alternate Title(s): Publicist

Salary Range: $20,000 to $88,000

Employment Prospects: Fair

Advancement Prospects: Poor

Prerequisites:
   Education—Undergraduate degree in communications, English, or liberal arts
   Experience—Background as publicity assistant or journalist essential
   Special Skills—Good writing and organizational skills; salesmanship

```
┌─────────────────────────────┐
│    Director of Publicity    │
└─────────────────────────────┘

┌─────────────────────────────┐
│      Publicity Manager      │
└─────────────────────────────┘

┌─────────────────────────────┐
│     Publicity Assistant     │
└─────────────────────────────┘
```

Position Description

Publicity managers have highly visible jobs in publishing houses. They represent their publishing houses to the media, and they are responsible for generating favorable press coverage of books and authors.

Most books receive minimal publicity support, but a certain few are identified for receiving special effort. The amount of publicity can vary from a mailing of review copies with press releases to a full-blown campaign that includes an author tour, as well as advertising and sales promotion.

Planning for publicity begins long before a book is finished and ready to be delivered to the stores. Publicity managers coordinate their plans with editorial, advertising, sales, and promotion staffs. Budgets and deadlines are set for materials, mailings, travel, and other expenses.

For a major campaign, the publicity manager works with the author to develop press-kit material, such as author's biography and photograph, questions for interviewers to ask, press releases, and clips of early reviews or other notable news coverage an author may have received previously.

Review copies and press releases are mailed to book reviewers in advance of publication. Publicity managers are responsible for maintaining up-to-date lists and for seeing that books are sent to appropriate reviewers. A technical book, for example, would require a different mailing list than a novel.

In addition to reviews, publicity managers try to generate news or feature stories in the media. They send press releases and follow up with phone calls to arrange interviews for the authors. They also book speaking engagements and autograph signings at bookstores, libraries, and other places.

For author tours, publicity managers may do the bookings themselves or may hire freelance publicists to make all arrangements. Tasks include deciding tour cities; contacting the media for interviews; setting up schedules; and arranging for transportation, accommodations, and travel advances for authors' out-of-pocket expenses. Tours are complicated, time-consuming, and involve a great many last-minute changes.

Publicity managers may be in charge of their publishers' entire publicity operation, or they may report to directors of publicity. They are likely to supervise assistants who handle much of the routine writing, stuffing, and mailing jobs.

In addition, publicity managers may:

- be responsible for maintaining clipping files on all authors and books;
- maintain good relations with the media through regular contact;
- plan and direct company publicity functions, such as dinner and cocktail parties.

Salaries

Salaries for publicity managers averaged $69,200 to $69,225 in 1998, in houses with revenues above $10 million, according to a survey by *Publishers Weekly*. (There were not enough respondents to provide accurate data for smaller houses.)

Employment Prospects

The job market in this field is very tight, due to the competitive nature of such desirable jobs and the fact that publicity is one of the first areas to be cut back in bad economic times. Many openings at this level are not openly advertised. The best bet is to start as a publicity assistant and make industry contacts.

Advancement Prospects

Opportunities for promotion are limited in this field. At some publishing houses, publicity manager is the top position, supervised by a director or vice president of sales and/or advertising. In others, the next highest position is director of publicity. Advancement is usually achieved by changing employers rather than being promoted from within. Competition is strong.

Education

An undergraduate degree in communications or journalism is preferred for publicity jobs in publishing. Also acceptable are degrees in liberal arts and social science.

Experience/Skills

Three to five years of experience usually is required for publicity-manager positions, either as a publicity assistant or journalist for a newspaper or magazine. Publicity managers should understand the needs of the media and know what constitutes good publicity material. They should have good newswriting skills, and be outgoing and personable in their relations with the media. Publicity managers also should be persuasive, as they must "sell" their ideas to the press.

Unions/Associations

Major professional organizations include the Public Relations Society of America, Inc.; and Association for Women in Communications. Local 2110 of the United Auto Workers represents some employees of large publishing houses.

PROMOTION MANAGER

CAREER PROFILE

Duties: Supervise promotional projects to help book sales

Alternate Title(s): Sales Promotion Manager

Salary Range: $29,000 to $69,000+

Employment Prospects: Poor

Advancement Prospects: Poor

Prerequisites:
   Education—Undergraduate degree in advertising or marketing preferred
   Experience—Two to five years in copywriting, promotion, or marketing
   Special Skills—Sales orientation; copywriting ability; marketing knowledge; supervisory skills

CAREER LADDER

```
┌─────────────────────────────────────┐
│   Director of Marketing or Sales     │
└─────────────────────────────────────┘

┌─────────────────────────────────────┐
│         Promotion Manager            │
└─────────────────────────────────────┘

┌─────────────────────────────────────┐
│       Copywriter; Researcher;        │
│        Publicity Assistant           │
└─────────────────────────────────────┘
```

Position Description

Promotion is an important part of the overall marketing support given books once they are published. Other elements of support include media advertising, publicity, and direct-sales efforts. The most visible work of the promotion department can be seen in bookstores, where certain titles are out in special floor displays or emphasized by shelf tags, wall posters, buttons, and bookmarks at the cash register.

Other promotion products include direct-mail brochures and order blanks, sales literature, exhibits at industry conventions, and tie-ins such as T-shirts, tote bags, caps, key rings, and other items that are given away to the public.

Promotion managers work with editorial, advertising, and sales staffs to identify the books that will be supported. They develop and coordinate promotion plans, including scheduling, deadlines, and budgets. They then delegate work to copywriters, researchers, and assistants, and approve the final products. If specialty items such as T-shirts and note pads are to be used, they supervise their purchase and distribution.

Promotion managers often play an instrumental role in determining whether certain manuscripts are purchased by publishers. If a book is not promotable, in terms of getting attention and attracting a big enough audience, it may be rejected. Promotion managers sometimes sit in on editorial meetings at which buying decisions are made.

Promotion managers usually report to directors or vice presidents of marketing or sales. They may work with outside advertising agencies, if their publishers use such agencies, in the development of copy and materials. They may also supervise freelance copywriters in addition to their own staff.

In addition, promotion managers may supervise publicity efforts, supervise jacket copywriting, and assist in the preparation of sales catalogs.

Salaries

The average salary for a promotion manager in 1998 ranged from $36,750 at smaller houses to $69,000 at larger ones, according to a survey by *Publishers Weekly*.

Employment Prospects

Not all publishing houses have separate job positions for promotional work. Duties may be folded into another job, such as advertising manager.

Advancement Prospects

Promotion managers face stiff competition from their peers in sales and advertising for promotion to director or vice president of sales/marketing. Sales experience is an asset for advancement.

Education

An education in marketing or advertising is preferred for sales-promotion work. Also acceptable are undergraduate degrees in communications, liberal arts, or social sciences.

Experience/Skills

Two years of experience in copywriting, market research, publicity, or sales is considered the minimum for sales-promotion manager; ideally, job candidates should have at least five years of experience.

Sales-promotion managers should be knowledgeable in advertising and marketing techniques, and should be skilled copywriters themselves. Managerial skills include preparing budgets and long-range plans, and hiring, training, and supervising staff.

Unions/Associations

Major organizations include the American Advertising Federation, Advertising Club of New York, Advertising Women of New York, and Association for Women in Communications.

PROMOTIONAL ASSISTANT— ELECTRONIC PUBLISHING

CAREER PROFILE

Duties: Write promotional copy about electronic publishing products such as on-line databases, data collections, and telephone information services

Alternate Title(s): Publicity Assistant

Salary Range: $17,500 to $35,000

Employment Prospects: Good

Advancement Prospects: Good

Prerequisites:

Education—Undergraduate degree in liberal arts, communications, English, or history

Experience—Familiarity with computer databases as a user of on-line services; any background in book promotion or publishing a plus

Special Skills—Ability to communicate technical information clearly and precisely; familiarity with products; computer literacy; ability to adjust to change

CAREER LADDER

```
┌─────────────────────────────────┐
│   Assistant Product Manager;     │
│       Promotion Manager          │
└─────────────────────────────────┘

┌─────────────────────────────────┐
│      Promotional Assistant       │
└─────────────────────────────────┘

┌─────────────────────────────────┐
│ College; Researcher; Library Clerk │
└─────────────────────────────────┘
```

Position Description

Because electronic publishing is a relatively new field, most jobs related to it still do not have well-defined descriptions.

Electronic publishing involves producing on-line versions of reference books, magazines, and other works traditionally found in print. There are several reasons to convert books into electronic products. Some books have been turned into electronic databases to overcome the limitations of print. Electronic versions of books can be continuously updated up until "loaded" onto a computer. Information in traditional books is generally at least one year old by the time it hits print.

Also, online information is not restricted to a specific number of pages. If a computer user wants to use information from a book in his or her computer, it does not have to be retyped into the machine.

More and more textbooks are now published with CD-ROM disks, since computers with CD-ROM drives are so popular in homes and schools. Special visual effects on a computer can help children learn. Sometimes an outside packager is hired to create such CDs. An increasing number of publishers are offering electronic material on the World Wide Web also.

Information can also be put into the format a customer needs, merged with information from other sources, or combined with a software product that allows a customer to rearrange it to suit him- or herself.

Other books naturally lend themselves to a computerized form because of their content. If a book is invariably used in conjunction with a computer program, it works best if published in a form that can integrate with the program.

Other electronic publishing products include full-text databases of magazines, journals, or books, complete with reference citations that can be used to produce the whole text of the article that was referenced; company databases, with information about companies and their business activities; financial wire services, with stock quotes and other financial information; fax and telephone information services; and others.

Most jobs in electronic publishing resemble traditional publishing jobs, but require a good knowledge of the target customer for on-line services and a familiarity with databases. As a result, it can be hard to find people with the right combination of skills to write promotional material about electronic products.

Promotional assistants in this field would work with the product manager to define who the target audience of the product might be, what features of the product might appeal to these customers, and how to present the product to them.

They might also become involved with using market research to develop project design, learning what customers want and adapting books to meet those needs.

Salaries

Pay varies according to the size of the publisher, the size of the electronic publishing operation within the company, and the actual job duties. Such a job would probably pay somewhere within the $20,000 to $30,000 range.

Employment Prospects

Many people now employed in nontechnical electronic publishing jobs come from print publishing. Those with the right background and skills might find it easier landing job in this area than in traditional publishing.

Advancement Prospects

The next step up for someone in this job might be to assistant product manager, project coordinator, or to another promotional job within the publishing house.

Education

A communications or liberal arts degree would be preferred. Formal education with computers is not necessary, but could be a plus.

Experience/Skills

While this may be an entry-level job, familiarity with computer databases and software is a must. This can be self-taught. Librarians or other researchers would have the type of familiarity with computer-aided research necessary. Experience in book promotion would also be a plus.

An ability to communicate clearly and translate technical information in everyday language is also necessary.

Unions/Associations

The Software & Information Industry Association is the main trade association for electronic publishing. The Association of American Publishers also has an electronic publishing division.

ELECTRONIC PUBLISHING PRODUCT MANAGER

CAREER PROFILE

Duties: See the idea for an electronic version of a book through to a completed product; decide how best to market and promote the product

Alternate Title(s): Varied

Salary Range: $35,000 to $50,000+

Employment Prospects: Good

Advancement Prospects: Fair

Prerequisites:

Education—Undergraduate degree in communications, liberal arts, history, or English; a master's degree in library science, with training in computer-aided research, would be a plus

Experience—Several years' experience as a promotional assistant, project coordinator, or assistant product manager within electronic publishing; experience working in a library or using computer databases in a corporation is also helpful

Special Skills—Familiarity with users of computer databases; an ability to see what books might lend themselves to electronic form; knowledge of what information users of computer databases might need and how that information should be packaged

CAREER LADDER

```
┌─────────────────────────────────────┐
│    Director of Marketing or Sales    │
└─────────────────────────────────────┘

┌─────────────────────────────────────┐
│           Product Manager            │
└─────────────────────────────────────┘

┌─────────────────────────────────────┐
│     Assistant Product Manager;       │
│        Promotion Assistant           │
└─────────────────────────────────────┘
```

Position Description

Because electronic publishing is still emerging, job descriptions within it are far less static than those in traditional publishing, and a lot of a product manager's job within electronic publishing is experimental.

This position could be described as a cross between promotional manager and editor. The product manager is responsible for cradling an electronic product along from the original idea for the product to promoting and marketing it.

The product manager also must ensure that the final product properly integrates writing with pictures and sound, so that the completed product looks finished. He or she must obtain the necessary permissions to use video clips or other features added to the book.

Many electronic products are online versions of books that benefit from continuous updating, or contain too much information for a traditional book format. Many reference works, such as encyclopedias and directories, lend themselves to database form and can be periodically updated with new CD-ROM disks (which subscribers can obtain by turning in their old disks), or be made available on-line via the World Wide Web.

Others are computerized versions of books designed to be used with computer programs, or computerized products designed to be used with books. Electronic publishers also produce audio versions of books.

The product manager needs to be familiar with who might use the company's products and what they need the product to do. Because libraries, schools, and major corporations are the largest customers for these products, a background in using databases or computer systems in one of these settings can be helpful.

The product manager also has to be familiar with market research or speak to users of computer databases directly to define who they are and what they need.

He or she must then determine what marketing approach would work best. Unlike traditional publishing, where there are several defined ways to promote a book, this area can be more experimental in electronic publishing. Familiarity with traditional book promotion is important, however.

Many electronic products can be cross-promoted with books. Others can be more difficult to promote because they require the use of computer bulletin boards and other outlets not traditionally used by publishers. Because advertising is discouraged on some computer services, the problem of reaching the customers for a product can be more complicated.

Salaries

Salaries vary according to the size of the publisher and the electronic publishing division. Typically, they fall in the $35,000 to $50,000 range.

Employment Prospects

With the right background, landing this type of job might be easier than getting a similar job in traditional publishing. Many people now employed in nontechnical electronic publishing jobs come from publishing backgrounds.

Advancement Prospects

Someone in this job might advance through the publishing company's traditional marketing department into a more conventional marketing job. The product manager might also advance within the electronic publishing unit to become the unit manager.

Education

A bachelor's degree in communications, English, journalism, marketing, advertising, or liberal arts is generally required. Formal knowledge of computer systems and computer-aided research is a must.

Experience/Skills

Several years' experience as an assistant product manager or another job within the electronic publishing unit is required for most product manager jobs. Experience in marketing, copywriting, market research, publicity, or sales may also be required.

Unions/Associations

Product managers may belong to the same associations that promotion managers do. In addition, the trade association for electronic publishing is the Software & Information Industry Association. The Association of American Publishers also has a division for electronic publishing.

ARTS AND ENTERTAINMENT

AUTHOR

CAREER PROFILE

Duties: Research and write nonfiction or fiction books and articles

Alternate Title(s): Writer; Novelist

Income Potential: $0 to no limit

Work Prospects: Fair

Prerequisites:

Education—None required; undergraduate or advanced degrees in specialized fields desirable for nonfiction credentials

Experience—Background as a journalist or professional writer helpful

Special Skills—Creativity; self-motivation; persistence; good writing ability

Position Description

Authors enjoy an envied, glamorous image. Many people think writers don't really "work" for a living, merely spending a few hours a day at their typewriters composing whatever strikes their fancy.

In truth, most authors work hard, spending long hours researching, writing, editing, and rewriting. A good portion of their work is done on speculation—that is, they don't get paid unless their finished work is accepted—and rejections are far more common than acceptances.

Most professional authors work on nonfiction books and articles, which in general earn more money than fiction. Nonfiction includes textbooks, encyclopedias, and academic works as well as topical books. Some authors also write novels, and a very few write nothing but novels.

The author's work is a solitary pursuit requiring strong self-discipline and motivation. Authors treat their writing like any other job—it must be done daily, and deadlines must be met. Authors do have an advantage in being able to choose their working hours. Some authors gauge their work by hours per day, while others measure it by numbers of pages or words written. They spend a great deal of time searching for ideas by reading periodicals and books, as well as by being naturally curious and observant.

Established authors seldom complete manuscripts before trying to sell them. They make a sale based on a proposal, which consists of an introductory pitch, an outline, and sometimes a sample chapter; or a partial, which is generally three or more chapters, a synopsis, and an outline. Beginners may be asked by publishers to complete their manuscripts before they are purchased, especially in fiction.

Most authors prefer to have agents handle their material. The agent sends manuscripts or proposals, called properties, to publishers. Agents also negotiate contracts, collect payments on behalf of the author, and often mediate in any problems that arise. Agents also find work for their clients by being aware of editors' interests.

The author's work is not done once a book is written and sold. Revisions must be completed and page proofs proofread. Authors often spend their own time and money in helping publishers promote and advertise their books.

Authors may work on more than one project at a time, including developing ideas for sale while working on books under contract. Authors essentially run a small business, and must keep track of tax deductible expenses.

In addition, authors may supplement book income with freelance writing or part- or full-time jobs, and speak or teach at writers' conferences, colleges, and universities.

Income Potential

Authors earn anywhere from nothing (if they cannot sell their work—and sometimes it takes years!) to $100,000 or more. The average author in the late 1990s earned about $8,000 annually.

Because most authors write part time, statistics on their earnings are hard to come by. Only the best-sellers garner the big money, however. Beginning novelists can earn advances of $500 to $10,000 or more, but most novels never earn royalties (a percentage of the retail price) beyond the advance.

Genre novels such as mysteries, science fiction, romances, and westerns fare the best. Authors of these types of novels can earn up to $50,000 a year or more.

Nonfiction books, especially if they are on "hot" topics, can bring high advances and earn royalties over a long period of time. Most books, however, are out of print within a year of publication. Scientific and technical authors are able to earn more money than many other nonfiction authors.

Work Prospects

More than 40,000 books are published every year in the U.S., but that number represents only a fraction of the total number of manuscripts, proposals, and queries submitted by authors. Most ideas are rejected. Authors can wait months, even years, to sell their books. It's not uncommon to collect dozens of rejections before making a sale, even with the help of an agent. Also, because so many publishers are under financial pressure to publish best-sellers, it is difficult to publish a second book if your first had only moderate sales.

Education

For nonfiction, an undergraduate degree of any kind is helpful. If the author is writing as an expert in a specialized field, an advanced degree is helpful. Fiction depends more on creativity and imagination than education.

Experience/Skills

Any kind of writing experience, such as school newspaper, a creative-writing class, or a media job, is good training. Professional writing experience as a news journalist or magazine staff writer is an asset for nonfiction credentials.

Authors must be imaginative, very self-disciplined, and able to spend long periods of time alone. They must possess a high degree of perseverance, both in perfection of craft and against the odds of rejection. They cannot afford to be easily discouraged.

Knowledge of publicity and promotion is helpful in aiding publishers in selling published books.

Unions/Associations

Major national authors' associations include the Authors Guild; PEN American Center; American Society of Journalists and Authors, Inc.; National Writers Union; Authors League of America, Inc.; and National Writers Association. Other organizations serve a wide range of specialized interests. Major women's groups include the International Women's Writing Guild and National League of American Pen Women. The Writers Guild of America is a union representing radio, TV, and film scriptwriters.

GHOSTWRITER/COLLABORATOR

CAREER PROFILE

Duties: Work with others to write, rewrite, and edit books and articles

Alternate Title(s): None

Income Potential: If ghostwriter gets no credit, $5,000 to $50,000 per project, plus expenses. For "as told to" projects (working with a celebrity): advance plus 50 percent of royalties, typically $15,000 to $25,000. If subject self-publishes, $25 to $85 an hour, or $125 to $175 per book page. Research time is charged extra.

Work Prospects: Fair

Prerequisites:

Education—High school diploma or undergraduate degree in communications, journalism, English, or liberal arts

Experience—Background as an author, journalist, or novelist helpful

Special Skills—Good organization and research; editing skill; ability to imitate another's style or "voice"

Position Description

Ghostwriting carries little glamour but can be very lucrative. Many books and articles that appear under celebrities' or experts' names are in fact written, rewritten, or edited by professional writers who receive little or no credit for their role. The celebrity or expert provides the raw material; the writer molds it into a salable work.

The amount of work performed by ghostwriters varies. They may do all the researching, interviewing, writing, and editing, or they may write only a first draft. Some ghostwriters are hired to fix manuscripts by rewriting and editing.

The job of the ghostwriter is to become the voice of the subject. Thorough research is required in order to become familiar with the subject's manner of expression.

Most ghostwriting is nonfiction, such as articles or papers written for business officials, politicians, professionals, or scientific and academic leaders who wish to gain prestige through authorship. Many celebrities hire ghostwriters to write their first-person autobiographies. The ghostwriter may also write a textbook and nonfiction book for publication under an expert's name.

Some ghostwriters write novels for well-known authors. This is much more difficult than nonfiction.

Ghostwriters may be acknowledged in the introduction for "help in preparing the manuscript," or receive credit on the cover and title page under the guise of "with" or "as told to." Many ghostwriters prefer to remain invisible or are required to do so by their contracts. While they receive scant public recognition for their work, they can build reputations within publishing circles.

Collaboration is a more visible form of ghostwriting, often involving working in a partnership with another writer or celebrity. Collaborators usually share the research, writing, and revising.

Ghostwriting or collaboration can be an excellent way for writers to break into publishing and earn book credentials. Some ghostwriters build big reputations and do no other kind of writing.

In addition, ghostwriters and collaborators may:

- write their own books and novels;
- write magazine articles, short stories, scripts, screenplays, or other freelance material;
- work as freelance editors.

Income Potential

Income varies according to the project, the celebrity or expert involved, and the experience of the ghostwriter. If a book is being ghostwritten but published under a celebrity's name, it generally earns more. Business articles for trade journals can earn from $300 to $3,000 if published under someone else's byline.

For books, fees vary according to whether the author is self-publishing or has a publisher lined up, and whether the ghostwriter receives an "as told to" line or not. For a book with "as told to" credit, the fee includes a portion of the advance and up to 50 percent of the royalties. If the subject is self-publishing, the fee is $25 to $85 per hour.

If the subject is either self-publishing or does not have a publisher lined up, a ghostwriter who is not getting "as told to" credit would charge a flat fee of $5,000 to $50,000, with payment at regular intervals throughout the project.

Work Prospects

The ongoing popularity of celebrity books, plus the increasing number of specialized and trade publications that require expertise, provide a fair number of opportunities for ghostwriters and collaborators. Most of these writers tend to live in major cities near publishing and entertainment centers.

Education

There are no minimum education requirements unless a writer is working in business, professional, or technical fields.

Experience/Skills

Most ghostwriters and collaborators are experienced journalists, freelance business and magazine article writers, or novelists. Even with a writing background, it can be difficult to get one's own book published. Many writers break into publishing by ghosting or collaborating, and then use the credentials to help sell their own books.

Good interviewing, researching, writing, and editing skills are necessary. Above all, collaborators and ghostwriters are able to mimic others' writing styles.

Unions/Associations

Major national authors' associations include the Authors Guild, Inc.; American Society of Journalists and Authors, Inc.; National Writers Union; Authors League of America, Inc.; and National Writers Association. Other organizations serve a wide range of specialized interests. Major women's groups include the International Women's Writing Guild and National League of American Pen Women.

SCRIPTWRITER/SCREENWRITER

CAREER PROFILE

Duties: Write scripts and screenplays for film, television, and radio

Alternate Title(s): None

Income Potential: $9,000 to $100,000+

Work Prospects: Poor

Prerequisites:
   Education—Undergraduate degree in fine arts, English, or communications
   Experience—Writing for any medium helpful
   Special Skills—Creativity; writing talent; production knowledge

Position Description

Writing scripts and screenplays for the entertainment industries, particularly for film and television, is prestigious and glamorous—and can be quite lucrative. The business also is extremely unpredictable, high-pressure, and intensely competitive. Many scripts and screenplays that are commissioned are killed before production, which means lower fees for writers, if any at all. And many scripts that are produced undergo so many changes by so many writers that the original writer may not be credited with the final product. (Some even request no credit, if they dislike the alterations.)

In the golden days of Hollywood, most screenwriters worked under contract to the big studios. Today, most screenwriters and scriptwriters are freelancers. They may work on a project-by-project basis, trying to interest producers in ideas for series or one-shot programs. Or, they may work under short contracts—13 weeks is standard for most serial shows on television, such as soap operas or comedy/variety programs.

A beginner usually must write an entire script or screenplay before a producer will consider it for option. Writers with more experience and good track records may be commissioned on the basis of less—a "treatment" or "story," which is an outline. According to Guild rules, writers are paid for all work, even outlines and the polishing of someone else's work, though rates are less than if a writer does all the work alone. Not every producer, however, recognizes Guild agreements. It's not uncommon, especially for beginners, to work on speculation—that is, they are paid only if their work is accepted.

Most scriptwriters and screenwriters employ agents to help them find work and negotiate contracts. They may attend special screenings of pilots for new television shows, at which networks solicit script ideas. They may meet with production executives to discuss ideas, a process called "pitching" or "spitballing." Such a session can lead to an assignment for a treatment.

Scriptwriters and screenwriters often work in stages, with many projects never seeing completion. Some projects never go beyond treatments; others are killed after a first draft is written. Frequently writers are called in to rewrite and polish someone else's work. Payments are negotiated for each step.

It's difficult to write ful time for the entertainment industry without living in its capital, Los Angeles. Day-to-day contacts and proximity to producers and studios are vitally important. Many writers also live in New York City.

Income Potential

Scriptwriters' and screenwriters' earnings vary widely. Some never sell anything. Others, especially if they author one hot script, can make a comfortable living even if they never get anything else produced. And some sell lots of scripts even if the first one turned into a terrible bomb of a movie.

The first step to selling a script is selling an option—the right to buy the script within a specific time period—to use the script, which generally pays the author 10 percent of the total fee. If the script is made into a production, they get the remaining 90 percent. After 18 months, the option generally expires. The script can be sold elsewhere or the option can be renewed for another 10 percent.

Some scriptwriters earn a comfortable living just selling options and never have a script produced. Others, if they author a screenplay or script that results in a successful production, receive additional money from the novelization of the script and television or videocassette presentations of the production.

Scriptwriters and screenwriters may also get a bonus if they receive credit on the final film. Because so many scripts are rewritten, receiving credit depends on how much rewriting occurs.

Income also varies according to the medium (TV, film, or radio), the length and type of script, and other services such as narrations, treatments, rewrites, and polishing. Income also depends on whether or not a writer is under contract to a network or studio to produce multiple scripts.

According to the 2000 edition of *Writer's Market,* freelance scriptwriters are typically paid from $50 to $85 per hour; or $300 per finished minute; or $3,000 per project for nontheatrical TV scripts. For theatrical scripts, they are paid $15,000 per 30-minute sitcom. A 1997 article in *Media Circus* reported that TV entry-level staff writers generally start at $2,500 per week for 13 episodes. (Most episodes take two weeks to produce.) From staff writer, they may move to story editor, then to assistant producer. In addition, writers receive additional pay for reruns and foreign sales.

Week-to-week and term employment for theatrical and television writers ranges from $1,950 to $4,642 per week, depending on the number of weeks employed in a given period of time.

Radio scriptwriters are paid according to the number and length of programs.

Work Prospects

In spite of the large number of films, television, cable TV, and radio programs produced every year, breaking into the business is very difficult—particularly in film or commercial television. An agent in Los Angeles is almost mandatory for most film and television work. Most scriptwriters and screenwriters live in Los Angeles or New York City. Steady work is unpredictable and highly competitive.

Most scriptwriters and screenwriters in the entertainment industry are white males; women far outnumber minorities. Since this is largely a freelance field, there are no affirmative-action policies. Opportunities depend on talent, contacts, and luck.

Education

Most scriptwriters and screenwriters have broad educations, such as undergraduate degrees in fine arts, English, or communications. Some have degrees in advertising and start their careers as ad copywriters.

Experience/Skills

It is possible for someone with little previous writing experience to write salable scripts and screenplays. Most scriptwriters and screenwriters have had seasoning in some medium, such as print or broadcast. Experience matters less than talent, creativity, and ability to write good dialogue. Good scriptwriters and screenwriters have an ear for how people talk. They also understand the visual aspects of their work—how their ideas will translate to the screen.

Unions/Associations

Writers who work for most major film studios and television networks are required to join the Writers Guild of America (WGA). Salaried writers for radio and television stations may also belong to the WGA; American Federation of Television and Radio Artists; or National Association of Broadcast Employees and Technicians—Communications Workers of America. Scriptwriters and screenwriters may belong to other professional writing groups as well.

PLAYWRIGHT

CAREER PROFILE

Duties: Write dramatic and comedic scripts for public performance

Alternate Title(s): Dramatist

Income Potential: Quite variable, ranging from a percentage of the gross receipts, a small fee per performance plus royalties and a percentage of the receipts, to $1,000 and up per performance plus royalties and a percentage of the receipts

Work Prospects: Fair to poor

Prerequisites:

Education—Undergraduate degree in drama, writing, English, communications, or other liberal or fine arts; advanced course work in drama and writing beneficial

Experience—None necessary to break in; acting experience considered a must by some

Special Skills—Excellent command of English; writing skills, particularly in dialogue; self-motivation; ability to withstand repeated rejection before finally achieving success

---

Position Description

Like working on a novel, writing a play is a labor of love. Unless commissioned to create a particular story, playwrights usually develop their plays in their spare time. Few can devote all their energies to playwriting unless receiving income from another source. Writing a play may be something that many writers dream of doing, but it is more hard work than glamour.

Formerly, a playwright knew the audience: a congregation of interested (he or she hoped) individuals enjoying the action at the time it was performed. The playwright received instant feedback about the play's success or failure. Now, however, playwrights may write initially for the stage, but the play may also appear as a TV movie, a miniseries, a film, or even on radio.

A play written for the stage is much less susceptible to change by directors, actors, or producers. If the playwright's work is covered by a contract approved by industry organizations such as the Dramatists Guild, no changes at all may be made in the script without the author's consent. He or she, along with the producer, also have approval of cast and director, full ownership of copyright and all other rights, and the right to formulate contracts for all other uses of the play. Works for TV or the movies may be rewritten, according to the dictates of commercial and moral standards.

On radio, playwrights must create "movies" of the imagination and are expected to be familiar with sound effects, music, narration, and dialogue. As on the stage, the power of the author's written word is so important that few producers choose to change it.

In addition, playwrights may be called upon to:

- act as agent to sell the play;
- perform in the production, either on stage or behind the scenes;
- represent the play at industry functions and be responsible for talking with the press.

Income Potential

Since writing a play is quite different from regular employment, payment is not so much a salary as consideration for a finished work. Radio scripts can bring from $75 to $900 for a half-hour, and from $1,000 to $2,000 for a full hour. Regional theater groups may pay a playwright a flat

$500 to $2,000 for a play, or negotiate a variety of payment schedules. Some theaters pay $50 a week against a percentage of the box office receipts; some offer $35 for the first performance and $15 for every performance thereafter; some offer a percentage of the receipts only; and some generously pay a flat rate, a percentage, and travel and/or living expenses for the playwright. Payment depends entirely on the size of the theater company, the support of the community, and the previous success or "bankability" of the playwright.

Work Prospects

Playwrights do not apply for jobs in the same manner as magazine editors, although there are established channels for getting a play published and performed. Contrary to popular belief, publishers and theater groups are seeking new works all the time; the best chances are with small and regional theaters. Another "given" that is no longer true: Playwrights do not have to live in New York (or Los Angeles).

The prospects of making a career out of playwriting can be quite good if the playwright enjoys a successful first play—or better yet, a successful second or third effort. Advancement is based on luck and skill; there is no established career path.

Education

While an undergraduate degree in English, drama, writing, or other liberal or fine arts field is preferable, there is no set educational requirement for playwriting. Course work in writing or acting is a plus. Sometimes education in the "school of hard knocks" gives a playwright as much fodder for drama as college might.

Experience/Skills

It is difficult to pinpoint exactly what experience a playwright should possess. Some authorities feel that work as an actor is almost a necessity in order to know how actors transmit words to an audience. Others merely want proof that the playwright can write plays—sort of a chicken-and-the-egg situation, but usually borne out by work for small, regional theaters or academic productions. A good knowledge of English is essential; so is the ability to write dialogue and visualize how the actor will express the playwright's words. One successful play does not guarantee a playwright a career in drama, but it does make him or her more likely to receive attention upon completion of the second effort.

Unions/Associations

Playwrights for radio join the Writers Guild of America—the union for TV, motion picture, and radio writers—upon selling a script. There is no union for stage dramatists, but most join the Dramatists Guild of America, Inc., to protect their rights to a play, to stay informed of standard business practices, and to learn who's looking for scripts. Guild membership also offers members help with emergency problems, access to health insurance, subscriptions to Guild publications, and participation in Guild workshops and symposia. The Dramatists Guild of America, Inc., is part of the Authors League of America, Inc. Playwrights may also join the National Writers Union.

LYRICIST/JINGLE WRITER

CAREER PROFILE

Duties: Write lyrics for musical compositions, whether for popular distribution or as commercial advertising vehicles

Alternate Title(s): Songwriter

Income Potential: $0 to no limit

Work Prospects: Fair to poor

Prerequisites:

Education—An undergraduate degree in music, writing, English, or other liberal or fine arts field is preferable but not required; knowledge of music theory, harmony, counterpoint, standard, and popular songs is necessary

Experience—Previous work as a lyricist; no experience necessarily required

Special Skills—Ability to write "singable" words; skill to take a commercial idea or motto and create singing verse around it; attentiveness; ability to take directions and compromise; business and public-relations skills; self-discipline; versatility; feel for current trends; poise and stamina

Position Description

As with playwright, employment as a lyricist or jingle writer is not quite definable. Fitting words to music is not a science or learned skill so much as a talent. Lyricists are employed by stage producers, record producers, movie companies, and struggling composers.

The lifestyle is anything but "normal." Lyricists keep no regular hours, have little or no job security, and can count on night and weekend work. Few lyricists become famous, but some achieve modest recognition after receiving industry awards.

For jingle writing, the important thing is to make sure the product's name and motto or slogan are incorporated prominently into the song. Being able to write jingles or little songs quickly is definitely a plus, as advertisers may request almost immediate turnaround.

Most jingle writers work for music production houses, although some may work for advertising agencies. Some freelance. Jingle writing is considered less "important" work than writing legitimate lyrics, yet a jingle is heard instantly by millions on television and may accompany a really catchy tune. Some jingles become part of American popular culture, such as "Join the Pepsi generation," "Have it your way," or "It's the real thing."

Most jingle writers also write song lyrics, and some see their jingles expanded into full-length songs. Many lyricists began their careers as jingle writers. Once a lyricist has sold a song lyric successfully, he or she is more likely to be called upon to write the words for other pieces of music. Occasionally a composer and lyricist work so well together that they collaborate on all future work.

A list of Web links useful to songwriters can be found on-line at http://www.songdemo.com/html/resources.html.

Income Potential

Lyricists can sell songs for one-time flat fees, or on a royalty basis. The average advance against royalties is $5,000 to $6,500. According to the Songwriters Guild of America, a good minimum contract should pay the songwriter 50 percent of the gross receipts earned from mechanical reproduction (royalties from sale of records, tapes, or sheet music), electrical transcriptions, and synchronization.

The three performing-rights organizations—American Society of Composers, Authors and Publishers (ASCAP); Broadcast Music Inc. (BMI); and SESAC, Inc.—monitor the performances of all members' music and handle payment of royalties. ASCAP uses a formula based on the number of performances within each media group (radio, TV, concert, restaurant music, etc.) and weights the performance by factors accounting for that medium's share of income among all media and the possibility of performances not accounted for. This formula yields "credits," which are then multiplied by a standard figure. ASCAP then distributes the member lyricist's royalties based on the fee negotiated in his contract. Both BMI, which is the largest performing-arts organization in America, and SESAC, which is the smallest, operate similarly.

If the lyricist is not the composer, his or her 50-percent share will be divided between the two songwriting partners. The more popular and successful a lyricist becomes, the higher a percentage he or she may negotiate, and the more money he or she earns. Successful songwriters earn $500,000 or more a year. A few earn more than $1 million a year.

Work Prospects

Breaking into the field is quite difficult. Many people want to write song lyrics. The field is highly competitive, but there are opportunities for talented people. As more television and film projects use music, whether for title songs or as background, the need for lyricists will grow. Check the business trade weekly magazines and newspapers such as *Songwriter* magazine, for the names of publishers interested in songs.

Becoming a jingle writer is most likely an intermediate stop for a serious lyricist; the best opportunities are in New York or Los Angeles, with the major advertising and music production companies. Getting your foot in the door usually works best through personal connections, individual contractors, studios, music reps, and your own sterling reputation. Other opportunities exist as staff writers for music publishing companies, or lyricists for TV or movie soundtracks.

There is no set career path. Once a lyricist has had success with a producer or advertiser, he or she is likely to continue. Good jingle writers can count on more and more work as companies put catchy words and tunes on television.

Industry recognition, such as a Clio award in advertising, an Oscar, an Emmy, or a Grammy, helps assure the lyricist of continued success and financial reward.

Education

There are no educational prerequisites for work as a lyricist or jingle writer, but a background in music or writing is definitely a plus. Undergraduate degrees in music, English, or other liberal or fine arts are the norm. One source believes that jingle writers must have a complete musical education, with a working knowledge of theory, harmony, and counterpoint. Talent alone is not quite enough. It is also important for any lyricist or jingle writer to remain familiar with the old standards and keep abreast of current pop tunes.

Experience/Skills

As with playwriting, success at writing song lyrics depends on the success of earlier efforts, but the trick is getting the first one accepted. Most producers of songs, movies, and television shows prefer previous work on other songs or productions. Spending time in a music or recording studio as an observer will give you a good grounding in how the system operates.

The best skills to have for this business are the abilities to write clearly, to work well with the music's composer, and to be willing to compromise. Jingle writers often begin with copy provided by the advertising agency or client, so he or she needs to be flexible. The ability to work fast, sometimes producing immediate turnaround, is also important. Business and public-relations skills, self-discipline, versatility, stamina, and poise help as well.

Unions/Associations

Most lyricists join one of the performing-rights organizations—ASCAP, BMI and SESAC—and/or guilds. Both the Songwriters Guild of America and the Dramatists Guild of America, Inc., are open to lyricists. Guild membership entitles members to review of contracts, health insurance, and participation in seminars and workshops. Membership in a performing-rights organization provides the lyricist with a valid tally of performances and distribution of royalties. Other groups include the National Association of Composers, USA, and Songwriters Resources and Services.

POET

Duties: Compose various forms of verse and poems for magazines and books

Alternate Title(s): None

Income Potential: Up to $2.00 per line, sometimes more

Work Prospects: Poor

Prerequisites:
Education—Undergraduate degree in English or liberal arts
Experience—Background in creative writing helpful
Special Skills—Thorough understanding of grammar and English language; knowledge of disciplines of poetry

Position Description

Poetry is an artistic form of expression of emotions, ideas, and visual images. There are three basic types of poetry: dramatic, which is action-oriented; narrative, which tells a story; and lyric, which describes first-person emotions and also includes verses for songs. Each of those types is broken down into specific forms. Free verse, for example, follows no meter but allows the poet to compose in lines of any length. A haiku poem has a rigid form of three lines with five, seven, and five syllables per line, respectively.

Many persons write poetry as a hobby. Professional poets publish their work in literary, academic, and a few general-circulation magazines, and occasionally in books, such as poetry anthologies.

Some write traditional, humorous, and inspirational verses for greeting-card publishers, while still others take their talent to music, writing lyrics for songs and plays (see "Lyricist," page 108). Whatever market is sought, a poet should be thoroughly familiar with the work being published and produced.

Most poets earn their livings teaching English, literature, creative writing, or poetry, or by freelance writing.

Income Potential

All but a handful of poets earn little or nothing for their work. Literary and academic magazines, even small book presses, often pay in free copies rather than money. Some magazines pay from $1 to $15 per poem, while others pay per line. A good rate range is $1 to $1.50 per line. Prestigious magazines pay up to $10 a line.

Books of poems do not sell well—a few hundred copies is considered excellent. Advances are negligible, perhaps several hundred dollars, or nonexistent. Many poets resort to self-publishing in order to see their works in print, or enter into cooperative arrangements with publishers to share production and distribution costs.

Typical advance pay for the lyrics to a song ranges from several hundred dollars to $1,000, plus royalties. Many music publishers pay no advance but will underwrite the costs of a demonstration tape.

Some poets can obtain foundation grants to subsidize their work.

Work Prospects

Selling poetry is hard work. Markets include literary and academic magazines, as well as general interest magazines and some newspapers. Poets in search of a book publisher will find their best chances with small presses or in self-publishing.

Songwriting and selling poems, gags, and ideas to greeting-card publishers are more lucrative areas for the poet but very competitive. Greeting cards for the Internet are a new area for poets to explore.

Education

Most accomplished poets have had extensive educations in English, poetry, literature, and creative writing. An undergraduate degree in English or liberal arts is good preparation. Graduate degrees—preferably a Ph.D.—are required for college-level teaching positions. Lyricists should have an educational background in music.

Experience/Skills

Many poets begin by joining writing groups and reading their work aloud for critiques. Command of the English language—a good vocabulary and grammar skills—is essential.

Unions/Associations

The Songwriters Guild of America and the American Society of Composers, Authors and Publishers represent music publishers, composers, and lyricists. Other associations for poets include the Academy of American Poets; PEN American Center; Poetry Society of America; and National Writers Union. The National Federation of State Poetry Societies can provide contacts for state poetry affiliates. The Greeting Card Association has an industry market list for artists and writers.

GREETING CARD WRITER

CAREER PROFILE

Duties: Write verse and sentiments for greeting cards

Alternative Title(s): None

Income Potential: $30 to $300 per sentiment, depending on size of the company and whether artwork is included

Work Prospects: Poor

Prerequisites:
Education—Undergraduate degree in English or liberal arts
Experience—Background in creative writing helpful
Special Skills—Understanding of what attracts a sender to a card; ability to be witty and innovative

Position Description

Greeting card writers compose verse and sentiments for inclusion in a wide variety of types of cards. Some bear traditional rhymed poems, others inspirational verse, others clever sayings or humorous phrases.

A good greeting card will attract the sender to the card. It expresses a universal sentiment but makes the sender think of the person who will receive it. Greeting card writers are constantly coming up with new ways to say "I love you" and "Happy Birthday."

While larger greeting card companies hire their own stable of writers, many buy freelance ideas for cards.

Card lines are being developed to reflect demographic changes, according to the Greeting Card Association. Trends in card design include cards for seniors, cards targeted at working women, cards about health and fitness, and cards about divorce, separation, terminal illness, and friendship.

Of the holidays, Christmas is the one that results in the most card sales. Next is Valentine's Day, followed by Mother's Day and Easter.

Some companies that buy freelance require illustrations to be submitted with card ideas. Others prefer to provide their own illustrations, although suggestions for artwork may be welcome.

The Greeting Card Association was founded in 1942. That year, total wholesale sales of greeting cards were $43 million. In 1998 they were $7.5 billion! Clearly this is a burgeoning industry with significant potential. However, writ-

ers must realize that more of that $7.5 billion is spent on artwork than on writing, and another chunk of it goes for paper and printing. Some messages stay the same from year to year, but are given a new, fresh-looking illustration.

The three largest greeting card companies command 85 percent of the market, and two of them do not accept writing from freelancers. However, there are over 1,500 greeting card publishers in all, many of which welcome freelance contributions.

A relatively recent development in the greeting card industry is the development of electronic greeting cards. The computer user chooses pictures, sometimes accompanied by animation and sound, and then writes a personal message. The card is sent electronically, like E-mail.

Income Potential

The greeting card industry is very competitive. Some companies prefer to receive a resume, business card, and client list along with card ideas; others like to get individual card ideas on index cards. Freelancers should contact the greeting card company first to see what their submission procedures require.

Most companies pay per idea; only a few pay royalties. Pay can be $30 to $250 per idea, depending on the company. Some companies maintain large writing staffs and do not purchase much freelance material.

Most greeting card writers, unless they are on staff, do other kinds of freelancing or have other jobs.

Work Prospects

About one idea in 10 ends up being purchased at most companies. Odds might be better at companies where cards are primarily freelanced.

Education

If your ideas are good, many companies are not interested in your background. However, most freelancers have undergraduate degrees in liberal arts, communications, journalism, or creative writing. Some companies ask for a resume.

Experience/Skills

Good command of the English language is essential. An ability to express an old sentiment in a fresh and new way is also important.

Unions/Associations

The Greeting Card Association has an industry market list for artists and writers.

BUSINESS COMMUNICATIONS AND PUBLIC RELATIONS

PUBLIC-RELATIONS ASSISTANT

CAREER PROFILE

Duties: Assist public-relations manager, director, editor, and others with public-relations activities

Alternate Title(s): Editorial Assistant; Publicity Assistant

Salary Range: Under $20,000 to $28,000

Employment Prospects: Good

Advancement Prospects: Good

Prerequisites:

Education—Undergraduate degree in communications, journalism, liberal arts, or English

Experience—School journalism experience helpful

Special Skills—Good writing and editing skills; knowledge of graphics; ability to work as part of team and independently; outgoing personality; secretarial skills

CAREER LADDER

```
+------------------------------------+
|   Internal Publications Editor     |
+------------------------------------+

+------------------------------------+
|     Public-Relations Assistant     |
+------------------------------------+

+------------------------------------+
|        College; Journalist         |
+------------------------------------+
```

Position Description

The role of the public-relations professional is to present a favorable image of the employer to its audience, which could include the general public, the investment community, lawmakers, or clients.

Public relations encompasses many image-building tasks, and the public-relations assistant gets exposure to all or nearly all of them. The job is entry-level and can be found in private business and industry, government, nonprofit associations, and education. Many of the job duties are menial, such as word processing on a computer, filing, running errands, and taking telephone calls. Most public-relations assistants get opportunities to work in a variety of public-relations functions. For example, they may contribute short articles to an internal newsletter or magazine, called the "house organ," or write and distribute bulletin board notices and paycheck stuffers.

They may also help develop and update mailing lists for news releases, write simple news releases for executive approval, assemble press kits, and stuff envelopes. They may handle certain media queries themselves.

In addition, a public-relations assistant may:

• update biographies of key company executives and photo files;

• help arrange speaking engagements;
• assist in community activities and fundraising drives;
• assist internal publication editors on production work.

Salaries

Salaries for public relations graduates employed full-time in 1996 were generally higher than for other recent journalism school graduates. *The Mississippi Business Journal* reported in 1996 that more print journalism graduates are entering corporate public relations because of low salaries in the print journalism field.

Salaries in public relations can range from under $17,000 up to the high $20,000s at the assistant level.

Women make less than men with comparable experience in public relations, but a recent salary survey showed the gap closing a little.

Salaries throughout the public-relations field vary according to employer. Public-relations professionals working for government, health care, or nonprofit organizations had a median salary of $43,260, considerably lower than the median for public-relations firms and corporations: $51,340 and $50,770, respectively. Public-affairs specialists in the federal government in nonsupervisory, supervisory, and managerial positions averaged about $52,540 in 1996.

(These statistics take into account higher positions than public-relations assistant, but they are still revealing.)

Salaries also vary widely according to size of firm, location of firm, and specialty area. A 1999 survey by New York–based firm Gould & Company found that the average salary of account executives surveyed was $40,647 in health care but only $35,111 in fashion and beauty.

Employment Prospects

More graduates of journalism schools in the last six years majored in public relations than in print journalism.

This does not mean that job prospects are better in public relations. The Bureau of Labor Statistics predicts that employment of public-relations specialists will increase rapidly through 2006, but competition for entry-level jobs will be keen. Opportunities should be best for college graduates with degrees in journalism, public relations, advertising, or other communications-related fields. Experience as an intern is also very helpful in competing for entry-level jobs.

Public relations seems to have captured the imaginations of students raised on media images, and demand for good public-relations specialists should continue as business grows more competitive.

Advancement Prospects

Public-relations assistants who perform well can expect good chances of advancement. The exposure to a wide range of activities is helpful for targeting a career path.

Education

Entry-level jobs generally require a college degree in communications, public relations, journalism, advertising, or liberal arts. In addition, some organizations have their own formal training programs for new employees.

Journalism school graduates are also combining specialties, leaving them qualified for more specialized public relations jobs.

Jobs that might use such combinations include public-relations assistant positions at newspapers, where the best opportunities might be within chains such as Gannett; at magazines, where planning press and trade parties can be part of the duties; at television stations; in advertising agencies, which often offer public-relations services to clients and maintain staff to provide them; in the federal government, where projecting public reaction to policies may be an important part of the job; or at nonprofit institutions, where lobbying in the state capital or Washington on behalf of the institution might be needed, in addition to the basic public-relations functions.

Experience/Skills

Public relations firms and departments once recruited former journalists. Now increasing numbers of journalism school graduates are going directly into public relations. While no experience may be necessary for entry-level jobs, the field is increasingly competitive. Internships or college newspaper experience is advantageous.

Public-relations professionals should be creative, outgoing, and able to motivate and persuade others. They should be good writers and editors, understand the needs of the media, and be knowledgeable in graphics and layout. Experience with video display terminals is helpful.

Unions/Associations

Major professional associations include the International Association of Business Communicators; the Public Relations Society of America, Inc.; and Association for Women in Communications.

INTERNAL PUBLICATIONS EDITOR

CAREER PROFILE

Duties: Write, edit, and produce employee magazine or newsletter

Alternate Title(s): Communications Specialist; Editor

Salary Range: $25,000 to $45,000+

Employment Prospects: Good

Advancement Prospects: Good

Prerequisites:
  Education—Undergraduate degree in communications, journalism, public relations, liberal arts, or English
  Experience—Background as news reporter or editor helpful
  Special Skills—Good writing and editing ability; photography and graphics skills; self-motivation; organizational skills

CAREER LADDER

```
┌─────────────────────────────────────┐
│     Manager of Editorial Services    │
└─────────────────────────────────────┘

┌─────────────────────────────────────┐
│      Internal Publications Editor    │
└─────────────────────────────────────┘

┌─────────────────────────────────────┐
│       Journalist; News Editor;       │
│  Public-Relations Assistant; College │
└─────────────────────────────────────┘
```

Position Description

Rare is the company, association, or organization that does not produce and distribute an employee newsletter or magazine. Management views internal publications as a pipeline for communication and a means to foster goodwill and boost morale. A publication may be a mere two-sided single sheet of paper or a slick, four-color magazine. Many employers have more than one internal publication; a slick magazine may come out quarterly, supplemented by monthly newsletters. Most publications, however, are monthly magazines.

The job of internal publications editor encompasses planning, writing, editing, editorial decision-making, photography, layout, and production. Most editors are able to put their personal stamp on their publications.

The editors usually work under the supervision of communications coordinators or managers of editorial services. The editors must plan issues in advance and submit outlines for managerial review and approval, then arrange for interviews and photographs. Editors must be able to meet deadlines and stay within their production budgets.

Some editors produce a publication alone, doing all the work or hiring freelancers to assist them. Some may have an assistant, and others may have a staff.

Editors are responsible for clearing all material for publication through management channels. They also spec type (decide typeface style and point size), do page layouts, or work with graphic artists. In addition, they instruct typesetters and printers.

Content depends on the nature of the publication. Articles usually include profiles of employees or departments; new hires and promotions; messages from senior executives; community projects; and other news and features.

In addition, an internal publications editor may write occasional press releases and speeches, or produce slide shows and films for internal audiences.

Salaries

An entry-level internal publications editor is generally paid between $25,000 and $45,000.

Employment Prospects

The job of internal publications editor is one of the most common public-relations positions, and is often the easiest way to break into a public-relations department. Turnover in this type of job is steady. The Bureau of Labor Statistics predicts that employment of public-relations specialists will increase rapidly through 2006.

Advancement Prospects

An employee publication provides a good showcase for talent, skill, and visibility. Prospects for advancement to higher-level positions are good.

Education

The minimum requirement is an undergraduate degree in communications, journalism, public relations, liberal arts, or English.

Experience/Skills

Some internal-publications-editor positions are entry-level, filled by college graduates. Others require several years of experience, preferably as a news reporter or editor, or in another aspect of public relations.

Excellent writing and editing skills plus leadership qualities are essential for any editing job. Editors should have good news judgment and organizational skills as well. They also must be able to work well with others and be able to take direction. Corporate editors have much less latitude than news media editors in determining content. Corporate interests are served first, and negative news is often downplayed or ignored.

Unions/Associations

Major professional associations include the Public Relations Society of America, Inc.; International Association of Business Communicators; and Association for Women in Communications.

EXTERNAL PUBLICATIONS EDITOR

CAREER PROFILE

Duties: Write news releases, articles, informational brochures, speeches, slide scripts, and letters for an external audience

Alternate Title(s): Communications Specialist; Communications Associate; Information Representative; Public Information Officer

Salary Range: $25,000 to $45,000+

Employment Prospects: Good

Advancement Prospects: Good

Prerequisites:
   Education—Undergraduate degree in public relations, communications, journalism, liberal arts, or English
   Experience—Background in news reporting helpful
   Special Skills—Strong newswriting ability; organizational and analytic skills

CAREER LADDER

```
┌─────────────────────────────────┐
│   Communications Coordinator;   │
│    Public-Relations Manager     │
└─────────────────────────────────┘

┌─────────────────────────────────┐
│   External Publications Editor  │
└─────────────────────────────────┘

┌─────────────────────────────────┐
│   Public-Relations Assistant;   │
│     Journalist; News Editor     │
└─────────────────────────────────┘
```

Position Description

External publications editor is a job that specializes in promoting the interests of the employer with the general public, media, or special-interest groups. In some cases, particularly small companies and organizations, job duties may be combined with others for more generalized job descriptions.

The external publications editor is responsible for educating and informing external audiences, such as the general public, stockholders, the news media, or special-interest groups. The job involves producing news releases, feature articles for the business and trade press, brochures, slide scripts, and speeches.

The communications could concern the announcement of new products; how ongoing programs are benefiting the economy or community; or the appointment of new executives. Feature articles are written for trade, industry, and professional publications. For example, a bank may describe a program to serve customers more quickly at teller windows, or a trucking firm might put together an article about how a computerized maintenance system has cut repair bills by a significant percentage.

External publications editors may also develop informational material, such as booklets that answer common questions for stockholders, or pamphlets that tell the histories of their companies or organizations.

In addition, external publications editors may write articles for internal publications and write community-relations letters for an executive officer's signature.

Salaries

An external publications editor with some experience either in public relations or journalism can expect to earn about $25,000 to $45,000 a year. Salaries can go as high as $50,000—and more—after several years of experience, depending on the level of the job.

Employment Prospects

Job opportunities in public relations are expected to increase rapidly through the year 2006, according to the Bureau of Labor Statistics. However, the profession is subject to cutbacks in economic downturns and recessions.

Advancement Prospects

External publications editors are in good positions to move into managerial jobs. They often work directly with upper management, which gives them visibility that helps them move through the ranks.

Education

An undergraduate degree in communications, public relations, journalism, liberal arts, or English is the minimum requirement. Degrees in finance or business can be advantageous, as can advanced degrees.

Experience/Skills

A journalism background is the best preparation for this type of public-relations work. An external publications editor must be able to write not only many types of material but for different audiences as well.

Good writing and editing skills are important, as is an understanding of the needs of the news media. A background in graphics is useful.

Unions/Associations

Major professional associations include the Public Relations Society of America, Inc.; International Association of Business Communicators; and Association for Women in Communications.

PUBLIC INFORMATION OFFICER

CAREER PROFILE

Duties: Handle media relations for company or organization; write and distribute news releases; place articles in news media

Alternate Title(s): Public-Relations Manager; Public Affairs Practitioner

Salary Range: $25,000 to $50,000+

Employment Prospects: Good

Advancement Prospects: Good

Prerequisites:

Education—Undergraduate degree in communications, journalism, English, or liberal arts

Experience—Newswriting, wire service, or previous communications experience essential

Special Skills—Newswriting; organizational ability; outgoing personality

CAREER LADDER

```
┌─────────────────────────────────┐
│   Director of Communications    │
└─────────────────────────────────┘

┌─────────────────────────────────┐
│   Public Information Officer     │
└─────────────────────────────────┘

┌─────────────────────────────────┐
│   Communications Coordinator     │
└─────────────────────────────────┘
```

Position Description

Public information officers act as liaison between the news media and the company or organization they represent. They answer questions from the news media; generate favorable news stories about the company or organization, then try to place these stories in newspapers, with the wire services, or on television and radio; keep management informed of issues that might result in media inquiries; and prepare in advance management's responses to anticipated questions.

A large part of the public information officer's job is to maintain regular contact and establish a relationship of trust with the news media. Trust is very important in getting a message or image across to the public. The public information officer also must be able to answer press questions immediately or within a set deadline. Other duties include coaching company executives on how to handle media interviews.

Public information officers must stay informed of all news developments that affect their employers so that they can act quickly to shield executives from unfavorable publicity or seize opportunities for favorable publicity. They

may be responsible for providing daily news digests and clips to management.

Most supervise a staff or one or more assistants; some may have only secretarial help. Depending on the employer, the public-information-officer position can be a mid-level position or a top position.

In addition, a public information officer may write speeches and slide show scripts or produce informational brochures.

Salaries

Salaries vary greatly according to professional experience, geographic location, type of employer, and where the public information officer fits into the hierarchy. Average salaries are in the thirties; nearly half of the professionals earn more than $45,000, depending on their expertise, special skills, and employer.

Employment Prospects

Public information officers have become increasingly important in recent years to many businesses, organizations, and government agencies, due largely to more aggressive reporting by the news media. According to the Bureau of Labor Statistics, job opportunities are expected to increase rapidly through the year 2006, especially in private industry. Job openings in education—school districts, colleges and universities—will be limited due to staff cutbacks.

Advancement Prospects

The public information officer is a front-line position with high visibility. Chances are good for promotion to higher-level, more responsible positions.

Education

Most public information officers have undergraduate degrees in communications, journalism, English, or liberal arts. Some have undergraduate or graduate degrees in business, economics, or political science.

Experience/Skills

Public information officers generally have previous experience working in the news media as well as in other public-relations positions. Some employers may require several years' experience.

Public information officers should have sound news judgment, as well as good writing and editing skills. They should be outgoing and able to mix well with a wide variety of people. In addition, they should be well organized and responsive to requests made on deadline.

Unions/Associations

Major professional associations include the Public Relations Society of America, Inc.; International Association of Business Communicators; American Business Communication Association; and Association for Women in Communications.

GOVERNMENT AFFAIRS SPECIALIST

CAREER PROFILE

Duties: Monitor government and public-affairs issues of concern to employer; prepare position papers for management; oversee company's political action committee

Alternate Title(s): Public Affairs Specialist

Salary Range: $30,000 to $60,000+

Employment Prospects: Good

Advancement Prospects: Good

Prerequisites:
Education—Undergraduate degree in communications, journalism, public relations, liberal arts, political science, or history; graduate degree helpful
Experience—Background in journalism, politics, or public relations essential
Special Skills—Strong analytical skills; good organizational ability; understanding of political process; speaking ability; salesmanship

CAREER LADDER

```
┌─────────────────────────────────────┐
│   Manager of Government Affairs      │
└─────────────────────────────────────┘

┌─────────────────────────────────────┐
│   Government Affairs Specialist      │
└─────────────────────────────────────┘

┌─────────────────────────────────────┐
│   Communications Specialist          │
└─────────────────────────────────────┘
```

Position Description

The government affairs specialist plays a very important role in many large companies and corporations, by monitoring the activities of various local, state, and federal government bodies and agencies whose activities might affect a company's business and operations. He or she may be part of a large public-relations department and assigned specific areas of responsibility, or else be the company's sole legislative watchdog.

Government affairs specialists keep track of such things as tax legislation, labor regulations, consumer rights regulations and legislation, and other related issues. They keep management apprised of pending issues that are of immediate or long-term concern. They often prepare position papers outlining the effect of proposed laws or regulations on a company's business.

Government affairs specialists also act as spokespersons for their companies when the media calls for information about their companies' stands on certain issues, such as proposed tax increases or regulations governing minority hiring. Occasionally, they testify on behalf of their employers

at government hearings; they may also lobby lawmakers and members of government agencies.

A government affairs specialist may also coordinate a company's political action committee, or PAC—the arm of the company that is allowed to contribute to political campaigns. As part of the job, a government affairs specialist may develop dossiers on various candidates for public office, evaluating which deserve support by his or her company; write letters or prepare newsletters for other PAC members to update them on pending issues; and answer queries from governmental agencies seeking information to help them formulate legislation or regulations.

In addition, a government affairs specialist may prepare speeches or testimony for management on a variety of issues.

Salaries

A government affairs position carries a great deal of responsibility in most companies and is not an entry-level job. Salaries typically begin in the low thirties and climb according to a person's experience and the size of the employer.

Employment Prospects

This is a crucial position for many companies because of the proliferation of governmental agencies, the activities of which need to be monitored, as well as ever-changing and complex regulations. Employment prospects are good for qualified individuals. The Bureau of Labor Statistics predicts that employment of public-relations specialists will increase rapidly through 2006.

Advancement Prospects

A government affairs specialist has a high-visibility job and often works closely with upper management, which enhances opportunities for advancement.

Education

An undergraduate degree in communications, journalism, public relations, liberal arts, political science, or his-

tory is the best preparation for this type of work. Advanced degrees may be advantageous.

Experience/Skills

Experience as a political journalist or legislative assistant or aide on the state or federal level are ideal backgrounds for government affairs specialists. A background in public-relations work is also good.

Government affairs specialists must be able to analyze complex information and explain it clearly to others. They should be well organized, personable, and outgoing. In addition, they should be persuasive and comfortable making speeches.

Unions/Associations

Major professional associations include the Public Relations Society of America, Inc.; International Association of Business Communicators; and Association for Women in Communications.

SPEECHWRITER

CAREER PROFILE

Duties: Write speeches for company executives on a variety of topics and for a variety of audiences

Alternate Title(s): Management Communications Specialist

Salary Range: $30,000 to $100,000+

Employment Prospects: Good

Advancement Prospects: Good

Prerequisites:
Education—Undergraduate degree in communications, journalism, liberal arts, English, or business
Experience—Background in journalism or public relations essential
Special Skills—Excellent writing ability; creativity; good research and organizational skills; persuasiveness

CAREER LADDER

```
┌─────────────────────────────┐
│   Director of Management     │
│      Communications         │
└─────────────────────────────┘

┌─────────────────────────────┐
│        Speechwriter         │
└─────────────────────────────┘

┌─────────────────────────────┐
│  Public Information Officer; │
│     Publications Editor      │
└─────────────────────────────┘
```

Position Description

Speechwriting jobs are found mainly in larger corporations with highly structured communications staffs and in companies whose executives make frequent public appearances. Speechwriters are responsible for developing speeches for corporate executives on a wide range of subjects and for a wide range of audiences. For example, an executive might address a group of Wall Street analysts one week and a community-fundraising organization the next.

Some executives work closely with speechwriters to develop content and tone, but in many cases, the speechwriter must research and write alone. Before beginning a draft, the speechwriter usually meets with the executive or his or her assistant to get preliminary information: the audience, topic, length of speech, and general content; whether anyone from the company has addressed this audience before and on what topic; who else is on the roster; whether the speeches will be before or after a meal; whether or not questions will be allowed; and the possibility of media coverage.

In some cases, the speechwriter may be able to rewrite or update a previously delivered speech. In most cases, he

or she will write from scratch, going through many drafts and revisions. There is little pride in authorship in speech-writing.

The speechwriter does extensive reading to stay abreast of news and trends that relate to his or her employer.

In addition, a speechwriter may write slide scripts and videotape presentations or write articles for industry or business publications, which will carry an executive byline.

Salaries

Speechwriters are paid according to experience and talent. A beginning speechwriter can expect to earn about $30,000; experience can bring salaries up to $100,000 or more. Some freelance speechwriters earn well over $200,000 a year.

Employment Prospects

Speechwriters are always in demand. The profession is noted for its high turnover, because of the pressure of the job and also because speechwriters tend to move from company to company. The best job opportunities are in private industry and business.

Advancement Prospects

Speechwriter is a highly visible position, and those who do well in the job have a good chance of being promoted to management.

Education

An undergraduate degree in communications, journalism, English, or liberal arts is essential. Some speechwriters have undergraduate or advanced degrees in business, economics, or political science.

Experience/Skills

Speechwriters come from all backgrounds. Many started in the news business; others have come from other public-relations jobs.

Speechwriters should have a flair for writing the spoken word. They should be able to easily mimic an individual's style of speaking. In addition, they need strong research skills and patience in dealing with extensive revisions.

Unions/Associations

Major professional associations include the Public Relations Society of America, Inc.; International Association of Business Communicators; and Association for Women in Communications.

COMMUNICATIONS COORDINATOR

CAREER PROFILE

Duties: Coordinate internal/external public and community-relations activities

Alternate Title(s): Public-Relations Specialist; Communications Specialist

Salary Range: $20,000 to $45,000+

Employment Prospects: Good

Advancement Prospects: Good

Prerequisites:
   Education—Undergraduate degree in public relations, communications, journalism, liberal arts, or English
   Experience—Background in public relations or journalism essential
   Special Skills—Strong writing and organizational skills; creativity; administrative ability

CAREER LADDER

```
┌─────────────────────────────────┐
│     Public-Relations Manager     │
└─────────────────────────────────┘

┌─────────────────────────────────┐
│    Communications Coordinator    │
└─────────────────────────────────┘

┌─────────────────────────────────┐
│    Internal Publications Editor; │
│           Journalist             │
└─────────────────────────────────┘
```

Position Description

Communications coordinator is a position usually found in a company or organization with three to four communications professionals reporting to a manager or director. The coordinator generally has decision-making authority and may supervise lower level employees, such as public-relations assistants or publications editors.

The communications coordinator has a broad range of responsibilities, almost all of which are writing-related. Duties fall into three categories: internal communications; external communications; and community relations.

Internal communications account for the greatest share of the communications coordinator's workload. He or she might be responsible for editing or supervising the editing and production of the employer's newsletter, magazine, company notices for the bulletin board or paycheck stuffers, and/or informational brochures on company benefits and programs. Other internal responsibilities might include managing an employee feedback program or assisting the personnel department in a recruiting program.

External communications include quarterly and annual stockholder reports; financial statements for the federal government; mailings to stockholders and the public; and all press materials and inquiries.

Community-relations activities might include coordinating a speakers' bureau or representing the company on communications committees of allied industry groups or trade associations.

In addition, a communications coordinator may write speeches for executives or write or supervise the writing and production of scripts for slide shows and films.

Salaries

This is not an entry-level position in most companies. Depending on previous experience, employer, and geographic location, salaries can range from $20,000 to $45,000 or more.

Employment Prospects

Employment opportunities for all public-relations jobs are expected to increase rapidly through the year 2006, according to the federal government. The best prospects for communications coordinator are in private business and industry, especially with large corporations that have big public-relations departments.

Advancement Prospects

A communications coordinator has a good chance of advancing to a higher managerial or supervisory position within the communications department.

Education

Most public-relations workers have undergraduate degrees in public relations, communications, journalism, liberal arts, or English. A degree or advanced degree in business or economics may be advantageous for employment and advancement.

Experience/Skills

A background in public-relations work is desirable for communications coordinator, though some persons may come directly from a journalism background.

Strong writing skills are a must, as is the ability to handle a diverse number of projects simultaneously with minimum supervision. Communications coordinators should be creative and able to direct and motivate others.

Unions/Associations

Major professional associations include the Public Relations Society of America, Inc.; International Association of Business Communicators; and Association for Women in Communications.

PUBLIC-RELATIONS ACCOUNT EXECUTIVE

CAREER PROFILE

Duties: Perform public-relations functions for and advise clients

Alternate Title(s): Consultant

Salary Range: $15,000 to $50,000

Employment Prospects: Good

Advancement Prospects: Good

Prerequisites:
    Education—Undergraduate degree in communications, public relations, journalism, liberal arts, or English
    Experience—Three to five years in public relations, journalism, or as assistant account executive
    Special Skills—Outgoing personality; salesmanship; good writing and organizational skills

CAREER LADDER

```
┌─────────────────────────────────┐
│      Account Supervisor          │
└─────────────────────────────────┘

┌─────────────────────────────────┐
│      Account Executive           │
└─────────────────────────────────┘

┌─────────────────────────────────┐
│  Assistant Account Executive;    │
│  Journalist; News Editor;        │
│  Public-Relations Professional   │
└─────────────────────────────────┘
```

Position Description

A large percentage of public-relations professionals work for agencies or consulting firms. These businesses function the same way as advertising agencies—they perform public-relations services for clients, create publicity campaigns and strategies, and advise clients on public-relations matters, for all of which they charge fees or commissions. Some clients have little or no public-relations staff, while others use agencies to handle projects that would be too big or time-consuming for their own staff.

The account executive is the liaison between the agency and client. He or she works under the supervision of an accounts supervisor or senior consultant. Beginners are usually called assistant account executives, and they perform mostly routine tasks.

Duties depend on the types of services requested by the client. These may include preparing and mailing press kits; conducting press conferences; arranging media interviews and tours for client executives; placing favorable news or feature stories in the media; handling arrangements for promotional luncheons and dinners as well as trade shows; and conducting opinion surveys.

Advisory duties concern planning publicity campaigns; setting up a public-relations department or program; evaluating such a program; and establishing a lobbying platform.

Account executives are likely to coordinate their work with advertising and marketing activities.

Many agencies or consultants specialize in certain areas, such as entertainment or government regulations.

In addition, public-relations account executives may canvass for new clients and write reports for senior staff.

Salaries

Salaried public relations specialists working full time earned a median salary of $34,000 in 1996, according to the federal government. The middle 50 percent earned from $25,000 to $54,000 annually.

Public-relations professionals working for government, health care, or nonprofit organizations had a median salary of $43,260, considerably lower than the median for public-relations firms and corporations: $51,340 and $50,770, respectively. Public-affairs specialists in the federal government in nonsupervisory, supervisory, and managerial positions averaged about $52,540 in 1996. (These statistics take into account higher positions than account executive, but they are still revealing.)

Salaries vary widely according to size of firm, location of firm, and specialty area. A 1999 survey by New York–based firm Gould & Company found that the average salary of account executives surveyed was $40,647 in health care but only $35,111 in fashion and beauty.

Employment Prospects

Employment prospects are best in large cities where communications facilities are based and businesses and trade associations have their headquarters. Cities such as New York, Los Angeles, Chicago, and Washington, D.C., house many public relations firms.

This field is expected to remain competitive, with more people applying for jobs than there are job openings. Employment is expected to increase faster than average for all occupations in the upcoming decade. The Bureau of Labor Statistics predicts that employment of public-relations specialists will increase rapidly through 2006. An increased awareness of the need for public relations should feed growth; corporate downsizing, however, could eliminate some jobs.

Advancement Prospects

The account executive is in a good position for advancement, either in the agency or by moving to a corporation or association. Some account executives become self-employed consultants.

Education

An undergraduate degree in communications, journalism, public relations, liberal arts, or English is the minimum requirement. For consulting, a graduate degree in business or finance is advantageous.

Experience/Skills

Most account executives have backgrounds in public-relations work or in the news media—as journalists or news editors. Skills include ability to work well with others; salesmanship; good writing; creativity; and self-motivation.

Unions/Associations

Major professional associations include the Public Relations Society of America, Inc.; International Association of Business Communicators; and Association for Women in Communications.

TECHNICAL COMMUNICATOR

CAREER PROFILE

Duties: Write and/or edit technical materials for technical and lay audiences

Alternate Title(s): Technical Writer; Technical Editor

Salary Range: $20,000 to $70,000+

Employment Prospects: Excellent

Advancement Prospects: Fair

Prerequisites:

Education—Undergraduate degree in English, technical communications, science, engineering, computer science, journalism, liberal arts

Experience—Previous work as writer or in some capacity in a technical or scientific field advantageous

Special Skills—Comprehension of field being served; ability to work with engineers, technicians, and scientists; ability to rewrite technical material for lay audiences

CAREER LADDER

```
┌─────────────────────────────────┐
│   Technical Communications      │
│   or Publications Manager       │
└─────────────────────────────────┘

┌─────────────────────────────────┐
│   Technical Communicator        │
└─────────────────────────────────┘

┌─────────────────────────────────┐
│   Writer                        │
└─────────────────────────────────┘
```

Position Description

Technical communicators write and edit a wide range of technical material for a variety of audiences. Depending on the industry in which they work, they might write software manuals for the lay computer user; technical manuals for the computer programmer; sales materials that will be aimed at engineers and technicians; repair manuals; in-house communications; specifications sheets; inserts for pharmaceutical products; speeches for industry conferences and meetings; scripts for slides and films, etc.

Their duties may extend into production, for which they work with graphic artists and oversee galleys, proofs, and mechanicals. They may supervise other writers, assistants, and freelancers. Some technical communicators work in education, preparing information and training materials.

Technical communicators often have prior experience in journalism or corporate communications, or in technical fields.

The typical member of the Society for Technical Communications (STC), the leading professional organization, has seven years' experience, lives in a major metropolitan area, works for the computer industry, and is female. About 70 percent are writers or editors.

Members also report a high level of job satisfaction. About 83 percent said they were satisfied with their jobs. Ninety-four percent said job satisfaction was very important to them; 80 percent cited adequate salary; 79 percent said creative opportunity was very important; 76 percent listed freedom as very important.

Salary Range

A 1998 survey by the Society for Technical Communication reported that the mean salary of its members in the United States—who are technical writers and communicators—was $48,250. Mean entry-level salaries were $36,100.

Technical communicators with a Ph.D. degree earned an average of $59,480, as opposed to $49,460 for those with a master's degree and $47,300 for those with a bachelor's degree. Pay varied widely by geographic location. For example, in some parts of California, the median salary was $61,500, but in Idaho and Wyoming, it was only $30,000.

The same study found that, as would be expected, pay increased dramatically with years of experience in technical communication and with age. Men's mean salary was $2,150 higher than women's.

A separate 1999 study by Abbott, Langer & Associates, published on the Internet by wsj.com, found that the median salary and bonus for technical writers was $40,236.

Employment Prospects

Demand for technical writers is expected to increase because of the continued expansion of scientific and technical information and the continued need to communicate it. Although many people are attracted to writing and editing jobs, technical writers and editors enjoy better opportunities than most because of the limited number of people who can handle technical material.

Advancement Prospects

About 20 percent of the members of the STC have managerial responsibilities. However, a survey of members showed that only 24 percent feel that managerial responsibility is very important. The majority valued job satisfaction, adequate salary, creative opportunity, freedom, professional development, and job security.

Education

Ninety-one percent of STC members graduated from a four-year college; a third hold master's degrees or higher. A third majored in English; 18 percent majored in technical writing. A majority of members were hired for their communications skills. Many technical writers picked up specialized knowledge on the job.

Degrees in science, engineering, computer science, graphic arts, mathematics, or economics can also be helpful when combined with good writing ability.

Experience/Skills

Many technical writers transfer to the field from jobs as scientists or engineers. Others start out in lower-level assistant or trainee jobs within a technical information department, learn about the technology, and assume writing jobs.

Technical communicators have to be able to cut through jargon to explain technical points or offer instruction in everyday language. Some jobs may require a technical background or degree. Attention to detail, precision, creativity, organization, and self-discipline are important attributes for these jobs.

Unions/Associations

The Society for Technical Communication is the primary professional association. Technical communicators also may belong to organizations in their areas of expertise, such as the American Medical Writers Association or National Association of Science Writers, Inc.

ADVERTISING

ASSISTANT ACCOUNT EXECUTIVE

CAREER PROFILE

Duties: Research and prepare materials pertaining to advertising agency account management

Alternate Title(s): Account Executive Trainee

Salary Range: $20,000 to $45,000

Employment Prospects: Fair

Advancement Prospects: Good

Prerequisites:
    Education—Undergraduate degree in advertising, liberal arts, journalism, business
    Experience—None
    Special Skills—Grasp of advertising and marketing; organization; salesmanship

CAREER LADDER

```
┌─────────────────────────────┐
│     Account Executive       │
└─────────────────────────────┘

┌─────────────────────────────┐
│ Assistant Account Executive │
└─────────────────────────────┘

┌─────────────────────────────┐
│      Trainee; College       │
└─────────────────────────────┘
```

Position Description

Assistant account executive is generally an entry-level position, though in some agencies it may be a step up from trainee, which is essentially a clerical and secretarial job.

Assistant account executives learn the advertising business by performing routine and low-level tasks for the account service department. They may work for one account executive on one or two accounts, or they may work for an entire department of account executives. In the process, they learn how to look after a client's interests, coordinate creative and production work, plan campaigns, and do market analyses.

Duties include research for client proposals and advertising campaigns; assistance in preparing reports and proposals, including writing and graphics; typing; proofreading; and errands. Assistant account executives may occasionally take part in meetings with clients or in presentations.

Assistant account executives often shoulder the bulk of the legwork on projects but share very little of the credit. Work hours are regular business hours, but overtime is not uncommon, especially on short notice.

Some public-relations agencies may also employ assistant account executives to work on public relations and publicity campaigns.

Salaries

A December 1997 survey done by *Advertising Age* found that beginning salaries for assistant account executives ranged between $20,000 and $25,000. The same survey found that the employee's level and quality of education, and previous industry experience, such as an internship, influenced starting position and salary considerably.

Survey respondents reported that raises were scant and benefits had been trimmed. The best raises went to those who changed jobs. Most increases were around 5 to 10 percent.

Younger employees with less experience were most concerned about pay levels, particularly those working in New York, where the cost of living eats up low pay. Those under 30 averaged $30,000 in assistant or junior-level jobs.

Employment Prospects

Mergers and consolidations of agencies make the field very competitive.

Advancement Prospects

An assistant account executive who is willing to work hard has a good chance of being promoted to a full-fledged account executive. Often promotion comes through turnover, which is high in the advertising industry.

Education

Assistant account executives generally have undergraduate degrees in advertising, business, journalism, or liberal arts. The work is marketing- and sales-oriented, so an educational emphasis on business and economic studies is helpful. Advanced degrees in business or advertising can give job candidates the competitive edge with many employers.

Experience/Skills

Some assistant account executives begin their careers as trainees, little more than clerical and secretarial assistants. Others come straight from college or from entry-level work in a related field, such as sales, public relations, or journalism. Writing and selling experience is helpful.

Skills include a flair for making favorable impressions and getting along well with others, clear writing ability, salesmanship, good organization, and persistence.

Unions/Associations

Major associations for advertising professionals include the American Advertising Federation; Business/Professional Advertising Association; American Marketing Association; and Association for Women in Communications.

ACCOUNT EXECUTIVE

CAREER PROFILE

Duties: Coordinate all advertising activities for advertising agency clients; maintain good client relations

Alternate Title(s): None

Salary Range: $27,500 to $65,000+

Employment Prospects: Fair

Advancement Prospects: Fair

Prerequisites:
Education—Undergraduate degree in advertising, business, liberal arts, journalism, or communications
Experience—One to three years as trainee or assistant account executive helpful
Special Skills—Leadership and salesmanship; copy judgment; knowledge of graphics, media, and marketing

CAREER LADDER

```
+-------------------------------------+
|        Accounts Manager;            |
|        Accounts Supervisor          |
+-------------------------------------+

+-------------------------------------+
|         Account Executive           |
+-------------------------------------+

+-------------------------------------+
|  Assistant Account Executive; Trainee |
+-------------------------------------+
```

Position Description

Most account executives work for advertising agencies; others work in the advertising or sales departments of businesses and media. The account executive is in charge of the advertising for one or more of an ad agency's clients (usually one large account or several small accounts). He or she determines and plans the nature of the advertising to be produced, relaying the client's expectations and needs to the agency's creative and media buying departments. The account executive coordinates the agency's activities and reviews the creative work produced before presenting it to the client. He or she is the agency's liaison with clients, and must work to maintain good communication and a good relationship.

Account executives must have a thorough knowledge of all operations within an agency, and understand their clients' businesses, marketing, and competition. They must be able to judge whether or not creative copy and proposed ad campaigns are on target. They must be able to understand market analyses and have a thorough understanding of all media, in order to plan the most effective ad campaigns. When campaigns are developed, account executives make formal presentations to the clients or management.

Account executives report to an account supervisor or account manager, who in turn reports to a director or vice president of account services. In large agencies, account executives may delegate research and clerical functions to assistants; in small agencies, they may do everything themselves.

Public-relations agencies also employ account executives, who are responsible for publicity campaigns and press relations.

Additionally, account executives may participate in campaigns and presentations to win new clients, and coordinate publicity and promotional activities along with advertising.

Salaries

A December 1997 survey done by *Advertising Age* found that beginning salaries for account executives ranged between $27,500 and $32,500. The same survey found that the employee's level and quality of education, and previous industry experience, such as an internship, influenced starting position and salary considerably.

Advertising Age reported that the average salary of account executives at advertising agencies in 1998 was $48,200: that is, $45,000 base pay plus a $3,200 bonus. With experience, pay can increase to $65,000 or more.

Those who change jobs more frequently may gain bigger raises. Many survey respondents reported no recent raises or raises in the 5 to 10 percent range; 20 percent reported changing jobs in the previous year.

Employment Prospects

Employment in advertising is projected to increase at a fast rate during the next 10 years, however. Competition between businesses will require greater marketing and promotional efforts, according to the federal government.

Advancement Prospects

Account executives who excel at their jobs can advance rapidly in responsibility and pay. The top executives of most advertising agencies came up through the ranks of account executives. Competition is fierce, however, and job security is low—it is not uncommon to be fired if an agency loses an account or if the economy is in recession.

Education

Most account executives have undergraduate degrees in advertising, business, liberal arts, or journalism. A graduate degree in advertising, business, or economics is not necessary but works to the candidate's advantage.

Experience/Skills

In most cases, account executives work as assistant account executives or trainees before being given full responsibility for clients. Some account executives have worked previously as journalists or in advertising sales.

Account executives must understand all aspects of an advertising campaign, from judging creative copy to coordinating the purchase of media space and time. Since they have highly visible positions as their agencies' representatives, they must be skilled in salesmanship and demonstrate leadership.

Unions/Associations

Associations include the American Advertising Federation; Business/Professional Advertising Association; and Association for Women in Communications.

ASSISTANT COPYWRITER

CAREER PROFILE

Duties: Assist in development and execution of creative ad copy; clerical tasks

Alternate Title(s): None

Salary Range: $16,000 to $35,000

Employment Prospects: Fair

Advancement Prospects: Good

Prerequisites:
Education—Undergraduate degree in advertising, liberal arts, journalism, communications, or art
Experience—None
Special Skills—Imagination; creativity; command of English

CAREER LADDER

```
┌─────────────────────────────┐
│        Copywriter           │
└─────────────────────────────┘

┌─────────────────────────────┐
│     Assistant Copywriter    │
└─────────────────────────────┘

┌─────────────────────────────┐
│      Trainee; College       │
└─────────────────────────────┘
```

Position Description

Assistant copywriter is an entry-level position, usually at an advertising agency, sometimes in the advertising or marketing department of a business. An assistant copywriter may be fresh out of college or may still be enrolled, working during summers or through class internships.

The position involves routine work assisting copywriters, as well as limited opportunities to handle creative projects. Routine work includes researching a client, product, service, or industry that will be used by the copywriter in developing an ad; proofreading copy; trafficking copy among departments; and running errands.

Assistant copywriters also may be assigned creative projects of their own. They work under the supervision of a copywriter or senior copywriter, sometimes the copy supervisor. Their position may enable them to receive career counseling or training. Opportunities to learn other aspects of the advertising business, such as production, media buying, or account services, may be offered them.

Salaries

According to a 1994 salary survey done by *Adweek,* assistants of all kinds in advertising agencies averaged $33,600. Employees in creative departments earned more than those in account services or media, averaging $85,900.

Women assistants averaged $32,700, while men averaged $41,100 in junior or assistant positions.

A 1992 survey of recent journalism school graduates, however, reported an average starting salary of $20,000 for those working in advertising agencies or departments.

Job-jumpers fared better with raises in 1994. Most *Adweek* survey respondents reported raises in the 5 to 10 percent range; raises of 20 percent or more were primarily reported by those who changed jobs.

Employment Prospects

Employment slowed and competition for jobs in advertising grew in the late 1980s and early 1990s as agencies consolidated. But government projections show employment in advertising growing at a fast rate during the next 10 years. Growth will be spurred by increased competition between businesses, which will then need to promote their products and services more vigorously.

Advancement Prospects

Once hired, advancement opportunities in the creative department can be good for those with talent and initiative. New and fresh ideas are always encouraged, and successful ideas are well rewarded in salary, bonuses, and other perks.

Education

An undergraduate degree in advertising, liberal arts, communications, or art is the minimum requirement. Education should include courses in writing and creative writing. Advanced degrees are not all that helpful for the creative side of the advertising business.

Experience/Skills

Any kind of writing experience, especially advertising-related, is advantageous for copywriting jobs. Aspiring copywriters should work on school publications, community projects, or for agencies or the media part time. Some journalists make the transition to advertising copywriting.

Copywriters should excel in their command of English and have a flair for persuasion. They should be able to write for different media.

Unions/Associations

Associations open to advertising professionals include the American Advertising Federation; American Marketing Association; Business/Professional Advertising Association; and Association for Women in Communications. The Writers Guild of America, a union, includes many copywriters who also write scripts and screenplays for television and film.

COPYWRITER

CAREER PROFILE	CAREER LADDER

Duties: Develop ideas and write ad copy and scripts for media, sales campaigns, and direct marketing

Alternate Title(s): None

Salary Range: $25,000 to $70,000+

Employment Prospects: Fair

Advancement Prospects: Fair

Prerequisites:
   Education—Undergraduate degree in communications, liberal arts, art, advertising, or business
   Experience—Background as a professional writer or journalist helpful
   Special Skills—Creativity, imagination, salesmanship, command of English

```
┌─────────────────────────────────┐
│         Copy Supervisor         │
└─────────────────────────────────┘

┌─────────────────────────────────┐
│            Copywriter           │
└─────────────────────────────────┘

┌─────────────────────────────────┐
│ Assistant Copywriter; Journalist; │
│             College             │
└─────────────────────────────────┘
```

Position Description

Copywriters write the text of print ads for radio and television ads, as well as text for promotional material, sales campaigns, and direct marketing campaigns.

Many copywriters work for advertising agencies, while others work for the in-house advertising departments or marketing departments of companies and corporations. Their jobs are highly demanding, because the success of the advertising depends greatly on the creativity and sales stimulus of the copy. Working hours generally are regular weekday hours, but overtime is often required to meet deadline pressures.

In a large agency or department, copywriters report to a senior copywriter or copy supervisor, who in turn reports to a creative director or advertising director. In a smaller environment, copywriters may report directly to the creative or advertising director.

The creation of an advertising campaign is a team effort. The creative staff works with the account service or marketing staff to execute an overall strategy or theme that will accomplish the client's goals. Any combination of media may be used: print, broadcast, point-of-sale, direct mail, billboards, transit, or specialty (giveaway premiums imprinted with the client's name).

In a small agency or department, one copywriter may do all the media copy for a particular client; in a large agency, the client's work may be divided among several copywriters who each specialize in one or two media, such as billboards or broadcast. Copy and scripts must convey information and persuade others to buy products or services, or accept ideas. Radio and television scripts must also include instructions for voice-overs and special effects.

In addition, copywriters may research information for ads, edit and rewrite copy, and be responsible for production and distribution of ad materials.

Salaries

Employees in creative departments of advertising agencies can expect to make slightly more than those in other departments. *Advertising Age* reported that the average salary of copywriters in 1998 was $50,900: that is, $48,000 base pay plus a $2,900 bonus.

Another survey by *Advertising Age* found that copywriters' base salaries grew by an average of over 6 percent during 1999, but the exact percentages varied by geographic region: 8 percent in the West, 7 percent in the East, and 6 percent in the Midwest and South.

Employment Prospects

Employment in advertising in the late 1980s and early 1990s became very competitive as agencies consolidated.

The job outlook for the next 10 years seems brighter, however. Government projections predict fast growth in advertising as businesses compete vigorously to promote their products and services.

Advancement Prospects

Advertising is a highly competitive field, but those with initiative, fresh ideas, and talent advance rapidly and are well rewarded. Good copywriters are given increasing supervisory responsibility and more prestigious accounts. Advertising is characterized by high turnover, and advancement often comes by moving to another agency or company.

Education

The minimum requirement is an undergraduate degree in communications, liberal arts, art, business, or advertising. Advanced degrees are of less value for copywriting than for account service. Education should include courses in copywriting or creative writing.

Experience/Skills

Education should be supplemented with writing experience, such as working on school or community publications. Part-time advertising jobs or advertising-related extracurricular work is helpful. Previous experience in journalism also is useful for copywriting.

The copywriter must have an excellent command of language and be able to visualize ad ideas. One should have a good knowledge of production, including typography and layout. Above all, he or she should be inventive and willing to experiment with unusual approaches or ideas.

Unions/Associations

The American Advertising Federation and the American Marketing Association are principal associations of interest to copywriters. Many belong to the Association for Women in Communications. Some copywriters are members of the Writers Guild of America, a union for television, film, and radio scriptwriters and screenwriters.

FEDERAL GOVERNMENT

EDITORIAL ASSISTANT AND CLERK

CAREER PROFILE

Duties: Edit and handle production of manuscripts; secretarial tasks

Alternate Title(s): None

Salary Range: $17,000 to $28,000

Employment Prospects: Fair

Advancement Prospects: Good

Prerequisites:
　Education—High school diploma minimum
　Experience—General office, clerical, or editorial support work required
　Special Skills—Knowledge of grammar, editorial production; clerical skills

CAREER LADDER

```
┌─────────────────────────────┐
│   Supervisory Editorial     │
│    Assistant or Clerk       │
└─────────────────────────────┘

┌─────────────────────────────┐
│  Editorial Assistant or Clerk │
└─────────────────────────────┘

┌─────────────────────────────┐
│   High School or College    │
└─────────────────────────────┘
```

Position Description

Editorial clerks and assistants perform a wide range of clerical and editorial support work, in preparing manuscripts for publication and in verifying information in copy. Basic duties include proofreading final copy and page proofs against the original manuscripts; specifying formats, type, and styles; editing for basic grammatical accuracy and structural clarity; and verifying references, footnotes, and tabular material.

Specific duties vary according to federal agency and grade level. Some editorial clerks and assistants work in groups under the direction of a supervisory editorial clerk or assistant. Others work directly for writers, editors, or subject matter specialists. Regardless of the work setting, editorial clerks and assistants usually all perform the same types of work. Most of their editing jobs concern accuracy and grammar, though they may suggest to editors changes to reorganize material.

They prepare the layout, including placement of graphics, and give typesetting and printing instructions. High-level clerks and assistants may perform more writing, as well as substantive editing tasks similar to those expected of writers and editors.

Special knowledge of subject matter isn't necessary, except for certain specialized and technical subjects. Editor-

ial clerks and assistants should be thoroughly familiar with grammatical rules and production procedures.

Employees frequently work under rigid deadlines, high pressure, and last-minute rushes. Accuracy is all-important. The editorial assistant/clerk also must have the ability to handle a high volume of work independently, follow detailed instructions, and interpret policies and regulations.

Salaries

Editorial assistant and clerk positions are among the few in the federal government in which women tend to earn more than men. Overall, salaries can range from $17,000 to $28,000. Most positions fall within the G54 to G57 range, around $20,000.

Jobs within the federal government are managed by the U.S. Office of Personnel Management (OPM), which has an informative web site at http://www.opm.gov/index.htm. Another web site, http://www.opm.gov/fedclass/index.htm, gives more detailed information about the OPM's federal job classification system.

Employment Prospects

Federal jobs are highly competitive. Growth in new positions has been slow and is expected to remain so due to budget cutbacks. Nearly 80 percent of all federal employees work outside of Washington, D.C., throughout the United States.

Advancement Prospects

Advancement by grade level brings additional responsibilities and pay. Editorial clerks and assistants may also move up to writer or editor positions, or other posts in communications.

Education

A high school diploma is the minimum education requirement for editorial assistant and clerk positions.

Experience/Skills

Two to five years of clerical or editorial support experience is considered minimal. College education may be substituted for experience in order to qualify. Experience includes responsibilities for grammatical editing, reviewing, and screening; fact-checking; research; proofreading; and editorial production.

Because of the detail of their work, editorial assistants and clerks must be meticulous, dependable, and accurate to a very high degree. The work also requires an unusual degree of patience and a liking for close and exacting work.

Unions/Associations

Major unions and associations that represent federal white collar employees are the National Association of Government Employees; American Federation of Government Employees; National Federation of Federal Employees; National Association of Government Communicators; American Federation of State, County and Municipal Employees; and Federally Employed Women, Inc. Editorial assistants and clerks may also belong to related professional associations outside of government.

WRITER AND EDITOR

CAREER PROFILE

Duties: Write and edit articles, news releases, publications, and scripts

Alternate Title(s): None

Salary Range: $19,000 to $65,000

Employment Prospects: Fair

Advancement Prospects: Good

Prerequisites:
    Education—High school diploma minimum; college degree preferred
    Experience—Two to six years' writing or editing experience for most positions
    Special Skills—Good writing, editing skills; originality; initiative

CAREER LADDER

```
┌─────────────────────────────────┐
│   Supervisory Writer or Editor   │
└─────────────────────────────────┘

┌─────────────────────────────────┐
│        Writer or Editor          │
└─────────────────────────────────┘

┌─────────────────────────────────┐
│ Editorial Assistant or Clerk; High │
│       School or College          │
└─────────────────────────────────┘
```

Position Description

Writers and editors communicate information for several purposes: to report research and investigations carried on by federal agencies; to explain laws and regulations, as well as changes in them; and to make public reports on the activities and plans of agencies. The forms of communication include articles, press releases, pamphlets, brochures, speeches, and radio, television, and film scripts.

Some writing and editing positions do not require substantial subject-matter knowledge; all positions, however, require the ability to adapt information to a particular style, format, or audience. Most positions do not involve formulating the policy or philosophy behind the content of the information.

Writers collect information through library research, reading, and interviewing subject specialists, policy officials, and others. They turn their manuscripts over to editors, who review, rewrite, and edit as necessary and in consultation with writers. Editors may supervise editorial assistants and clerks to do routine checking and editing.

Most positions are either wholly writing or editing, but some combine the two functions. Those employees are called writer-editors. Writers and editors may specialize according to media, working predominantly in print, radio, film, or television.

The overall scope of a writer or editor's responsibilities depends on the grade level of the job. At lower grade levels, assignments are specific, and detailed instructions cover scope and content. There is limited opportunity for creativity. At higher levels, the writer or editor has greater opportunity to influence the scope of the assignment.

Salaries

Salaries for federally employed writers and editors depend on the job grade and years of experience. Most fall between the pay scales GS5 and GS12 or GS13, with pay ranging from $19,000 at entry level to $65,000 at the top. The highest-paying positions may require 10 or more years of experience. The average salary for writers and editors in the federal government in 1992 was $39,077.

Jobs within the federal government are managed by the U.S. Office of Personnel Management (OPM), which has an informative web site at http://www.opm.gov/index.htm. Another web site, http://www.opm.gov/fedclass/index.htm, gives more detailed information about the OPM's federal job classification system.

Employment Prospects

The chances of getting a federal writing or editing job are only fair, due to budget cutbacks and lack of growth.

Advancement Prospects

Writers and editors have a good chance of advancing to more responsible grade classification positions or to supervisory jobs. Other communications jobs exist outside of writing and editing.

Education

The minimum requirement is a high school diploma. Undergraduate degrees in English, journalism, or communications may be preferred for many higher level posts. College study may be substituted for job experience in meeting minimum hiring qualifications.

Experience/Skills

Persons without college degrees must be experienced in professional, administrative, technical, or other work that requires the ability to analyze information and present it in written form. Specialized experience in writing or editing jobs in a particular medium may also be required.

Basic skills include researching, analyzing, and organizing information; good writing and knowledge of grammar; editing ability; self-motivation; and the ability to work independently and, at times, under deadline pressure.

Unions/Associations

The National Association of Government Employees; National Association of Government Communicators; American Federation of Government Employees; National Federation of Federal Employees; American Federation of State, County and Municipal Employees; and Federally Employed Women, Inc., are the major unions and associations for federal white-collar workers. Employees may also belong to related professional organizations outside of federal government.

TECHNICAL WRITER AND EDITOR

CAREER PROFILE

Duties: Write and edit technical manuals, specifications, and publications for federal agencies

Alternate Title(s): Technical Publications Writer or Editor; Technical Manuals Writer or Editor; Specifications Writer or Editor

Salary Range: $19,000 to $100,000+

Employment Prospects: Poor

Advancement Prospects: Fair

Prerequisites:
 Education—Undergraduate college degree preferred
 Experience—Two to six years' writing or degree with courses in science, engineering, or computer science
 Special Skills—Understanding of and ability to explain technical subjects; writing and editing skills; self-motivation

CAREER LADDER

```
┌─────────────────────────────┐
│   Supervisory Technical      │
│     Writer or Editor         │
└─────────────────────────────┘

┌─────────────────────────────┐
│   Technical Writer or Editor │
└─────────────────────────────┘

┌─────────────────────────────┐
│   College; Other Technical   │
│    Writing or Editing Job    │
└─────────────────────────────┘
```

Position Description

There are three general categories of technical writers and editors in the federal government: publications, specifications, and manuals.

Technical publications writers and editors are involved in government activities that carry on programs of research, investigations, or operation in natural and social sciences, engineering, medicine, law, and the like. They are responsible for disseminating findings and information to the general public as well as to scientific and administrative communities. Their work involves preparation of papers, articles, reports, summaries, and digests based on interviews, research reports, and their own reading.

Many agencies combine technical writing and editing assignments. Some editors may be assigned to groups or committees, and be responsible for assembling individual reports into a single document reflecting the total viewpoint of the group.

Both technical manual and specifications positions are found in federal activities that carry on programs of applied scientific research and development of weapons, communications systems, equipment, and devices. Job duties include writing, editing, and disseminating basic instruction materials, maintenance and operation instructions, design information, and training guides. Equipment specifications are used for purchasing and inventory control.

Most technical writing and editing jobs require substantial knowledge of a particular subject or field. Those technical writers and editors who have educations or specializations in journalism or English usually have had additional training or education in technical subjects.

About three-fourths of the technical writers and editors work for the Department of Defense, writing manuals on weapons and instruments for military personnel. The departments of Agriculture, Interior, and Health and Human Services, as well as the National Aeronautics and Space Administration, also employ many technical writers and editors.

Salaries

Technical writer was listed as one of 20 hot job tracks by *U.S. News & World Report* in its 1999 annual guide to best jobs. A specialized background like engineering or business helps, but on-the-job training is often available. Government salaries vary widely, depending on the complexity of the job, geographic area, and other factors. Some government technical writing jobs pay in the low $20,000s; others pay $100,000 or more.

Jobs within the federal government are managed by the U.S. Office of Personnel Management (OPM), which has an informative web site at http://www.opm.gov/index.htm. Another web site, http://www.opm.gov/fedclass/index.htm, gives more detailed information about the OPM's federal job classification system.

Employment Prospects

Few federal job openings are expected through the 1990s. Most vacancies will occur due to retirements or transfers to other jobs.

Advancement Prospects

Chances of advancement are limited, due to the small number of openings that occur every year. Rising in job grade classification levels brings increasing responsibilities and salaries. Other advancement may be possible by moving to related communications jobs.

Education

Job candidates should have undergraduate degrees, preferably in a science. Those with nonscience degrees should have had studies in science, engineering, or com- puter science. In this field, a graduate degree in a science is likely to be very advantageous.

Experience/Skills

Job experience is not necessary for some entry-level positions; a year or more of experience can qualify a candidate for a higher level job with more pay.

Technical writers and editors must be able to understand complex subjects and be able to write clearly about them. They are often required to write for different audiences, explaining the same topic to a sophisticated professional group and to the general public, for example. Their job requires accuracy and an orientation to detail. Editing, production, and supervisory skills may be necessary for many positions.

Unions/Associations

Major unions and associations include the American Federation of Government Employees; National Association of Government Communicators; National Association of Government Employees; American Federation of State, County and Municipal Employees; National Federation of Federal Employees; and Federally Employed Women, Inc. Technical writers and editors may also belong to the Society for Technical Communication, as well as to related writing or scientific professional associations.

PRESS SECRETARY

CAREER PROFILE

Duties: Respond to press inquiries; write press releases; ghostwrite speeches, newspaper columns, letters to constituents and other materials for legislators; arrange press conferences; write and produce material for radio shows and release to radio reporters; stay abreast of news developments and try to anticipate their impact

Alternate Title(s): Public Affairs Specialist

Salary Range: $20,000 to $90,000+

Employment Prospects: Fair

Advancement Prospects: Good

Prerequisites:

Education—Bachelor's degree

Experience—Several years working in news (print, radio, or television); familiarity with media in legislator or political figure's home state, if working for an individual

Special Skills—Ability to imitate employer's writing style; ability to anticipate what issues or news events will prompt questions from the media; good organizational skills

CAREER LADDER

```
┌─────────────────────────────────┐
│  Private Industry; Press         │
│  Secretary at Federal Agency     │
└─────────────────────────────────┘

┌─────────────────────────────────┐
│        Press Secretary           │
└─────────────────────────────────┘

┌─────────────────────────────────┐
│          Journalist              │
└─────────────────────────────────┘
```

Position Description

Press secretaries perform a wide range of duties, depending on how much emphasis their employers place on media visibility and whether they work for a legislative committee or political figure.

Some politicians do not like to write, and rely heavily on their press secretaries to compose speeches, letters, newspaper columns, and other written material in addition to press releases. While press releases are generally straightforward and written like news, other materials may require the press secretary to know how his or her boss thinks and speaks to be able to ghostwrite in that style.

A press secretary must also monitor the news—television shows, newspapers, wire services, and magazines—and anticipate what impact events may have upon the policies and public stances of his or her employer. Responses to anticipated questions from the media need to be assembled and information gathered.

Some press secretaries may also act as chiefs of staff or administrative assistants, making personnel decisions or influencing a politician's legislative agenda.

While most press secretaries confine their work to Washington, almost all of them visit the legislator's home district from time to time. It is important for press secretaries to meet with the reporters back home who will be reading the releases and calling with questions.

Press secretaries also sometimes produce short radio programs, during which they ask the congressman five or six questions, in the house recording studio. Tapes and scripts are then sent out to radio stations.

Part of the job also involves getting publicity for the legislator's pet projects and bills he or she may be sponsoring.

Workdays can be long. During times of heavy political activity, or if a particular issue of concern to the employer comes to the fore, 12-hour days are not uncommon. As in the news business, events often dictate the workload. Press secretaries for high-profile figures may also have heavier workloads.

Salaries

Salaries vary widely according to the priorities of each legislator. Each congressman and senator receives a budget for his or her office staff to spend as he or she sees fit.

A high-profile politician may hire a press secretary with impressive credentials for a higher salary, and cut back on staff in some other area. Some highly paid press secretaries also double as the administrative assistant, who oversees the office staff and is in charge of hiring and firing. Legislative committees and subcommittees employ press secretaries and have more money at their disposal to hire staff.

Public affairs positions within government agencies range from about $17,000 to $65,000. The average press secretary in the House makes about $38,200. The average salary for a press secretary to a senator is $54,000.

Employment Prospects

Prospects are best in Washington, D.C., where there might be a dozen press secretary openings at any given time. Jobs turn over regularly, either due to the defeat of incumbents at the polls or because seasoned press secretaries leave for less pressured jobs.

However, competition is stiff, and many legislators prefer to hire people with a familiarity with the media in their home state rather than those versed in the mores of Washington power politics.

Related positions, public affairs jobs in federal agencies, account for the highest number of communications-related jobs in the federal government, and many press secretaries cross over into these jobs.

Advancement Prospects

The wide range of public affairs–related jobs within the federal government makes for good advancement prospects.

Press secretaries can become chiefs of staff or administrative assistants, take jobs with higher-profile legislators or ones they get along with better, work for legislative committees or federal agencies.

Most press secretaries work in the legislature for a few years and then move on to less-pressured, more stable jobs, either with government agencies or in the private sector.

Education

Most press secretaries have undergraduate degrees in communications, journalism, English, or liberal arts.

Experience/Skills

A background in one of the news media or public relations is generally required, although there is no one unifying characteristic among press secretaries. A familiarity with news organizations in a legislator's home state is very helpful.

Creativity, intelligence, the ability to analyze information and to communicate clearly are also key attributes of successful press secretaries.

Unions/Associations

Each political party has its own professional organization for public affairs specialists and press secretaries in Washington, D.C., such as the Republican Communications Association. In addition, press secretaries may also belong to the Public Relations Society of America, Inc., or the Association for Women in Communications.

Some also belong to the National Association of Government Communicators; the National Association of Government Employees; American Federation of Government Employees; National Federation of Federal Employees; American Federation of State, County and Municipal Employees; and Federally Employed Women, Inc. Many find it advantageous to belong to the National Press Club.

POLITICAL SPEECHWRITER

CAREER PROFILE

Duties: Research, draft, and edit speeches for political figures or bodies

Alternate Title(s): Special Assistant for Communications

Salary Range: $20,000 to $100,000

Employment Prospects: Fair

Advancement Prospects: Fair

Prerequisites:
   Education—Bachelor's degree in liberal arts, communications, or journalism; some jobs may require a law degree or other advanced degree
   Experience—Experience varies; can include backgrounds in law, journalism, public relations, legislative research, political campaigning, public policy
   Special Skills—Must know where to find information; must understand the substance of the speech and whom it is targeting; must be able to work under pressure and imitate style of person who will be delivering the speech

CAREER LADDER

```
┌─────────────────────────────────┐
│   Director of Communications    │
└─────────────────────────────────┘

┌─────────────────────────────────┐
│         Speechwriter            │
└─────────────────────────────────┘

┌─────────────────────────────────┐
│  Public Information Officer; Press │
│  Secretary; Legislative Director  │
└─────────────────────────────────┘
```

Position Description

Political speechwriters are generally people interested in politics who have had some other contact with political life. Often they are hired for their expertise in a specific area and frequently write speeches on related topics. In some offices, speechwriters divide the workload according to topic; sometimes the division can be as broad as foreign and domestic policy.

In smaller offices, speechwriting duties may be handled by a press secretary or legislative director. The work is often high pressure with little advance warning. Speeches often have to be prepared in response to news events, and information has to be gathered quickly.

Speeches also have to be prepared for a wide range of audiences. The speechwriter needs to know if questions from the media and the audience will be allowed, how long the speech should be, the topic, and general content.

Speechwriters may also be moved between staff jobs and campaign jobs. A staff speechwriter cannot work on his boss's campaign; a campaign speechwriter must be paid from campaign funds.

Salaries

Because speechwriting is such a visible job, experienced and talented speechwriters can earn $100,000 or more. Those hired with little experience to work for a low-profile legislator or committee may only make $20,000; others may find speechwriting just one of a number of public relations duties within an office.

Employment Prospects

Demand for speechwriters is growing as more professional speechwriting is being used both by politicians and private businesses. Within the federal government, political offices, committees, and federal agencies hire speechwriters.

Advancement Prospects

Just as people come to speechwriting from all kinds of backgrounds, they move into all different types of careers from speechwriting. Some move into private-sector speechwriting, drafting speeches for company executives. Others become newspaper columnists, bookwriters, or political consultants.

Speechwriters may move from less-visible offices to those of higher-profile political figures or agencies. They may become press secretaries or legislative directors.

Education

An undergraduate degree in communications, journalism, English, or liberal arts is essential. An advanced degree in political science, government, public policy, law, or journalism is a plus.

Experience/Skills

A wide variety of backgrounds can be found among speechwriters. Public policy, campaigning, legislative research, journalism, or public relations are generally good preparation for this field.

Speechwriters should have an ear for the spoken word and an ability to mimic the style of the person who will deliver the speech. Strong research skills, an ability to work under pressure, and a tolerance for revisions are also important attributes.

Unions/Associations

Major professional associations include the Public Relations Society of America, Inc., and the Association for Women in Communications. Some speechwriters may also belong to unions for federal employees.

SCHOLASTIC, ACADEMIC, AND NONPROFIT INSTITUTIONS

JOURNALISM TEACHER

CAREER PROFILE

Duties: Teach secondary-school classes in journalism, creative writing, and English; advise student publications

Alternate Title(s): None

Salary Range: $15,000 to $45,000+

Employment Prospects: Fair

Advancement Prospects: Fair

Prerequisites:
  Education—Undergraduate degree in communications, journalism, education, liberal arts; graduate degree preferred
  Experience—None to several years
  Special Skills—Ability to help and motivate others; organization; speaking skills; ability to handle problems

CAREER LADDER

```
┌─────────────────────────────┐
│        Administrator        │
└─────────────────────────────┘

┌─────────────────────────────┐
│           Teacher           │
└─────────────────────────────┘

┌─────────────────────────────┐
│           College           │
└─────────────────────────────┘
```

Position Description

A journalism teacher in a junior or senior high school usually has a wide range of responsibilities. Only one or two classes may be devoted to teaching news gathering, writing, and editing, or work on student publications. The teacher may also conduct classes in English and creative writing, plus supervise study hall, homeroom, or lunch periods.

Journalism teachers are responsible for all or most student publications, such as newspapers, creative writing magazines, and yearbooks. They advise the student staffs on content and layout, and give final approval to the finished product before it is published.

Disciplinary problems must be handled with sensitivity and tact. Classroom presentations must be designed to meet the individual needs and abilities of students. Instructional materials can include films, slides, and computer terminals, as well as books. Teachers may bring in journalism and editorial professionals as guest speakers, as well as arrange field trips to visit local newspapers, magazines, or printing companies.

In addition to developing and teaching regular classes, teachers supervise extracurricular activities, meet after hours with students and parents, and are expected to participate regularly in classes and workshops to stay current in their field. Most teachers work more than 40 hours a week, but have at least two months off during summer break.

Salaries

In the 1997–98 school year, the national average beginning teacher salary was $25,735, and the national average teacher salary was $39,347. Graduate degrees bring higher pay. Earnings in private schools are generally lower.

Employment Prospects

Overall job prospects at the secondary school level are expected to increase through the next decade due to the corresponding growth in the population of 14- to 17-year-olds.

Advancement Prospects

Experienced teachers with additional preparation may move into positions as school librarians, reading specialists, curriculum specialists, or guidance counselors. Teachers may also move into administrative or supervisory jobs. In some schools, experienced teachers may become senior or mentor teachers, helping less experienced teachers while continuing to teach.

Advancement opportunities may be improved as the high school age population grows; however, pressure from taxpayers to limit spending on education could reduce advancement opportunities.

Education

An undergraduate degree, preferably in English, liberal arts, communications, or journalism, is the minimum educational requirement. Approximately half the states in the nation require graduate degrees. In addition, teachers must be certified by state boards of education.

Experience/Skills

Beginning teachers start right after graduation from college. Previous work as a journalist or editor is helpful for specializing as a journalism teacher. Teachers should be comfortable speaking to groups, able to organize class content, materials, and tests, and interested in helping and instructing others.

Unions/Associations

The National Education Association and American Federation of Teachers are the major professional and wage-bargaining unions for secondary-school teachers. The AFT is affiliated with the AFL-CIO.

ASSISTANT PROFESSOR

CAREER PROFILE

Duties: Teach college-level classes in all or various aspects of communications

Alternate Title(s): None

Salary Range: $27,000 to $50,000+

Employment Prospects: Good

Advancement Prospects: Fair

Prerequisites:
   Education—Ph.D. usually required
   Experience—Four to five years working in the field
   Special Skills—Skill in instructing and helping others; speaking ability; organization

CAREER LADDER

```
┌─────────────────────────────┐
│    Associate Professor       │
└─────────────────────────────┘


┌─────────────────────────────┐
│    Assistant Professor       │
└─────────────────────────────┘


┌─────────────────────────────┐
│         Instructor           │
└─────────────────────────────┘
```

Position Description

Assistant professor is an entry-level untenured teaching position in colleges and universities. Candidates have worked several years as journalists or advertising or public-relations professionals, and have earned graduate degrees, usually Ph.D.s.

Assistant professors teach undergraduate courses, many of them large lecture classes of several hundred students. They may specialize in certain areas of communications, such as print or broadcast journalism, advertising, or public relations. Their courses may include introductions to mass communications and mass-communications law and theory, as well as practical instruction in news or copywriting, editing, composition, and layout. They may coordinate course materials and lectures with other faculty members. Teaching loads average nine to 12 hours a week. Besides lecturing, assistant professors make reading and writing assignments, and develop and grade exams.

College enrollment is projected to grow from 14 million in 1996 to 16 million in 2006, an increase of 14 percent. The demographic breakdown of the nation's college students is changing; there are more 18- to 24-year-old students, along with a growing number of female, part-time, and older students.

Assistant professors, as well as their colleagues, are expected to stay abreast of developments in the field and to write and publish articles or books. They may also supervise or help supervise intern programs and have advisory roles on student publications. The proportion of time spent on research, teaching, administrative, and other duties varies by individual circumstance and type of institution. Assistant professors usually spend a smaller portion of their time conducting research than do full professors.

Assistant professors should enjoy instructing and helping others in their career preparation. Their schedules are flexible and change from one quarter or semester to another. Their days can be long, from morning classes to night ones. In addition, they maintain office hours for consultations with students.

Salaries

A 1995–96 study by the American Association of University Professors found that salaries for full-time assistant professors averaged $40,100. Faculty in four-year institutions earn higher salaries in general than at two-year institutions.

Employment Prospects

The Bureau of Labor Statistics projects that employment of college and university faculty will increase about as fast as the average for all occupations through the year 2006.

Faculty retirements should increase significantly from the late 1990s through 2006, because a large number of faculty who entered the profession during the 1950s and 1960s will reach retirement age. In an effort to cut costs, some educational institutions are expected either to leave these positions vacant or to hire part-time, nontenured faculty as replacements. This could create more jobs for assistant professors while reducing the number of jobs available for tenured full professors. An increasing number of jobs for assistant professors are part time, partly because of reduced state funding for higher education. Part-time faculty usually are not eligible for benefits, including health insurance, retirement benefits, or sabbatical leave.

Advancement Prospects

Assistant professorship is an untenured position. Tenure-continued employment and freedom from dismissal without cause may be granted after several years of employment and a review of an assistant professor's teaching and research record. During the probationary period, usually seven years, assistant professors work under term contracts. Failure to receive tenure generally means they must leave the institution.

Tenure is required to become an associate and full professor.

Education

Assistant professors must have earned graduate degrees, preferably in communications, English, or liberal arts. Doctorates are usually preferred for most positions.

Experience/Skills

In addition to advanced degrees, assistant professors must have had four to five years working in the field as journalists, editors, or advertising or public-relations professionals. Knowledge of computers and the Internet is essential.

Assistant professors (like professors at all levels) now use computers increasingly in their work. They may use the Internet, CD-ROMs, and software programs as teaching aids in the classroom. Some assistant professors also teach satellite courses that are broadcast to students off campus through closed-circuit or cable television.

Skills include the abilities to organize course direction and materials, to instruct and help others, and to speak to large audiences.

Unions/Associations

Associations and unions include the American Association of University Professors and National Education Association.

ALUMNI COMMUNICATIONS SPECIALIST

CAREER PROFILE

Duties: Prepare fliers, newsletters, letters, invitations, and other materials for distribution to alumni

Alternate Title(s): Donor Relations Specialist; Gift Recognition Specialist; Information Officer

Salary Range: $20,000 to $35,000

Employment Prospects: Good

Advancement Prospects: Good

Prerequisites:
   Education—Undergraduate degree in communications, liberal arts, journalism
   Experience—Knowledge of word processing, desktop publishing, and professional writing experience all helpful
   Special Skills—Ability to write and edit well very important

CAREER LADDER

```
┌─────────────────────────────────┐
│      Alumni Office Director      │
└─────────────────────────────────┘

┌─────────────────────────────────┐
│ Alumni Communications Specialist │
└─────────────────────────────────┘

┌─────────────────────────────────┐
│            College               │
└─────────────────────────────────┘
```

Position Description

Alumni communications require many of the same skills needed for public-relations work. A person in this job must promote the university and its activities to alumni and also solicit donations to support university programs.

Jobs in alumni communications take on a variety of forms. Some involve helping local alumni clubs plan events and contacting members with newsletters, fliers, and invitations. Others in alumni communications write thank-you letters to alumni who have made gifts to the university or write letters soliciting donations.

The alumni office also promotes educational programs for alumni, generally cruises or other trips that feature one of the university's professors. A person in this job would not be involved with continuing education, which is generally a separate department, but rather serve as a liaison between the faculty and alumni.

The alumni office may also plan speaking engagements and graduation activities. It attempts to make contact with recent graduates and to track the whereabouts of all graduates.

Salaries

A beginner with no experience can expect a salary close to, or perhaps even below, $20,000. Salaries range up to about $35,000.

Employment Prospects

Because turnover in alumni offices can be high, the prospect of getting a job is good. In addition, because alumni donations provide significant revenue to the university, this job might be less susceptible to cutbacks in a bad economy.

Advancement Prospects

A communications specialist who performs well can expect good chances at advancement within the alumni office, although many staffs are small. A person in this field may also be able to move into public relations, performing similar functions at a public relations agency or working in private industry.

Education

A bachelor's degree is essential to this job. In addition, if the school has a specialized program, a degree in that subject might be required. A person working in the alumni office of a particular school does not necessarily need to be an alumni of that school. A degree from a comparable school should be sufficient. A journalism degree, with a specialization in public relations, might also be appropriate.

Experience/Skills

No experience is necessary for an entry-level job. For a more advanced position, knowledge of desktop publishing and word processing systems may be needed. A person in an alumni office should also be creative and outgoing, and be able to write well.

Unions/Associations

Alumni communications specialists can receive career development information from the Council for the Advancement and Support of Education.

In addition, many of them belong to the same groups that serve other public relations professionals, including the Public Relations Society of America, Inc., and Association for Women in Communications.

ALUMNI MAGAZINE EDITOR

CAREER PROFILE

Duties: Supervise magazine preparation; manage staff; rewrite and edit

Alternate Title(s): Alumni Magazine Editor-in-Chief; Editorial Director

Salary Range: $35,000 to $80,000+

Employment Prospects: Fair

Advancement Prospects: Poor

Prerequisites:

Education—Undergraduate degree in liberal arts, journalism, or communications (does not have to be from institution issuing the magazine)

Experience—Background as an editor, journalist, or writer essential

Special Skills—Ability to identify different readership groups and be sensitive to their concerns; tactful handling of controversial subjects without compromising the magazine's editorial integrity

CAREER LADDER

```
┌─────────────────────────────┐
│           Editor            │
└─────────────────────────────┘

┌─────────────────────────────┐
│       Managing Editor       │
└─────────────────────────────┘

┌─────────────────────────────┐
│      Associate Editor       │
└─────────────────────────────┘
```

Position Description

The editor has complete responsibility for the editorial content and production of the magazine. He or she assigns stories, oversees the budget, and may perform day-to-day editing and production tasks.

At smaller alumni magazines, the editor may have other responsibilities as well, handling some public relations functions. However, the best magazines maintain an editorial integrity separate from public relations and do not see themselves as a promotional vehicle for the college but a forum for information.

Duties are similar to those for a mainstream magazine, but with the additional task of remaining sensitive to the concerns of alumni, faculty, administration, students, parents of students, and other magazine readers. An alumni magazine might choose to do a story on a controversial professor but must be aware of the possible reaction of different groups to such a story. These points of view should be sensitively represented.

Editorial integrity must also be closely guarded so university groups know the magazine's policies and respect them. Those who question why the magazine might choose to do a story should have their point of view represented, but should not have the power to censor the magazine.

The magazine editor plans issues, assigns photographs and stories, and edits manuscripts. He or she also hires and fires employees, answers letters from readers, and oversees placement of articles within the magazine.

He or she also has to operate within the magazine's budget. The magazine may rely solely on advertising revenue, donations from alumni, or a combination of the two, plus a sum allocated by the university.

Salaries

Editors earn between $35,000 and $80,000, depending on the size of the magazine. Prestigious colleges with larger endowments may pay more.

Employment Prospects

Alumni magazines provide opportunities away from New York, where many business and consumer magazines are based. Employment prospects are fair, but the field is competitive. Some editors and writers who have worked in New York or other large cities are attracted to alumni magazines in order to live in college communities.

Advancement Prospects

Editor is the top position at many alumni magazines. Advancement can be made by going on to larger magazines, either mainstream publications or at larger colleges.

Education

A bachelor's degree in liberal arts, communications, or journalism is required. Most alumni magazines do not require the degree to come from the employing college. If the college is highly specialized, such as an engineering or scientific school, some graduate-level education may be required.

Experience/Skills

The amount of experience required to be editor varies with the publication. Three to five years may be necessary for some jobs; 10 years or more for others. Experience can include news reporting, reporting jobs at magazines, and other magazine experience.

Unions/Associations

Major professional associations that serve the magazine industry in general are the American Society of Journalists and Authors, Inc.; American Society of Magazine Editors; and Association for Women in Communications. Other writer associations as well as trade and industry groups are open to magazine editors.

In addition, alumni magazine editors can receive career development information from the Council for the Advancement and Support of Education.

LIBRARIAN

CAREER PROFILE

Duties: Acquire, catalog, and maintain collections of books, records, and other sources of information

Alternate Title(s): Information Specialist; Information Scientist; Information Manager

Salary Range: $11,000 to $90,000+

Employment Prospects: Fair to good

Advancement Prospects: Fair

Prerequisites:
  Education—Graduate degree in library science
  Experience—None to several years for entry-level jobs
  Special Skills—Knowledge of book publishing and computer data bases; attention to detail; good organization

CAREER LADDER

```
┌─────────────────────────────┐
│      Senior Librarian       │
└─────────────────────────────┘

┌─────────────────────────────┐
│         Librarian           │
└─────────────────────────────┘

┌─────────────────────────────┐
│   Library Assistant/Clerk   │
└─────────────────────────────┘
```

Position Description

Librarians perform a vital role of information management. They acquire, catalog, maintain, and provide access to collections of information, either to the general public or to business, scientific, and technical professionals. In addition, they may develop media and educational programs.

Most librarians work either in schools, colleges, and universities, or in public or special libraries. A growing number work in business and industry, managing computerized databases of highly specialized information.

Tasks are varied. Some librarians specialize in certain areas, such as acquisitions or media development, but most handle a wide range of responsibilities.

After materials are acquired, they must be cataloged, indexed, and shelved or filed. Much information is transferred to microfilm. Librarians must be able to handle many requests to locate specific information. They may assist teachers in developing educational programs, or compile bibliographies for researchers. They may prepare computer abstracts for scientists and engineers. Librarians also may develop community programs and speakers' forums on issues and topics of interest. They often develop their own publicity materials.

Many librarians have access to remote databases, as well as maintaining their own computerized databases. Database searching skills have become very important to the librarian's job.

Most librarians work a five-day week of 35 to 40 hours, including evenings and weekends for public and college libraries.

Salaries

The Special Libraries Association Salary Survey for 1999 found that the mean salary for librarians was $45,162. However, there are many kinds of libraries and librarians. The more specialized the job, the higher the pay.

The Association of Research Libraries (ARL) is an organization whose members include libraries of North American research institutions (not *all* libraries). Still, the data from the ARL's 1998–99 annual salary survey are interesting. The median salary of university librarians was $45,775 during that fiscal year. For nonuniversity research librarians, the median figure was $56,000. The same study found that the overall gender balance in the 110 Canadian and U.S. university libraries studied was 35.05 percent male and 64.95 percent female. In 97 U.S. university libraries, there were 854 minority librarians, who accounted for 11.1 percent of ARL's U.S. library professionals. Minority research librarians continue to be disproportionately distributed across the country, with the Middle Atlantic, Pacific, and South Atlantic states showing better distributions. Average minority salaries are $2,054 lower than overall averages, or 4.5 percent lower—a slight improvement over 1997–98.

An earlier study by the ARL compared 1997 median librarian salaries by type of institution. Processed foods and pharmaceuticals research institutions were among the highest-paying, in the high $50,000s, while public libraries paid $35,750.

Some states have library associations that recommend minimum pay rates for librarians. However, libraries within those states are not obligated to pay salaries that high; some don't have high enough budgets.

Employment Prospects

The Bureau of Labor Statistics predicts that there will be slow employment growth in this field and an increasing number of MLS graduates through the year 2006, resulting in slower-than-average employment growth. This is partly due to budget constraints in school, public, and college and university libraries. Applicants for librarian jobs in large cities or suburban areas will face more competition than those applying for work in rural areas.

Specialties or concentrations that might increase opportunities for library school graduates include chemistry, engineering, sciences, math, foreign languages, music, cataloging, medicine, computer science, and information systems.

Of the placements of new library school graduates in special libraries, about half went to audiovisual and media centers or to youth services. Law, nonlibrary information services, medicine, rare books, and business were the next most popular choices.

According to the federal government, employment of librarians is expected to lag behind other jobs in growth during the next 10 years. Opportunities are expected to be best in nontraditional settings, including information brokerages, private corporations, and consulting firms. Companies need librarians to do research and organize information. Familiarity with on-line computer databases and computer-assisted research could be especially valuable in the job market.

Many librarians working in nontraditional settings are known by other job titles such as systems analysts, data base specialists, managers, and researchers.

Job prospects may also be better for those willing to relocate. Due to the closing of several accredited library school programs, there are fewer graduates of library science. Large areas of the country have no accredited library school programs.

Advancement Prospects

Advancement to senior librarian, manager, and director depends heavily on the area of work. Business and technical fields offer the best opportunities for promotion.

Education

Education should include an undergraduate degree in liberal arts, English, social sciences, or business, plus at least a master's degree in library science (M.L.S.) The M.L.S. includes advanced courses in cataloging, indexing, computer automation, abstracting, and library administration. A Ph.D. is advantageous for teaching or academic administration. Specialized technical or research work requires additional education.

Experience/Skills

For entry-level positions, experience or internships as a library assistant are helpful. In some localities where jobs are few and applicants many, several years' experience is required for entry-level positions. Public librarians must be state-certified, and requirements vary widely in each state.

Skills include attention to detail; knowledge of publishing, current events, or specialized subjects; and ability to work with the public. Computers revolutionized libraries during the 1990s. Some libraries no longer have physical card catalogs at all, but instead have computerized databases listing the books in their collection. Most libraries also offer access to the Internet for research purposes. Librarians must be able to help patrons navigate the Internet to find the information they are seeking.

Unions/Associations

The American Library Association, American Society for Information Science, and Special Libraries Association are major support groups serving the profession. Specialized associations and groups serve educational, technical, music, medical, and other library fields.

NEWS DIRECTOR

CAREER PROFILE

Duties: Distribute news about the college to newspapers, faculty, and staff members

Alternate Title(s): None

Salary Range: $20,000 to $80,000+

Employment Prospects: Good

Advancement Prospects: Good

Prerequisites:
   Education—Undergraduate degree in liberal arts, communications, journalism
   Experience—None for entry-level jobs at smaller colleges; several years at larger schools
   Special Skills—Ability to identify different groups to which the school disseminates information and develop a specific approach to each

CAREER LADDER

```
┌─────────────────────────────────┐
│   Director of Public Relations  │
└─────────────────────────────────┘

┌─────────────────────────────────┐
│         News Director           │
└─────────────────────────────────┘

┌─────────────────────────────────┐
│   Assistant News Director;      │
│      Reporter; College          │
└─────────────────────────────────┘
```

Position Description

College news directors distribute information about the college to the public through news releases. They also provide information about newsworthy campus events to the school's faculty, staff, and students.

To do this effectively, news directors need to identify what the college is all about and how it wants to be perceived. Messages to different groups can be adjusted to help promote the college.

News directors also need to be aware of how the different groups view them and their role. Who is in each group and what information they need helps determine the messages the news director sends.

Salaries

Salaries vary widely, depending upon the size of the institution and the amount of money allocated for the news office. Some schools prefer to put more money into admissions or fundraising. Others hire experienced professionals to serve as news directors and pay top dollar.

The range can be from $20,000 at an entry-level job requiring no experience to $80,000 or more at a prestigious school interested in promoting itself effectively.

Employment Prospects

The need for public relations professionals is expected to grow throughout the next decade.

Advancement Prospects

Advancement prospects are good. Advancement could be by moving up within the college to director of public relations or director of development or by moving to a larger college to take a similar job.

Education

An undergraduate degree in liberal arts, communications, or journalism is required.

Experience/Skills

Experience required varies with the job market and the institution. None may be required, or several years as a newspaper reporter or a public relations professional may be necessary. Additionally, a college news director must be sensitive to how the college wants to present itself to the public and the college community, and tailor the news accordingly for each group.

Unions/Associations

Many college news directors belong to the same groups other public relations professionals join: the Public Relations Society of America, Inc.; Association for Women in Communications. They also may belong to the Council for the Advancement and Support of Education.

FREELANCE SERVICES AND SELF-PUBLISHING

FREELANCE WRITER

CAREER PROFILE

Duties: Write nonfiction articles for magazines and businesses, or publicity, promotion, and ad copy

Alternate Title(s): Writer

Income Potential: $12 to $100 per hour+; $200 to $2,000 per 2,000-word magazine article; $40 to $500 for a feature article for a daily newspaper; $15 to $25 per hour for small associations and up to $85 per hour for larger groups; $20 to $35 per hour for a brief annual report for a business; various flat fees for projects

Work Prospects: Excellent

Prerequisites:

Education—No minimum education required; undergraduate degree in journalism, communications, or liberal arts preferred

Experience—Background as a journalist helpful

Special Skills—Good writing ability; persistence; self-motivation; salesmanship

Position Description

Freelance writing is a difficult way to make a living, but the rewards are great for those who succeed: the satisfaction of bylines and credits, ongoing relationships with editors, perhaps even retainers, and increasing income as one's reputation is established.

Most freelance writers begin their freelancing part time while holding full- or part-time jobs. They send queries and manuscripts to magazines, or write brochures or slide show scripts for businesses. Eventually, business builds to a point where the writer is able to begin freelancing full time.

General-interest magazines are a very tough market to crack, and many rejection slips may be collected before a sale is made. Freelancers who approach magazines with ideas for articles must first study a publication for its content, style, and slant. With the exception of a very few publications, most magazines do not pay well for the time a writer invests in researching, writing, and revising an article.

Trade and special-interest magazines that cover such topics as home computing, advertising, and business often are easier to break into than general-interest magazines, but they require that the writer have a background in the subject area.

Many freelancers rely heavily on business writing for regular income, which pays much better than most magazines. Business writing for corporations includes press and publicity material, trade stories, speeches, film scripts and slide shows, and internal newsletters and magazines. Some freelancers are able to work on retainers for businesses—a flat monthly fee in exchange for a specified amount of work, such as production of a newsletter. Many advertising and public-relations agencies also rely on freelancers.

Freelance writers must be highly self-disciplined to work on their own. Most put in long hours, and work tends to come unevenly, bringing frequent deadline pressures at the same time. Writers usually have many projects going concurrently in various stages of development—queries or proposals sent out for consideration, researching and interviewing for assignments, writing, and revising. It is essential to maintain a constant pursuit of assignments, because writers never know how long it will take to sell a particular idea. It could sell to the first magazine queried, or it could sell to the tenth after many months.

Many freelance writers find steady work contributing to textbooks, encyclopedias, and other reference books. This work usually is "work for hire," that is, the writer receives a flat fee from the publisher in exchange for all rights. No royalties are paid.

Writers must keep their own business records. They bill clients and keep track of tax deductible expenses.

Additionally, freelance writers may:

• write fiction stories or novels;
• write plays or screenplays;
• work as public-relations consultants;
• edit manuscripts.

Income Potential

A freelance writer's income depends on his or her geographic location and type of projects. Major cities, where more business, magazine, and publishing headquarters are located, offer more fruitful hunting grounds. Yet many freelance writers earn a fair amount of money by sending manuscripts through the mail to distant publications.

Many successful freelance writers earn $20,000 or more, and some who work mostly for businesses and industries earn $40,000 and up.

Pay for trade and general-interest magazine articles can range from $50 to $3,000; top-rated freelancers who work for prestigious publications can command more.

Many freelancers, especially those serving corporate clients, charge by the hour or by day; rates vary according to the job. Typical day rates range from $200 to $800, and hourly rates range from $10 to $100.

Work Prospects

Thousands of trade and general-interest periodicals and businesses rely on freelance writers, yet competition remains stiff, especially for the premium markets. The best bet for beginners is to look to small publications or businesses with which to build the experience and credentials sought by larger markets. It usually takes a freelance writer several years to become established and build a fairly steady income.

Education

Most freelance writers have undergraduate degrees in liberal arts, journalism, or communications. Specialized fields may require certain educational or work credentials. In general, however, a magazine editor looks for good ideas and good writing, not for degrees.

Experience/Skills

Many freelance writers start with no experience other than school writing courses. Others begin freelancing after spending several years as journalists, public-relations writers, or editors. To succeed against the competition, freelancers must be good writers and deliver on time. They must be persistent in selling themselves and should not be easily discouraged by rejections. Freelancers must have a strong entrepreneurial drive.

Unions/Associations

Major national associations include the Authors Guild, Inc.; American Society of Journalists and Authors, Inc.; Associated Business Writers of America, Inc.; National Writers Association; Public Relations Society of America, Inc.; and Association for Women in Communications. The Writers Guild of America is a union that represents scriptwriters for radio, television, and film; the National Writers Union represents writers and authors.

TECHNICAL WRITER

CAREER PROFILE

Duties: Interpret technical and scientific information for technical and nontechnical audiences; research and write a wide variety of material

Alternate Title(s): Publications Engineer; Staff Writer; Communications Specialist; Communicator; Industrial Writer; Instructional Materials Developer

Income Potential: $20–$30 per manuscript page or $35 to $75 per hour, depending on the complexity of the topic and the type of audience

Work Prospects: Excellent

Prerequisites:

Education—Undergraduate degree in technical communications, science, engineering, computer science, journalism, or liberal arts

Experience—Previous work as a technician, scientist, engineer, or writer is helpful

Special Skills—Understanding of complex technical subjects; logic; good writing and layout skills; curiosity

---

Position Description

Technical writing is a highly specialized field that combines technical, scientific, or engineering backgrounds with the ability to write. Technical writers use their specialized knowledge to translate complex information into readily understandable terms. Their audience may or may not have technical backgrounds.

Technical writing covers a wide variety of tasks. Technical writers prepare instruction manuals for equipment or computer software programs; catalogs and other materials used by industrial sales representatives; equipment specifications and instruction manuals for persons who assemble, operate, or repair machinery; or training aids. They write printed materials or scripts for films, filmstrips, or cassettes, and also write books.

Technical writers also prepare reports on scientific research; write papers and speeches for scientists and engineers; draft articles for technical publications; and write news releases, advertising copy, promotional brochures, and corporate annual reports. They also prepare exhibits for museums and trade shows.

Technical writers usually work closely with scientists and engineers. They research their subject by studying blueprints; diagrams; technical documents, studies, and journals; and the actual products. They become thoroughly familiar with their subject before writing about it.

Once they collect sufficient information, they prepare a draft for review by technical professionals—computer programmers, engineers, or scientists. A technical editor oversees changes and coordinates artwork and production.

Most technical writers do not begin work in the profession directly out of college. First they gain experience in their areas of expertise, or as writers or research assistants. Those with writing ability gradually move into technical writing jobs, first by doing library research and drafts for established technical writers.

Technical writers are concentrated in the electronics, computer manufacturing and software development, aircraft, and chemical and pharmaceutical manufacturing industries. Many freelance for research laboratories and hospitals. Others work for the federal government, technical publications, pharmacological and health-related industries, academic institutions, advertising and public-relations agencies, and technical publishing firms.

Income Potential

Freelance technical writers typically are paid by the hour. Some charge day rates. Hour rates are generally about $35 to $75, depending on the writer's credentials, the project, and the employer. Businesses generally pay more than publishers.

Technical writer was listed as one of 20 hot job tracks by *U.S. News & World Report* in its 1999 annual guide to best jobs. For staff positions, that article quoted average entry-level salary as $35,500, mid-level as $41,300, and top as $54,510. A specialized background like engineering or business helps, but on-the-job training is often available.

Work Prospects

Freelance opportunities for technical writers are expected to be strong through the year 2006, particularly in the electronics, computer, pharmaceutical, and health-related industries, and in research and development. The Society for Technical Communication reports that the number of freelancers and consultants has been increasing significantly since 1985. Most work opportunities are in major metropolitan areas.

Education

Most technical writers have undergraduate degrees in science, engineering, technical communications, journalism, or liberal arts. Some have advanced degrees. Most employers prefer thorough technical backgrounds.

Experience/Skills

Many employers look for freelance technical writers who have gained experience working in jobs related to their profession.

Technical writers should be curious, well-organized, and able to explain complicated information. They must be consistently accurate. Technical writers should have the patience and persistence to work long hours sifting through great quantities of details. They should be able to work well as part of a team and on their own.

Unions/Associations

The Society for Technical Communication represents technical writers, editors, scientists, engineers, educators, and others. Other major professional groups include the National Association of Science Writers, Inc., and American Medical Writers Association.

TECHNICAL EDITOR

CAREER PROFILE

Duties: Supervise preparation of technical information material; coordinate artwork; supervise production

Alternate Title(s): Technical Information Editor; Technical Communications Editor; Publications Editor; Instructional Materials Editor

Income Potential: $20 to $60 per hour or more; $150 to $1,000 per day

Work Prospects: Excellent

Prerequisites:

Education—Undergraduate degree in science, computer science, technical communications, engineering, journalism, communications, or liberal arts

Experience—Several years' experience as technical writer

Special Skills—Ability to translate technical material into understandable terms; sense of layout and graphics; copyediting skills; supervisory ability

---

Position Description

Technical editors are responsible for the content, accuracy, and production of a wide range of technical information materials. Many such editors freelance for technical and scientific journals and book publishers. Other technical editors work for businesses, industries, health professions, or the federal government, producing instruction manuals, sales and promotion literature, advertising copy, books, news releases, speeches, films, film scripts, and cassettes.

Freelance technical editors edit the work of technical writers. They may proofread page proofs. Their work requires adherence to production schedules and deadlines.

Technical editors work closely with scientific and technical professionals, who review their material.

Technical editors must have thorough backgrounds in their specific areas. Many begin their careers as engineers, scientists, or other technical professionals before becoming technical writers and editors.

Income Potential

Freelance/technical editors generally are paid between $15 and $60 or more an hour, depending on their expertise and the assignment.

Work Prospects

The demand for technical editors is expected to be strong through 2008, especially in major metropolitan areas. Major growth areas include computer manufacturing and software development, health professions, electronics, and pharmaceutical manufacturing. Research and development organizations also should provide good opportunities.

Education

While there are no rigid requirements for technical writing and editing, most technical editors have at least an undergraduate degree in science, engineering, or computer science, or in English, liberal arts, or journalism. Many have undergraduate degrees in science or engineering, and graduate degrees in journalism or English. A degree in almost any field is often acceptable with a good technical background and writing skills.

Experience/Skills

A professional background as a technician, scientist, engineer, or programmer is helpful for technical writing and editing. Most editors have had several years' additional experience as technical writers.

Creativity and interest in problem solving are important traits of technical editors. They must be able to supervise others and work as part of a team. They must always be conscious of deadlines, production schedules, and budgets. They should be good editors as well as writers, and be knowledgeable in graphics and layout.

Unions/Associations

The Society for Technical Communication is the professional association for this profession. The National Association of Science Writers, Inc., and American Medical Writers Association are two other organizations to which many technical editors belong.

COPY EDITOR

CAREER PROFILE

Duties: Edit manuscripts and copy for book and periodical publishers, trade and industry publications, and corporate communications and publications

Alternate Title(s): None

Income Potential: $17 to $75 per hour for books, magazines, and newspapers; $14 to $100 per hour for editing book content; $25 to $500 per day for general magazine editing; business copyediting, $25 to $85 per manuscript page; copyediting for nonprofit organizations, $15 to $25 per hour; copyediting for advertising, $25 to $35 per hour

Employment Prospects: Good

Prerequisites:

Education—Undergraduate degree; graduate degree may be preferred for technical subjects

Experience—Background and previous employment in communications helpful

Special Skills—Grammar, spelling, and style skills; knowledge of subject areas helpful or may be required

---

Position Description

Freelance copy editors edit a wide range of copy for grammar, style, spelling, punctuation, consistency, and clarity. They work within the house style guidelines provided by the employer. They improve awkwardly written sentences, correct spelling, and flag suspected errors or inconsistencies in numbers, dates, context, and content for double-checking by the author. Their work requires them to be familiar with numerous standard reference works, which they consult frequently when verifying facts.

Copy editors are hired to review book manuscripts (including appendices, indices, and bibliographies), periodical articles, newsletters, and copy for manuals, advertisements, press kits, in-house communications, and more. They work primarily from manuscripts or typeset galleys or proofs and mark corrections directly on the pages. With the increase in electronic text preparation, some copy editors edit on-line or with a disk.

Income Potential

Freelance copyediting fees usually are based on an hourly rate. Freelancers set their own rates for various types of jobs, but generally are limited to going rates established by industry or employer. The average rate range in book publishing, magazines, journals, and packaging ranges from about $10 to $40 per hour. Copy editors who work in advertising, public relations, and corporate communications command up to $100 an hour or more.

Employment Prospects

Work prospects for freelance copy editors are consistently good, for employers can cut staff costs by contracting work out. Good copy editors can build ongoing relationships for steady work.

Education

Copy editors should have an undergraduate degree, preferably in English or communications. Advanced degrees may be preferred or required for technical and scientific work.

Experience/Skills

Previous employment as an editor, copy editor, proofreader, or writer is desirable, or may be required, for freelance copyediting work. Technical or scientific backgrounds may be required for specialized work (see Technical Writer).

Copy editors are meticulous, good at detail work, and have a good command of grammatical rules and spelling. They are versed in production symbols and language and use them in editing. They are quick to grasp content and to spot weaknesses, errors, and inconsistencies. They use good judgment and do not impose their own prejudices on the writing. They are diplomatic in pointing out errors and inconsistencies. Copy editors frequently must work under great deadline pressure.

Unions/Associations

Editorial Freelancers Association is open to freelance copy editors. Those who also are writers may belong to a variety of writers' organizations, such as the American Society of Journalists and Authors, Inc., and National Writers Union.

PROOFREADER

CAREER PROFILE

Duties: Check typeset galleys, page proofs, mechanicals, and blue lines for errors prior to printing

Alternate Title(s): None

Income Potential: Proofreading books and magazines, $15 to $55 per hour; proofreading business publications, $15 to $55 per hour

Work Prospects: Fair to good

Prerequisites:

Education—Undergraduate degree in communications or other field; technical or scientific study for work in these areas

Experience—Prior work as writer, editorial assistant, editor, production assistant helpful

Special Skills—Good command of grammar and style; eye for detail

---

Position Description

The proofreader provides the final check for errors before copy and text of all kinds—from books to periodicals to annual reports to brochures to advertisements—are sent to the printer. Thus, the proofreader carries a great deal of responsibility.

Proofreaders may be called in at different or multiple production stages: when copy is typeset in galleys (or, more often nowadays, directly into page proofs); when copy and art are pasted onto boards (mechanicals), though this is rarely the case now that most publications are produced electronically using desktop publishing tools; or when a dummy is printed (typically in blue ink, hence the name "blue line" or "blues"). They check the typeset copy against the corrected manuscript or corrected galleys to make sure that all changes have been executed as marked. They also look for typographical errors, unevenness in printed lines, and other typesetting or printing imperfections. In addition to text, proofreaders make sure that captions, tables, etc. are correct, and that all pieces of art are in the right places. They mark all corrections on their proofs using printer's symbols. Proofreaders also may find inconsistencies or factual errors, which they bring to the attention of the editor.

Freelance proofreaders usually are writers and editors who perform other services, of which proofreading may be

a part. Proofreading may be done on an employer's premises or out of a freelancer's home or office.

Income Potential

Proofreaders usually charge an hourly rate that varies according to industry and the type of material being proofed. Book and magazine publishers typically pay the lowest rates, from about $8 to $30 an hour. Corporations and advertising and public relations agencies pay up to $50 or more an hour. If proofreading is part of an overall job done by a freelancer, especially for a corporation, the work may be billed at much higher rates.

Work Prospects

Freelancers have fair to good chances of frequent or steady proofreading work, especially in business and industry, where much communications production work is contracted out. Publishing work opportunities are greatest in the East, but exist wherever there are book and periodical publishers.

Education

Proofreaders usually are communications professionals who hold undergraduate degrees in communications or related fields. Scientific and technical employers may require graduate degrees.

Experience/Skills

Proofreaders must be careful readers and be meticulous in attention to detail. They should have a thorough knowledge of the rules of grammar, punctuation, and style. Since they may work directly with typesetters and printers, they should be versed in production procedures.

Proofreading is largely clerical in nature and can be tedious work. Proofreaders should be careful not to move through type too quickly or cut corners, as they may miss errors.

Unions/Associations

Depending on other communications services provided, proofreaders may belong to a variety of organizations, such as Editorial Freelancers Association, American Society of Journalists and Authors, Inc., Association for Women in Communications; National Writers Union, etc.

FACT CHECKER

CAREER PROFILE

Duties: Check the accuracy of manuscripts prior to publication

Alternate Title(s): Researcher

Income Potential: $26 to $75 per hour

Employment Prospects: Fair

Prerequisites:
  Education—Undergraduate degree in journalism, mass communications, or other field
  Experience—None required, but prior work as writer or researcher helpful
  Special Skills—Attention to details; knowledge of how to use library and reference works

Position Description

The publishers of articles, reports, and books rely heavily upon the author's accuracy, but many pass manuscripts on to fact checkers to double-check for errors. The depth of fact checking varies from verification of dates and spellings of names, titles, and places to verification of nearly every detail.

Fact checkers work from a copy of the manuscript and may be given all the author's original notes and tapes. They make heavy use of libraries and reference works. For example, if a writer states that a battle took place on a certain date and at a certain place, a fact checker would look it up, perhaps in an encyclopedia, to verify the information. Fact checkers also call persons interviewed to verify the accuracy of their quotes and statements, and research topics to ascertain whether or not the statements and claims in a manuscript can be validated. They may query the author to find out the sources of certain facts. They report their findings back to the editor.

Fact checking carries a great deal of responsibility but can be tedious work.

Income Potential

Freelance fact checkers typically earn $26 to $75 per hour. Some may work on a flat fee basis, or on retainer.

Employment Prospects

Work opportunities are fair at book publishing houses and magazines. However, fact checking is seen as expendable by many publishers, who are constantly looking for ways to cut costs. Increasingly, publishers rely on authors' statements that information in their manuscripts is accurate. Fact checking is still rigorously pursued at some publications, such as *Reader's Digest*, which has fact checkers on staff who immerse themselves in every article the *Digest* seeks to publish. Articles that do not stand up to fact checking are killed. Other publishers check only selected manuscripts. Sometimes freelance copy editors are expected to do minimal fact checking as well.

Education

There are no specific educational requirements for fact checking. An undergraduate degree in journalism, mass communications, English, or other field is desirable.

Experience/Skills

Prior experience as a writer, editor, researcher, or librarian's assistant is advantageous to obtaining freelance fact checking work.

Fact checkers must be diligent in their search for verifications and unwilling to let minor discrepancies go by. Their attention to detail is required to catch inconsistencies. They must be polite and sensitive in dealing with sources. In some cases, knowledge of the subject at hand is advantageous.

Unions/Associations

There is no professional association of fact checkers, but freelancers who offer this service usually provide other communications services, and may qualify for membership in the Editorial Freelancers Association; American Society of Journalists and Authors; Society for Technical Communications; or Association for Women in Communications, among others.

INDEXER

CAREER PROFILE

Duties: Compile indices to books, newspapers, periodicals, journals, databases, maps, and software

Alternate Title(s): None

Income Potential: $15 to $95 per hour, with higher rates charged if using computer indexing software programs that take fewer hours; $1.50 to $6.00 per printed book page; 40 cents to 70 cents per line of index; or flat fee of $250 to $1,000 per book, depending on length

Employment Prospects: Fair to good

Prerequisites:
Education—Undergraduate degree in humanities, social science, or liberal arts; graduate degree in library science or in scientific or technical areas may be required
Experience—Background in scholarly research or as librarian helpful
Special Skills—Organization, grammar, detail, logic, accuracy, reading skills, perception, ability to make connections, predictive ability

Position Description

Indices are the road maps of information—they guide a reader in a direct manner to a logical sequence of information and help the reader discover new information. Without indices, it would be difficult, if not impossible, to conduct research efficiently, and vast quantities of information would go unexplored and unused.

There is a misconception that indexing is clerical work and can be done with little or no experience. On the contrary, indices are complex constructions that require skill and training to produce. A poor index that confuses the reader is worse than no index at all.

Indices are compiled by professional indexers, many of them freelancers, who work for libraries, publishers, databases, and corporations. They are familiar with the different formats of indices and with international style standards. Rules and practices are in constant change, and professional indexers must stay abreast of them.

Prior to beginning work on an index, an indexer finds out the job requirements. The length and depth of the index is determined by the number of pages allotted, the number of columns per page, the type size, and the format and style rules to be followed. Ideally, the length of the index should be between 2 percent and 5 percent of the length of the text. Large reference works such as encyclopedias require the most complex indices, with up to 100,000 or so entries. A short and simple index, on the other hand, may have fewer than 1,000 entries. The more complex the index, the greater the skill required on the part of the indexer, who must cross-reference and spot associations that will lead readers to specific information.

Once the job requirements are known, the indexer carefully reads the entire text and begins compiling entries. The indexer keeps track by marking the text, by keeping alphabetical lists manually, or by using a computer software program. Numerous changes are made as work progresses and the indexer gets new ideas for referencing the information. In the final edit, the indexer checks the index to make sure that all entries lead the reader to the right information, and that the length fits the publisher's requirements. Sometimes indexers can obtain more space for an index by convincing the publisher to increase the number of pages or, more likely, to decrease the type size and leading (space between lines).

Indexers also provide a valuable service by spotting inconsistencies and errors in the writing and typographical errors overlooked by editors.

The average book index is compiled in one to four weeks. Large reference works may take months of work. Indexers often work under a great deal of pressure, as they are called in at the last minute to provide an index as quickly as possible. (The index cannot be done until the book's entire pagination is final, and by that late stage of production, deadlines are crucial!)

With the proliferation of personal computers and software programs, many indexers now compile indices electronically. Some, however, still prefer to work manually, constructing indices with a stack of 3 x 5-inch cards and a shoebox, and typing the final copy. In fact, some indexers believe that any index with fewer than 9,000 entries need not be done on computer. Increasingly, however, publishers are requiring indices to be submitted on disk or transferred electronically via modem.

In addition to indexing, some indexers provide other services, such as researching, abstract writing, updating databases, writing, editing, and proofreading.

Income Potential

Earnings depend on the type of indexing and one's expertise. Technical and scientific work pay more than consumer work. Freelance fees are negotiated according to the project, the employer's pay scales, and the indexer's scale of fees. Indexers may be paid by each line in an index, by the manuscript page indexed, by the hour, or by a flat fee. The average consumer book brings a fee of $250 to $500. Some indexers work on retainer and give that employer first priority. Court rulings on work-for-hire have enabled many indexers to retain rights to their work, and thus to earn additional monies for new editions, reprints, and foreign translations.

Employment Prospects

There is an increasing need for indexers due to the proliferation of information and the need to organize and manage it. More and more, people want speedy access to information and do not want to wade through texts in search of facts. In book publishing, some publishers still forgo an index as an optional expense, but book reviewers are paying more attention not only to the inclusion of indices, but their quality as well. Databases, libraries, corporations, newspapers, and periodicals require indexes to keep track of their collections.

Education

In addition to an undergraduate degree, many indexers have graduate degrees in library science. Some also have advanced degrees in technical or scientific areas. Graduate degrees, especially in library science, may be required for highly complex indexing work.

Experience/Skills

A background in library science and information management is helpful to a freelance career as an indexer. Indexing is precise work and should not be undertaken without some training. Graduate schools of library science may offer noncredit or credit seminars, workshops, and courses for the novice indexer.

Indexers bring a wide range of skills to the job. They must be careful readers who get a quick grasp of material. They must be able to anticipate how a reader might look for a specific piece of information. Though indices are logical, the reader does not always approach them logically. Indexers also must be knowledgeable on the latest rules and practices concerning index formats and grammatical style. In addition, indexers are good at seeing patterns, organizing information, paying attention to detail and accuracy, and working under pressure.

Unions/Associations

The American Society of Indexers is the only professional association in the U.S. devoted to the advancement of indexing; it is affiliated with professional indexing societies in Canada, the United Kingdom, and Australia. Membership is open to anyone interested in the field. Indexers who provide other freelance communications services may belong to societies for authors, writers, editors, technical writers and editors, public relations professionals, etc.

STRINGER

CAREER PROFILE

Duties: Provide frequent copy to newspapers and/or magazines

Alternate Title(s): Correspondent; Contributing Writer; Contributing Editor

Income Potential: Newspapers: $10 to $40 per piece; $1 per column inch; sometimes mileage paid extra. Magazines: 20¢ to $1 per word based on circulation

Work Prospects: Fair

Prerequisites:

Education—Undergraduate degree in communications, journalism, English, or liberal arts, or at least a high school diploma

Experience—Background as a journalist helpful

Special Skills—Ability to work independently and meet deadlines; good writing; sense for news

---

Position Description

Many newspapers and magazines cover broad geographic areas but are not able to maintain writing staff to monitor far-flung events. Instead, they rely on stringers or correspondents, writers who are expected to monitor local news of interest to the publication and provide timely, frequent stories. Some magazines pay writers to provide copy on specialized topics for columns and departments, such as computer technology or personal health. These writers are usually called contributing writers or contributing editors.

Stringers are expected to keep abreast of news developments and inform their editors of important or special events, or ideas for in-depth or feature stories. Their duties may include reporting on local government and school-board meetings, providing local material for roundup stories and reader surveys, and filing reports on conventions, exhibits, and conferences.

Deadlines depend on publication frequency. A newspaper stringer may be expected to cover an evening meeting and then dictate a story over the telephone. Some transmit copy by telecopier or other facsimile device, and others may only be required to mail articles. A stringer may be required to submit a certain number of stories a week or month, or just report on an as-needed basis. Assignments are given by home-base editors.

If a disaster strikes, such as a flood or tornado, stringers may be called on short notice to provide news coverage. Occasionally they may be asked to travel.

Stringers may hold writing or reporting jobs on other, noncompetitive publications, or they may be part- or full-time freelancers. Their editors depend on them the same way they depend on their immediate reporting or writing staff.

Income Potential

Most stringers do not earn a great deal of money, but the pay can be steady and can lead to other work. Major national news magazines pay hourly rates to stringers, from about $10 to $35 an hour, or daily rates of about $150 to $250 plus expenses. Other publications pay per story, $25 and up, and some pay by the published inch, usually $1 to $5. Some stringers can earn flat monthly retainer fees of $50 to $500 and up, depending on the publication and the work involved.

Work Prospects

Publications covering broad areas, particularly newspapers, and weekly trade and newsmagazines, are the best bets for stringing.

Education

Most stringers, like other journalists and writers, have undergraduate degrees in communications, journalism, or liberal arts. Those who specialize may have advanced degrees.

Experience/Skills

Stringers generally are established writers, either freelance or employed by another, noncompetitive publication, with several years' experience as journalists. They must be dependable, accurate, and self-motivated.

Unions/Associations

Major national associations include the Society of Professional Journalists, Sigma Delta Chi; American Society of Journalists and Authors, Inc.; National Writers Union; National Association of Black Journalists; National Federation of Press Women, Inc.; and Association for Women in Communications.

BOOK REVIEWER

Duties: Write book reviews for newspapers, periodicals, and newsletters

Alternate Title(s): Columnist

Income Potential: For a byline and the book only at small newspapers; $35 to $200 at larger publications; $22 to $750 for magazines

Work Prospects: Poor

Prerequisites:
Education—Undergraduate degree in communications, English, liberal arts, or in area of specific expertise; graduate degree may be preferred in some cases
Experience—Recognition as expert in subject areas or in literature; knowledge of other and current books
Special Skills—Good writing ability; criticism skills

Position Description

Book reviewers help readers choose books by providing summaries of their contents, plot synopses (without giving away surprises and endings), and opinions on their merits and flaws.

Reviewing books can provide a small but often steady source of income for freelance writers and authors. Most newspapers, consumer and trade periodicals, and industry newsletters carry book review columns in each issue; many rely on freelancers to provide the reviews. The column itself may be produced on a regular basis by a freelancer, or an editor may assign reviews to a variety of writers. Since the majority of publications are specialized and thus limit reviews to books of specific interest to their audiences, expertise in a subject area is often required of book reviewers. Some writers work regularly or often as reviewers, while others write occasional reviews upon invitation by publications.

Unless a writer is given responsibility for developing a book review column and generating his or her own material, a publication will ask a writer to review a certain book. The writer is given the book as well as instructions on length and format, and a deadline.

There are several types of review, which depend upon the publication and the importance of the book. Straight descriptive reviews are short and give the reader the title, author, publisher, price, and a brief description of the contents with no evaluation. Short reviews of several paragraphs provide the pertinent information with a brief evaluation. Essay reviews can be up to 1,000 or 2,000 words in length and include comparisons of the book to previous works by the same author and similar works by other authors, and an evaluation on the part of the reviewer. Critique reviews are even broader in scope, discussing an entire genre or literary movement.

Income Potential

Most writers are paid small fees for individual book reviews—$10 to $25 are typical fees. In some cases, a free book and a byline are the sole compensation. Large and prestigious consumer publications pay up to several hundred dollars for essay and critique reviews, but rely primarily upon well-known writers and experts.

Work Prospects

Many book reviews are assigned on the basis of the reviewer's credentials, expertise, and sometimes name recognition. The best prospects for regular work as a reviewer are in local markets, and through establishing a relationship with a publication by writing articles first. Aspiring reviewers also can query publications with a letter outlining credentials and expertise and, if available, sample review clips.

Education

No education is required to become a book reviewer. Most writers have an undergraduate degree in communications, liberal arts, English, or other subjects. Graduate degrees may be preferred for certain specialized areas or publications.

Experience/Skills

Book reviewers should be knowledgeable about the subjects covered in a book, if nonfiction, or the genre, if fiction.

One need not be an expert to write straight descriptive and short reviews, but expertise enhances the prospects for higher-paying reviews. Reviewers should be objective, fair, and sensitive and have good criticism skills.

Unions/Associations

There are no associations specifically for book reviewers. Those who are writers may belong to one or more writers' organizations, such as the Authors Guild, Inc.; American Society of Journalists and Authors; Mystery Writers of America, Inc.; PEN American Center; National Writers Union; etc.

CONTRIBUTING EDITOR

CAREER PROFILE

Duties: Suggest and write articles for periodicals

Alternate Title(s): Contributing Writer; Correspondent

Income Potential: Up to $50,000+

Work Prospects: Poor

Prerequisites:

Education—Undergraduate degree preferred; graduate degree may be preferred or required for specialized areas

Experience—Extensive published credits or name recognition with audience; thorough knowledge of subject areas

Special Skills—Excellent writing; dependability; self-discipline

Position Description

Contributing editors are hired by periodicals to write an article for every issue, or a certain number of articles per year. They generally are not part of the periodical's staff, but work on a freelance, contract basis. Pay is set per article or annually, depending on the contributing editor's responsibilities.

Contributing editors usually have extensive experience as writers. They have an established expertise and a reputation for dependability. They are invited to become contributing editors by writing regularly for periodicals. Some well-known or celebrity writers may be invited by a periodical to become contributing editors in order to draw readers. Many small periodicals use contributing editors as a way of stretching their staffs, particularly if they require coverage of faraway areas.

Contributing editors may be responsible for providing coverage of certain topics or geographic areas, or may be roving. They suggest their own ideas and are given assignments by their superior editors. Duties can range from writing articles, reviews, and columns to attending staff meetings to supervising other 'writers. (Distant contributing editors usually are not expected to attend staff meetings.)

A contributing editorship usually is but one of several sources of income for a writer.

Income Potential

Earnings depend on the size and nature of the publication, the responsibilities of the position, and the contributing editor's credentials and reputation. Contributing editors can earn as little as a few thousand dollars a year to $50,000 a year or more at prestigious publications. Celebrity writers may earn more.

Work Prospects

A solid track record of published credits and a good reputation as a writer usually are required to become a contributing editor at major periodicals. A writer may work into this position over time by writing regularly on a topic or for a periodical, and developing a good working relationship with the staff. However, small periodicals in need of dependable, freelance contributors may provide the best prospects for writers in the early stages of their careers.

Education

Most writers have an undergraduate degree in communications, liberal arts, English, or social sciences. Graduate degrees may be advantageous or required in technical and specialized areas.

Experience/Skills

Contributing editors usually have demonstrated their expertise over a period of years before becoming contributing editors. They must be creative, self-disciplined, reliable, knowledgeable about their areas, and good writers.

Unions/Associations

Contributing editors can belong to organizations for writers, such as the American Society of Journalists and Authors, Inc.; the Society for Technical Communication; the National Writers Union, and Association for Women in Communications. They may also belong to trade or professional associations related to the areas and topics they cover.

SYNDICATED COLUMNIST

CAREER PROFILE

Duties: Write, self-edit, and deliver columns to client newspapers; prepare sales material; sell columns

Alternate Title(s): None

Income Potential: $5 to $10 each for weeklies; $10 to $25 per week for dailies, based on circulation

Work Prospects: Poor

Prerequisites:

Education—Depends on need for expertise; most have undergraduate degrees

Experience—Background as journalist or writer helpful; knowledge of subject area important

Special Skills—Concise writing; self-editing; sales and entrepreneurial ability; self-discipline; perseverance

Position Description

All newspapers publish columns on a wide variety of subjects, including self-help pieces, feature articles, news analyses, and puzzles. Some of the columns are written by the newspaper's own staff, but most are purchased through syndication.

Writers who have ideas for columns can try to market them to syndicates—organizations that in turn sell to the newspapers—or market them directly to newspapers in self-syndication.

The proliferation of columns makes it appear deceptively easy to become syndicated. Almost anyone with a novel idea, it seems, can become wealthy and famous. In reality, syndication, by either route, is difficult and highly competitive work; few columnists become famous or wealthy.

A prospective columnist must be able to offer something new, or be able to write about a subject better than established columnists. The idea should be strong enough to generate interesting material at least once or twice a week over a long period of time. Syndicates and newspapers are not interested in fads. What's more, the columnist should have experience in writing and a background in the subject area.

Most columns are short, 500 to 1,000 words or so. They must be tightly written and deliver good information.

There are more than 60 major syndicates that handle all kinds of columns. A prospective columnist should submit to such syndicates at least six sample columns, along with a pitch letter that describes the writer's qualifications, the potential audience, and the column's appeal. Syndicates keep anywhere from 40 to 60 percent of the gross revenues of a column.

In addition to columns, syndicates also purchase single articles, called "one-shots," that have wide appeal and can be sold to newspapers for one-time use. A typical one-shot might be a feature story on a prominent person, or a topic or issue of great current interest. The author is usually paid a flat fee of about 20 to 50 cents a word.

Self-syndication is much costlier and more time consuming, but the writer keeps all of the profits. Sample columns and pitch letters are sent directly to newspaper editors and usually followed up by phone calls. Several hundred newspapers may have to be approached in order to net a few dozen clients. Some columnists start out by establishing themselves with one or two newspapers, and then expanding.

The self-syndicated columnist is responsible for writing, editing, and delivering the copy to all clients by their deadlines, and for billing them. Self-syndication can easily be a full-time job or more, requiring 40 to 80 hours of work per week.

Income Potential

Most columns are sold for $5 to $75 per piece to each client. Rates depend on the popularity of the column and writer. A few columnists earn over $100,000 a year, including Jack Anderson (well over $200,000), William Safire, Russell Baker, Art Buchwald, Abigail Van Buren (Dear Abby), Ann Landers, and others. A self-syndicated columnist who is published in about 60 or 70 newspapers and charges $10 per piece can clear about $30,000 a year. Most columnists earn far less than that.

Work Prospects

Syndicates and newspapers receive far more queries for columns than they can possibly use. Writers who can identify new and developing trends in popular interest have the best chances for successful sales. Self-syndication is an alternative for those willing to put in long hours to get established, a process that usually involves giving columns away on free trials. Most aspiring columnists will find their best bets in their own local markets, and among the nation's many small daily and weekly newspapers.

Education

Little attention is paid to education unless it is necessary to establish the columnist as an authority. However, an undergraduate degree in journalism or any other subject is desirable.

Experience/Skills

Most columnists are already established writers or journalists with several to many years of experience. Regardless of previous writing experience, columnists must demonstrate good writing ability. They must be able to research and develop fresh, concisely written material on a regular schedule. Persistence and a flair for sales and promotion is helpful to self-syndicators.

Unions/Associations

There are no associations specifically for syndicated columnists. Related groups include the Society of Professional Journalists, Sigma Delta Chi; Association for Women in Communications; American Society of Journalists and Authors, Inc.; and National Federation of Press Women, Inc.

COMMUNICATIONS CONSULTANT

CAREER PROFILE

Duties: Advise clients on ways to improve writing and communications skills, or editorial operations

Alternate Title(s): Editorial Consultant

Income Potential: $25 to $85 per hour; $250 per day plus expenses for nonprofit, social services, and religious organizations; $600 per day and up for others

Employment Prospects: Fair

Prerequisites:
  Education—Undergraduate degree in communications, liberal arts, or related field; graduate degree advantageous
  Experience—Sufficient background to provide expertise
  Special Skills—Excellent written and oral communications skills; teaching ability; salesmanship; self-motivation

Position Description

Consulting is viewed as a highly glamorous, prestigious occupation. Consultants enjoy a reputation for high compensation relative to work performed, as well as complete independence. While it is true that consultants can earn high pay, most work very hard for it, putting in long hours searching for and pitching clients. Their work and reputation must be good enough to earn repeat clients, for it is virtually impossible to stay in business on one-shot efforts.

Consultants exist in just about every profession, discipline, and occupation. In communications, consultants perform a variety of services. They assist businesses, publications, and newspapers in special projects, in streamlining and improving editorial operations, and in launching new publications. They conduct research and studies of potential advertisers, markets, and subscribers. They help pinpoint weaknesses. They conduct seminars for staff on how to improve writing and editing skills, or training sessions on new technology. Consultants may also assume responsibility for such publications as corporate newsletters, handling the editing and production involved.

To be successful, consultants must have expertise and credentials to attract and satisfy clients. Such a reputation usually comes after years of work in the field as a writer, editor, or publishing executive. Some people enter consult-

ing on a part-time basis, handling projects that are not conflicts of interest with their jobs. Part-time consulting allows for a base of clients and references to be built with a minimum of financial risk; however, it does limit the types of assignments that can be accepted. Part-time consulting can be built into a full-time occupation.

Most consultants have a strong desire to be self-employed and are highly motivated to succeed. Building a client base requires persistence and good sales skills. They must identify their target audience and develop direct-mail, telephone, and advertising campaigns to promote their particular skills and abilities.

Hours can be very long, especially in the beginning. Consultants spend a great deal of time prospecting for clients by attending professional meetings and conferences, accepting speaking engagements, and soliciting on the telephone. Work loads are seldom spread evenly, which creates many deadline pressures. Some consultants travel extensively.

Income Potential

Consultants usually work on a per diem or project basis. Per diem rates range from $250 to $2,000 and up. Rates depend on experience and expertise; the average is about

$800 per day. Flat fees for projects depend on the nature of the work and time spent.

Other common types of fees include: retainer fees (a flat monthly rate in exchange for a specified amount of time); percentage fees (a percent of the value of a product that is to be offered for sale); and equity fees (an interest in a business in lieu of cash).

Employment Prospects

Overall, there are some 50,000 full-time consultants in all fields, with an additional 2,000 persons setting up shop every year. The industry totals more than $32 billion a year. About half of all consultants are sole proprietorships.

In communications, the best employment prospects are among corporations, many of which use consultants regularly for ongoing staff education and training. Many newspapers also use consultants. In addition to editorial experience, many newspaper consultants also have some background in production, advertising, or circulation.

Education

High academic credentials carry weight in consulting. An undergraduate degree in communications, liberal arts, or a specialized area is the minimum requirement. A master's degree won't guarantee success, but it can help attract clients. A background in finance or accounting is advantageous in all areas of consulting.

Experience/Skills

Besides expertise, consultants should possess good problem-solving ability. They should be quick at grasping situations and in seeing solutions.

Excellent writing and speaking skills are a must for consultants. Pitch letters, proposals, reports, and studies must be well researched, organized, and written. Consultants do a great deal of public speaking, either in instruction to small groups or to larger audiences at conventions and professional meetings.

Sales skills also are essential to success. Consultants must sell themselves to potential clients, and sell their ideas and proposals to existing clients. Consultants must be well organized, ambitious individuals with a strong desire to succeed on their own.

Unions/Associations

Membership in professional associations and organizations is wise because of the contacts and referrals that can be made. Which organizations to join depends on the individual's area of expertise.

DESKTOP PUBLISHER

CAREER PROFILE

Duties: Produce or publish newsletters, magazines, brochures, reports, and other small publications

Alternate Title(s): Communications Consultant; Freelance Publisher

Income Potential: For 1,000 dots-per-inch type, $5 to $15 per camera-ready page of straight type; $30 per page of camera-ready page with illustrations, tables, maps, charts, or photos; $100 to $150 per oversize page with art. Also, $25 to $50 per hour depending on graphics, number of photos, and amount of copy to be typeset. Packages often include writing, layout and design, and typesetting.

Work Prospects: Fair to good

Prerequisites:
    Education—Undergraduate degree in mass communications, journalism, English, art, or graphic design
    Experience—Prior work in writing, editing, and publications production essential
    Special Skills—Good writing and editing skills; knowledge of desktop publishing software; management skills; organization; ability to meet deadlines; salesmanship

---

Position Description

Sophisticated computer technology has enabled the freelance writer and editor to expand in new directions and produce a finished product end to end. With an investment in the right computer hardware and desktop publishing (DTP) software, the freelancer becomes producer or publisher.

The desktop publisher works with businesses, associations, agencies, and organizations to produce publications that have a professionally published look. These usually are newsletters, magazines, and reports for either an in-house or external audience.

Desktop publishers work with a staff editor or communications manager who provides specifications for the publication's content, design, size, and length. The desktop publisher may be given the copy, produced in-house or by freelancers, or may have to generate it in accordance with an assignment list. If the copy is hard (printed on paper), it is keyed or scanned into the computer. Some copy may be provided on disk or transferred by modem or E-mail. The copy is edited, and the pages are formatted on-screen to accommodate graphics and design. The pages can be printed out exactly as they appear on the screen. Art must be screened and added.

Simple documents such as a single-sheet newsletter can be printed in quantity directly on a high-quality printer (laserjet is preferred). The printer also can be used to produce proofs, which are mounted on mechanicals and sent to a printer. The desktop publisher either delivers the finished product or the mechanicals, sends the mechanicals to a printer, or sends the printer a computer disk.

Desktop publishers wear all hats—writer, editor, copy editor, designer, typesetter—or supervise others who perform those tasks. All facets of producing a publication must be coordinated in order to meet deadlines. The task involves periodic meetings with the in-house person in charge of the publication to review progress and get the necessary in-house approvals on content and design.

Some desktop publishers found their own newsletters and periodicals. The success of these ventures relies in the astute meeting of a market need and the marketing of the product to paying subscribers. Fulfillment—the management of mail lists and the mailing of the publication—is time-consuming, as is collecting money and keeping track of accounts. New publications may operate in the red for a considerable period of time. If successful, self-published newsletters can be rewarding in terms of income and creative satisfaction.

Income Potential

Desktop publishers set individual fees, usually by establishing a day rate and estimating the time required to complete a job. Certain expenses may be billed in addition to the fee. The production of even a simple quarterly newsletter can bring in several thousand dollars annually.

An initial investment in equipment and software is necessary, however. One needs a personal computer with sufficient built-in memory to handle Desktop publishering programs, a word processing program, a Desktop publishering program and a high-quality printer that can handle different fonts.

Work Prospects

Opportunities for desktop publishers are fair to good and are increasing due to downsizing in the business world. Businesses are trimming their staffs or keeping them small, yet their need to communicate remains the same or increases. It's more economical for many businesses to hire freelance desktop publishers than to assign staff to produce certain publications. The desktop publisher is to business communications what the packager is to book publishing.

The best desktop publisher opportunities are at corporations of all sizes, professional or trade organizations, and associations, and the nonprofit sector, though pay is lower at the latter.

Education

An undergraduate degree in mass communications, journalism, English, art, or graphic design is desirable. Although some desktop publishers have no design background, with some training in design desktop publishers can produce a higher-quality, more professional-looking product.

Experience/Skills

Previous experience as a writer or editor, and knowledge of production, are essential. Though DTP programs do not require graphics design skill, some knowledge of layout and design is helpful, and may be essential for larger and more complex publications.

Desktop publishers must be well organized and able to coordinate people and tasks to bring the pieces together into a whole. Personal interaction skills are important, as desktop publishers typically work with a variety of people who must provide material, art, or approvals. Desktop publishers also must have good sales skills to sell their services.

Unions/Associations

DTPers may belong to a number of communications organizations, such as the International Association of Business Communicators; Public Relations Society of America, Inc.; Association for Women in Communications; the American Society of Journalists and Authors, Inc.; Editorial Freelancers Association; and more.

PACKAGER

CAREER PROFILE

Duties: Create books for publishers

Alternate Title(s): Book producer

Income Potential: $0 to no limit

Work Prospects: Poor to fair

Prerequisites:

Education—Undergraduate degree in English, communications, liberal arts, humanities; publishing and marketing courses desirable

Experience—Prior work as author or editor essential

Special Skills—Creativity; innovation; ability to sense marketing opportunities; salesmanship; marketing and finance savvy; familiarity with production

Position Description

Packagers provide complete book preparation services to publishers, from the outline to the finished product. Some also provide marketing and distribution services. By offering package deals to publishers, packagers save publishers money and reduce staff time. Most publishers pay packagers according to a percentage of the book's retail price and the number of copies ordered. The usual percentage is 20 percent. Thus, a packager is paid $5 for a book that will sell to the public for $25. To make a profit, the packager must hold production costs to less than $5 per book. Mistakes can make the difference between profit and loss.

Packagers conceive ideas for books and then write proposals, which they use as sales tools to interest editors. The proposal includes a summary of the book's contents, sample material, market potential, and, if the packager provides the finished product, the production specifications (number of pages, trim size, type of paper, etc.). The editor and packager then negotiate a price. The packager must take into account anticipated production expenses and build in a profit margin.

Some packagers write, edit, and produce their own books. Others work with authors, whom they pay on a flat fee or royalty basis. Unless a packager has production equipment, work is subcontracted to typesetters and print shops. The services of a graphic artist or illustrator usually are necessary. The packager consults with the editor at numerous points along the way. Depending on the contract, the editor may have a significant voice in how the book is produced.

Packagers devise production schedules and must coordinate a variety of personnel and activities. They are familiar with production. Many packagers retain rights to their books, which they sell piecemeal to publishers, periodicals, and other outlets. Selling these rights is time-consuming and requires knowledge of the publishing marketplace. Some packagers have agents to help them sell proposals and rights.

Most packagers have had extensive prior experience as authors or editors. They know the business and have numerous contacts in the publishing world. They may opt to specialize in certain kinds of books, such as art books or lavishly illustrated coffee-table and gift books, or in serial fiction.

Packaging can provide the satisfaction of self-publishing without the distribution worries, unless the packager opts to provide marketing and distribution services. However, it can be difficult to get started, and vagaries in cash flow from typically slow-paying publishers can strain a tight budget.

Income Potential

Earnings depend on the type of books packaged, the end product provided (finished books fetch more money but consume more money to produce), and the success of books sold. Profit margins vary depending on individual negotiations. The profit from a book may be only a few thousand dollars. Big sellers can go on to earn hundreds of thousands of dollars over a period of time.

Packaging requires startup investment on the part of the packager. In a typical contract, a packager is paid in thirds by the publisher (one-third on signing, one-third on delivery, and one-third on publication) or in halves (half on signing, half on delivery). Payment from a publisher can come months after signing or delivery; meanwhile, work must be done on the book and suppliers and authors expect to be paid. Packagers who work out of an office must factor in rent and other office expenses.

Work Prospects

It is difficult to get started in packaging without personal contacts in the publishing world, but it can be done. Packagers can work anywhere, but the overwhelming majority are concentrated near New York City, where they can have easy access for face-to-face meetings with major publishers.

A good-quality, professional product is paramount to success.

Education

Most packagers have an undergraduate degree in liberal arts, English, communications, humanities, or other area. They may have taken additional courses in publishing, business administration, marketing, advertising, and promotion.

Experience/Skills

Prior work as an author or editor is virtually essential to packaging. The packager functions almost as a publisher, and must be familiar with the market. The ability to make convincing proposals, both in writing and in person, is important. Packagers must manage cash flow, staff, and suppliers, and juggle tight deadlines.

Unions/Associations

The American Book Producers Association is the primary organization for packagers. Some may also belong to the Association of American Publishers, Inc., or various writers' organizations.

SELF-PUBLISHER

Duties: Write and publish one's own books, monographs, periodicals, etc.

Alternate Title(s): Independent publisher, private publisher

Income Potential: $0 to no limit

Work Prospects: Fair

Prerequisites:

Education—Undergraduate degree in English or communications; courses in business and finance helpful

Experience—Work as writer and editor helpful; familiarity with production essential; sales experience, financial acumen desirable

Special Skills—Innovation; willingness to take risks; ability to predict trends and market opportunities; salesmanship and marketing skills; self-promotion; organization; financial planning; good record keeping

Position Description

In times past, self-publishing once carried a stigma—it was the mark of an author who failed to sell his or her work to a publisher. That stigma no longer exists. In fact, many a self-published author is considered a savvy businessperson, someone who retains total control over the product and stands poised to keep all the profits, not a small percentage of them.

Self-publishing became viable with the explosion in personal computing and desktop publishing software. For a moderate investment, an individual can purchase the equipment and programs needed to produce manuscript copy, galleys, and page mechanicals ready for the printer. At the same time, the consolidation of large publishing houses has left openings in the market to be filled by small presses (many of which began as self-publishing operations and expanded) and self-publishers. The Internet and printing-on-demand technology may make self-publishing an even more viable option. Self-publishing is not to be confused with vanity publishing, in which an author pays a publisher to publish a work.

Self-publishing requires a great deal of business planning and organization, for the self-publisher bears all the expenses of producing and marketing a book. The author wears many hats, and must plan and budget for every step along the way. Prior to writing the book, the self-publisher must try to estimate production costs and market potential. A marketing plan is drawn up. The book is then written, and then must be typeset, proofread and corrected, paginated, and made ready for mechanicals for the printer. The self-publisher must be familiar with production shop operations and able to work with those personnel. A cover must be designed, which may require hiring a graphic artist. If the text is illustrated, the art must be collected or commissioned and positioned in the text. Any legal questions must be resolved with the help of an attorney.

Once the book is produced, the self-publisher takes delivery and must be able to sell the copies through channels of distribution, which include book and specialty stores, catalogs, direct mail, and wholesale distributors. Orders are placed; prices and terms must be negotiated; books must be delivered and monies collected. In addition, publicity and reviews must be solicited and advertisements, if desired, placed. Many of these activities are time-consuming, and authors find themselves working more as business managers than as writers. Furthermore, not all markets are eager to do business with self-publishers, and it is at the point of distribution that many self-publishers fail and lose money.

Success, however, is a heady experience. Sufficient profits enable self-publishers to produce other books. Once track records of sales are established, distribution becomes easier. Many authors who have been published by large publishing houses have found great satisfaction in self-publishing, even if profits are small or modest. They enjoy having complete control and in seeing immediate financial results, instead of waiting months to years to earn royalties.

Income Potential

A successful self-published book is one that earns at least enough income to cover production costs. Profits may range from several hundred dollars to several thousand dollars, depending on the profit margin per copy and the number of copies sold. Some very successful self-published books have made hundreds of thousands of dollars in profits. A trade paperback of about 155 pages with no illustrations and a simple cover might cost about 21¢ per copy to produce, and could sell for up to $9.95 or $10.95.

Minimum press runs typically are 1,000 or more copies. Depending on costs, the self-publisher must invest up front an average of $8,000 to $12,000 or more for a typical book. Depending on how quickly a book sells, recovering costs and making a profit may take several months to years. Those who succeed have researched in advance the potential market for their books and potential distribution channels.

Additional income may come from the sale of subsidiary rights, such as foreign sales, audiotapes, condensations, serializations, film and television production, etc. Occasionally a successful self-published book is purchased for larger distribution rights by a major publisher.

Nonfiction self-published books, especially those that are self-help, guides, or subjects for specialty markets, are much more likely to succeed than fiction and poetry.

Work Prospects

The ranks of self-publishers have swelled since affordable desktop computing arrived in the early 1980s. Market opportunities depend upon trends and perceived needs as seen by the aspiring self-publisher. It is possible to get started in self-publishing on a part-time basis while one continues to work at a full-time job, though the time demands can be grueling. Successful self-publishing can lead to the establishment of a small press, which publishes several titles a year, including the works of others. Thousands of small presses operate in the U.S. alone.

Education

Most self-publishers are authors-turned-publishers and have undergraduate degrees in communications, English, liberal arts, and the humanities. Additional courses in business, marketing, and finance are recommended prior to launching a self-publishing venture.

Experience/Skills

Self-publishers are good writers who are creative and innovative. They are not afraid to take risks. Editing skills are advantageous, though self-publishers can always hire editors on a project basis. Self-publishers also have a working knowledge of production and printing requirements and procedures. Financial, sales, and promotion skills also are necessary. A great deal of advance business planning must be done in order to be successful.

Unions/Associations

Many self-publishers belong to the Publishers Marketing Association, a national nonprofit cooperative, and to various regional small-press associations. Self-publishers also may belong to local business organizations and writers' organizations, such as the American Society of Journalists and Authors; Authors Guild, Inc.; National Writers Union; etc.

ADVERTISING COPYWRITER

CAREER PROFILE

Duties: Write advertising copy for advertising agencies, businesses, corporations, and design studios

Alternate Title(s): None

Income Potential: $50 to $100 per hour, $250 and up per day, $500 and up per week, $1,000 to $2,000 as a monthly retainer; $400 to $2,000 flat fee for full-page ad, depending on the client

Work Prospects: Excellent

Prerequisites:

Education—Undergraduate degree in communications, liberal arts, art, advertising, or business

Experience—Background as a professional writer or journalist helpful; proven track record as a copywriter required

Special Skills—Creativity, imagination, salesmanship, persistence, self-motivation, reliability

Position Description

Freelance copywriting can be frustrating, isolating, and erratic. It can also give you control over your own schedule and the satisfaction of running your own business.

To get started in the business, you must already have a strong portfolio of work. Clients hire freelancers to fill in when the in-house staff is swamped. As a consequence, freelancers are expected to come in and hit the ground running, delivering assignments of professional quality on time.

Freelancers are also expected to turn out assignments to meet deadline pressure, even if it means working over weekends or at night. An advertising agency in the middle of an important campaign may not call back if the freelancer turns down an emergency assignment.

A freelance copywriter must be able to manage time well, because he or she will most likely be handling several assignments at once. Assignments are best cultivated through contacts—repeat business from a former employer, word-of-mouth referrals, or networking within professional organizations. Some areas even have tip clubs—groups of people in different professions who meet and give one another leads.

Advertising agencies often need part-time help in busy seasons. Newspapers, radio, and television stations may also need copywriters for clients who do not have their own advertising agencies.

Advertising freelancers base their charges on hourly rates, but experienced freelancers can often estimate how long a job will take and quote a flat project rate or price range.

Doing business with repeat customers or referrals can also help cut down on problems receiving payment. Freelancers have to be prepared for uneven cash flow, sometimes waiting 90 days for checks. They also keep their own business records, bill clients, and keep track of tax-deductible expenses.

Income Potential

Hourly rates generally range from $50 to $100. Daily rates are $250 and up; weekly, $500 and up. Monthly retainers can be from $1,000 to $2,000.

Many experienced copywriters base their fees on an hourly rate, but quote the client a flat project rate based on how much time they expect the job to take. Rates vary with the size and type of client.

Work Prospects

A copywriter with some business contacts and a reputation for doing good work on deadline has a good chance of building up a healthy client list. Getting established, however, could take some time.

Education

Most advertising copywriters have an undergraduate degree in communications, liberal arts, advertising, or business. Courses in copywriting or creative writing are also helpful.

Experience/Skills

A solid background in advertising is essential for someone trying to become a freelance copywriter. Reliability, professionalism, and creativity are key attributes of freelancers in this field.

Unions/Associations

The American Advertising Federation and American Marketing Association are the major groups of interest to copywriters.

Other groups include the Association for Women in Communications and The Writers Guild of America, Inc, a union representing scriptwriters for radio, television, and film.

APPENDIXES

APPENDIX I
EDUCATIONAL INSTITUTIONS

Unlike careers in many fields—for example, health care or teaching—most careers in writing, publishing, or broadcasting do not require a specific degree in order to get a foot in the door. Most people who enter the fields described in this book have at least an undergraduate degree, often in journalism or communications. A postgraduate degree is useful for obtaining certain higher-level positions. Such college majors as English, dramatic arts, creative writing, foreign languages, or comparative literature often lead to the types of careers listed in this book. In fact, book editors may have majored in anything from mathematics to philosophy or geology, depending on the topics of the books they edit. A teaching background is helpful for writers of textbooks, but is generally not required for textbook editors. Many professionals in the publishing and media fields supplement their original undergraduate degree by taking courses at night in specific aspects of their field, and not necessarily for a postgraduate degree. For example, they might have a B.A. in English and later take night courses in management or marketing.

That being said, a degree in journalism or communications is certainly one good step toward becoming qualified for most of the jobs described in this book. Of course, years of work experience are also required for the higher-level jobs. Some educational institutions allow a student to emphasize a particular specialty (sometimes called a sequence) within the field, such as print journalism, broadcasting, or advertising/public relations.

The following is a list of some of the American four-year colleges and universities that offer such undergraduate degrees in journalism and/or communications. Many of these schools also offer master's degrees. The listings include addresses, telephone numbers, fax numbers where available, and web sites. Also listed are each school's majors or specialties related to journalism and communications, in alphabetical order. For more information about course descriptions, admissions requirements, and the availability of scholarships, contact the institutions of interest. In many cases you can obtain relevant, up-to-date E-mail addresses from the web site (e.g., the dean of the journalism department).

In addition, the institutions whose programs have met the standards set by the Accrediting Council on Education in Journalism and Mass Communications (ACEJMC) have been marked with an asterisk (*). The ACEJMC does not necessarily accredit *all* the degree programs listed here for an asterisked school. For example, the ACEJMC might have accredited only communications and journalism at a particular school even though advertising, film arts, and public relations are also listed in this book. Check the ACEJMC's web site at http://www.ukans.edu/~acejmc to see exactly what programs it has accredited and how recently. Each educational institution is normally reviewed for accreditation every six years.

Many major professional associations have information on scholarships and internships; consult Appendix III. The Dow Jones Newspaper Fund publishes a comprehensive annual Journalist's Road to Success booklet, which contains information about journalism careers and scholarships. Copies can be obtained for $3 each from:

The Dow Jones Newspaper Fund
P.O. Box 300
Princeton, NJ 08543-0300
phone: 609-452-2820

ALABAMA

Alabama State University
Montgomery, AL 36101-0271
phone: 334-229-4291
fax: 334-229-4984
http://www.alasu.edu
Broadcasting, communications, journalism, public relations

University of Alabama*
Tuscaloosa, AL 35487-0172
phone: 205-348-5520
fax: 205-348-3836
http://www.ua.edu

Advertising, journalism, public relations, speech/debate/rhetoric, telecommunications

Auburn University*
Auburn University, AL 36849-5206
phone: 334-844-4607
fax: 334-844-4665
http://www.auburn.edu

Communications, journalism, public relations, speech/debate/rhetoric

Jacksonville State University
Jacksonville, AL 36265
phone: 205-782-5400
fax: 205-782-5121
http://www.jsu.edu

Communications

Samford University
Birmingham, AL 35229
phone: 205-870-2011

fax: 205-726-2171
http://www.samford.edu

Communications, journalism, speech/debate/rhetoric

Spring Hill College
Mobile, AL 36608
phone: 334-380-3030
fax: 334-460-2186
http://www.shc.edu

Advertising, broadcasting, journalism, public relations

Troy State University
Troy, AL 36082
phone: 334-670-3179
fax: 334-670-3134
http://www.troyst.edu

Broadcasting, communications, journalism, speech/debate/rhetoric

University of South Alabama
Mobile, AL 36688-0002
phone: 334-460-6141
fax: 334-460-7023
http://www.usouthal.edu

Communications

ALASKA

University of Alaska—Anchorage*
Anchorage, AK 99508
phone: 907-786-1480
fax: 907-786-4888
http://www.uaa.alaska.edu

Communications, journalism

University of Alaska—Fairbanks*
Fairbanks, AK 99775-7840
phone: 907-474-7500
fax: 907-474-5379
http://www.uaf.edu

Journalism, speech/debate/rhetoric

ARIZONA

Arizona State University*
Tempe, AZ 85287-1305
phone: 602-965-5011
fax: 602-965-7041
http://www.asu.edu

Broadcasting, communications, journalism, media arts

Northern Arizona University
Flagstaff, AZ 86011-5619
phone: 520-523-5511
fax: 520-523-6023
http://www.nau.edu

Advertising, broadcasting, communications, journalism, speech/debate/rhetoric, telecommunications

University of Arizona*
Tucson, AZ 85721
phone: 520-621-3237
fax: 520-621-9799
http://www.arizona.edu

Communications, journalism, media arts

ARKANSAS

Arkansas State University*
State University, AR 72467-0540
phone: 870-972-2468
fax: 870-972-3856
http://www.astate.edu

Journalism, radio/TV technology, speech/debate/rhetoric

Arkansas Tech University
Russellville, AR 72801-2222
phone: 501-968-0343
fax: 501-964-0522
http://www.atu.edu

Journalism, speech/debate/rhetoric

Harding University
Searcy, AR 72149-0001
phone: 501-279-4407
fax: 501-279-4076
http://www.harding.edu

Advertising, broadcasting, communications

Henderson State University
Arkadelphia, AR 71999-0001
phone: 870-230-5028
fax: 870-230-5144
http://www.hsu.edu

Communications, speech/debate/rhetoric

John Brown University
Siloam Springs, AR 72761
phone: 501-524-9548
fax: 501-524-4196
http://www.jbu.edu

Broadcasting, journalism, public relations

University of Arkansas at Fayetteville*
Fayetteville, AR 72701-1201
phone: 501-575-3601
fax: 501-575-4314
http://www.uark.edu

Communications, journalism

University of Arkansas at Little Rock*
Little Rock, AR 72204
phone: 501-569-3250
fax: 501-569-8371
http://www.ualr.edu

Advertising, journalism, radio/TV technology, technical and business writing

University of Central Arkansas
Conway, AR 72035-0001
phone: 501-450-5000
fax: 501-450-5228
http://www.uca.edu

Communications, journalism, speech/debate/rhetoric

CALIFORNIA

California Polytechnic State University*
San Luis Obispo, CA 93407
phone: 805-756-2508
fax: 805-756-5744
http://www.calpoly.edu

Journalism

California State Polytechnic University
Pomona, CA 91768-4019
phone: 909-869-2000
fax: 909-869-4529
http://www.csupomona.edu

Communications

California State University, Chico*
Chico, CA 95929-0600
phone: 530-898-4779
fax: 530-898-4839
http://www.csuchico.edu

Communications, journalism

California State University, Dominguez Hills
Dominguez Hills
Carson, CA 90747-9960
phone: 310-243-3613
fax: 310-516-3609
http://www.csudh.edu

Communications

California State University, Fresno*
Fresno, CA 93740-8029
phone: 209-278-2087
fax: 209-278-4995
http://www.csufresno.edu

Communications, speech/debate/rhetoric

California State University, Fullerton*
Fullerton, CA 92834
phone: 714-278-3517
fax: 714-278-2209
http://www.fullerton.edu

Advertising, broadcasting, communications, journalism, speech/debate/rhetoric

California State University, Hayward
Hayward, CA 94542-3000
phone: 510-885-2624
fax: 510-885-3816
http://www.csuhayward.edu

Communications, speech/debate/rhetoric

California State University, Long Beach
Long Beach, CA 90840-0106
phone: 310-985-4141
fax: 310-985-4973
http://www.csulb.edu

Broadcasting, film arts, journalism, speech/debate/rhetoric

California State University, Los Angeles
Los Angeles, CA 90032
phone: 213-343-3901
fax: 213-343-3888
http://www.calstatela.edu

Broadcasting, journalism, radio/TV technology, speech/debate/rhetoric, telecommunications

California State University, Northridge*
Northridge, CA 91330-8311
phone: 818-677-3135
fax: 818-677-3438
http://www.csun.edu

Broadcasting, journalism, speech/debate/rhetoric

California State University, Sacramento
Sacramento, CA 95819-6048
phone: 916-278-3901
fax: 916-278-5603
http://www.csus.edu

Communications, journalism

Humboldt State University
Arcata, CA 95521-8299
phone: 707-826-4402
fax: 707-826-6194
http://www.humboldt.edu

Communications, journalism

Menlo College
Atherton, CA 94027-4301
phone: 650-833-3305
fax: 650-617-2395
http://www.menlo.edu

Advertising, broadcasting, communications, journalism, media arts

Pacific Union College
Angwin, CA 94508
phone: 707-965-6336
fax: 707-965-6432
http://www.puc.edu

Communications, journalism, public relations

Pepperdine University
Malibu, CA 90263-4392
phone: 310-456-4392
fax: 310-456-4861
http://www.pepperdine.edu

Advertising, communications, journalism, public relations, speech/debate/rhetoric, telecommunications

Point Loma Nazarene University
San Diego, CA 92106-2899
phone: 619-849-2519
fax: 619-849-2601
http://www.ptloma.edu

Communications, journalism, speech/debate/rhetoric

Saint Mary's College of California
Moraga, CA 94575-4800
phone: 510-631-4224
fax: 510-376-7193
http://www.stmarys-ca.edu

Communications

San Diego State University
San Diego, CA 92182
phone: 619-594-6871
fax: 619-594-6246
http://www.sdsu.edu

Broadcasting, journalism

San Francisco State University*
San Francisco, CA 94132

phone: 415-338-1689/2663
fax: 415-338-3111
http://www.sfsu.edu

Broadcasting, film arts, journalism, speech/debate/rhetoric

San Jose State University*
San Jose, CA 95192-0055
phone: 408-924-3240
fax: 408-924-3229
http://www.sjsu.edu

Advertising, broadcasting, film arts, journalism, speech/debate/rhetoric

Santa Clara University
Santa Clara, CA 95053
phone: 408-554-4700
fax: 408-554-5255
http://www.scu.edu

Communications

Stanford University
Stanford, CA 94305
phone: 415-723-2091
fax: 415-725-2846
http://www.stanford.edu

Communications

University of California at Berkeley*
Berkeley, CA 94720-5800
phone: 510-642-3383
fax: 510-643-9136
http://www.berkeley.edu

Communications, film arts, speech/debate/rhetoric

University of La Verne
La Verne, CA 91750-4443
phone: 909-593-3511, ext. 4026
fax: 909-596-1451
http://www.ulaverne.edu

Broadcasting, communications, journalism

University of the Pacific
Stockton, CA 95211-0197
phone: 209-946-2211
fax: 209-946-2413
http://www.uop.edu

Communications

University of San Francisco
San Francisco, CA 94117-1080
phone: 415-422-5555
fax: 415-422-2217
http://www.usfca.edu

Communications

University of Southern California*
Los Angeles, CA 90089-0281
phone: 213-740-3914
fax: 213-740-8624
http://www.usc.edu

Broadcasting, communications, film arts,
journalism, public relations

COLORADO

Adams State College
Alamosa, CO 81102
phone: 719-587-7712
fax: 719-587-7522
http://www.adams.edu

Advertising, journalism

Colorado State University*
Fort Collins, CO 80523-0015
phone: 970-491-6310
fax: 970-491-2908
http://www.colostate.edu

Journalism, speech/debate/rhetoric, technical and business writing

Mesa State College
Grand Junction, CO 81502-2647
phone: 970-248-1083
fax: 970-248-1973
http://www.mesastate.edu

Communications

The Metropolitan State College of Denver
Denver, CO 80217-3362
phone: 303-556-3058
fax: 303-556-6345
http://www.mscd.edu

Communications, journalism,
speech/debate/rhetoric

University of Colorado at Boulder*
Boulder, CO 80309-0030
phone: 303-492-4364
fax: 303-492-0969
http://www.colorado.edu

Communications, film arts, journalism

University of Denver
Denver, CO 80208
phone: 303-871-2036
fax: 303-871-3301
http://www.du.edu

Communications, journalism, telecommunications

University of Northern Colorado
Greeley, CO 80639
phone: 970-351-2881
fax: 970-351-2984
http://www.unco.edu

Advertising, communications, journalism,
public relations, telecommunications

University of Southern Colorado
Pueblo, CO 81001-4901
phone: 719-549-2461
fax: 719-549-2419
http://www.uscolo.edu

Broadcasting, communications, journalism, speech/debate/rhetoric

CONNECTICUT

Southern Connecticut State University
New Haven, CT 06515
phone: 203-392-5644
fax: 203-392-5863
http://www.scsu.ctstateu.edu

Communications, journalism

University of Bridgeport
Bridgeport, CT 06601
phone: 203-576-4552
fax: 203-576-4941
http://www.bridgeport.edu

Communications, journalism

University of Connecticut
Storrs, CT 06269
phone: 860-486-3137
fax: 860-486-1476
http://www.uconn.edu

Communications, journalism

University of Hartford
West Hartford, CT 06117
phone: 860-243-4296
fax: 860-768-4961
http://www.hartford.edu

Audio technology, communications, film
arts, technical and business writing, video

University of New Haven
West Haven, CT 06516
phone: 203-932-7319
fax: 203-931-6093
http://www.newhaven.edu

Audio technology, communications

DELAWARE

University of Delaware
Newark, DE 19716
phone: 302-831-2000
fax: 302-831-6905
http://www.udel.edu

Communications, journalism

DISTRICT OF COLUMBIA

American University*
Washington, DC 20016-8001
phone: 202-885-2058
fax: 202-885-2099
http://www.american.edu

Audio technology, communications, film
arts, journalism

The George Washington University
Washington, DC 20052
phone: 202-994-6040
fax: 202-994-0325
http://www.gwu.edu

Broadcasting, communications, journalism

Howard University*
Washington, DC 20059
phone: 202-806-2755
fax: 202-806-9227
http://www.howard.edu

Broadcasting, communications, film arts,
journalism

FLORIDA

Edward Waters College
Jacksonville, FL 32209
phone: 904-366-2715
fax: 904-366-2706
http://www.ewc.edu

Communications

Florida A&M University*
Tallahassee, FL 32307-3100
phone: 850-599-3718
fax: 850-599-3086
http://www.famu.edu

Journalism

Florida International University*
North Miami, FL 33199
phone: 305-348-2363

fax: 305-348-3648
http://www.fiu.edu

Communications

Florida Southern College
Lakeland, FL 33801-5698
phone: 941-680-3912
fax: 941-680-4120
http://www.flsouthern.edu

Advertising, communications, journalism, public relations

Jacksonville University
Jacksonville, FL 32211
phone: 904-745-7000
fax: 904-745-7012
http://www.ju.edu

Communications, speech/debate/rhetoric

University of Central Florida
Orlando, FL 32816-0111
phone: 407-823-3000
fax: 407-823-3419
http://www.ucf.edu

Advertising, broadcasting, communications, film arts, journalism, public relations

University of Florida*
Gainesville, FL 32611-8400
phone: 352-392-0466
fax: 352-392-3919
http://www.ufl.edu

Advertising, journalism, public relations, speech/debate/rhetoric, telecommunications

University of Miami*
Coral Gables, FL 33124-2030
phone: 305-284-3420
fax: 305-284-2454
http://www.miami.edu

Advertising, audio technology, broadcasting, communications, film arts, journalism, public relations, speech/debate/rhetoric, technical and business writing, telecommunications, video

University of North Florida
Jacksonville, FL 32224
phone: 904-620-2624
fax: 904-620-2414
http://www.unf.edu

Communications

University of South Florida*
Tampa, FL 33620
phone: 813-974-3350
fax: 813-974-9689
http://www.usf.edu

Communications, speech/debate/rhetoric

University of West Florida*
Pensacola, FL 32514-5751
phone: 904-474-2230
fax: 904-474-3360
http://www.uwf.edu

Communications

GEORGIA

Berry College
Mt. Berry, GA 30149-0159
phone: 706-236-2215
fax: 706-290-2160
http://www.berry.edu

Communications

Brenau University
Gainesville, GA 30501
phone: 770-534-6299
fax: 770-538-4306
http://www.brenau.edu

Corporate communications, mass communications

Clark Atlanta University
Atlanta, GA 30314
phone: 404-880-8918
fax: 404-880-6174
http://www.cau.edu

Communications, speech/debate/rhetoric

Georgia Southern University
Statesboro, GA 30460
phone: 912-681-5532
fax: 912-681-5635
http://www.gasou.edu

Communications, journalism

Georgia State University
Atlanta, GA 30303-3083
phone: 404-651-2000
fax: 404-651-4811
http://www.gsu.edu

Film arts, journalism, speech/debate/rhetoric

University of Georgia*
Athens, GA 30602-3018

phone: 706-542-1704
fax: 706-542-3113
http://www.uga.edu

Advertising, broadcasting, communications, film arts, journalism, public relations, speech/debate/rhetoric, telecommunications

HAWAII

University of Hawaii at Manoa*
Honolulu, HI 96822-2217
phone: 808-956-8881
fax: 808-956-5396
http://www.uhm.hawaii.edu

Communications, journalism, speech/debate/rhetoric

IDAHO

Boise State University
Boise, ID 83725
phone: 208-385-1156
fax: 208-385-3765
http://www.idbsu.edu

Communications

Idaho State University
Pocatello, ID 83209-0009
phone: 208-236-2475
fax: 208-236-4231
http://www.isu.edu

Communications, speech/debate/rhetoric

University of Idaho
Moscow, ID 83844
phone: 208-885-6326
fax: 208-885-9061
http://www.uidaho.edu

Communications, journalism, telecommunications

ILLINOIS

Bradley University
Peoria, IL 61625
phone: 309-677-1000
fax: 309-677-2797
http://www.bradley.edu

Communications

Columbia College Chicago
Chicago, IL 60605-1996

phone: 312-663-1600
fax: 312-663-5543
http://www.colum.edu

Advertising, audio technology, film arts, journalism, media arts, radio/TV technology

DePaul University
Chicago, IL 60604
phone: 312-362-8300
fax: 312-362-5749
http://www.depaul.edu

Communications

Eastern Illinois University*
Charleston, IL 61920-3099
phone: 217-581-5000
fax: 217-581-7188
http://www.eiu.edu

Communications, journalism

Illinois State University
Normal, IL 61761
phone: 309-438-2181
fax:309-438-3932
http://www.ilstu.edu

Communications, public relations, speech/debate/rhetoric, telecommunications

Loyola University Chicago
Chicago, IL 60611
phone: 312-915-6500
fax: 312-915-6449
http://www.luc.edu

Communications

Northern Illinois University
De Kalb, IL 60115
phone: 815-753-1000
fax: 815-753-8312
http://www.niu.edu

Communications, journalism

Northwestern University*
Evanston, IL 60208
phone: 847-491-3741
fax: 847-491-5565
http://www.nwu.edu

Broadcasting, communications, journalism, radio/TV technology

Roosevelt University
Chicago, IL 60605
phone: 312-341-3500
fax: 312-341-3523

http://www.roosevelt.edu
Broadcasting, journalism, public relations, telecommunications

Southern Illinois University at Carbondale*
Carbondale, IL 62901-6601
phone: 618-536-3361
fax: 618-453-5200
http://www.siu.edu/cwis

Advertising, broadcasting, journalism, speech/debate/rhetoric

Southern Illinois University at Edwardsville
Edwardsville, IL 62026-1045
phone: 618-692-3705
fax: 618-692-5013
http://www.siue.edu

Communications, speech/debate/rhetoric

University of Illinois at Urbana-Champaign*
Urbana, IL 61801
phone: 217-333-2350
fax: 217-333-9882
http://www.uiuc.edu

Advertising, broadcasting, communications, journalism, media arts, speech/debate/rhetoric

University of Saint Francis
Joliet, IL 60435
phone: 815-740-3360
fax: 815-740-4285
http://www.stfrancis.edu

Communications, journalism

Western Illinois University
Macomb, IL 61455-1390
phone: 309-298-3157
fax: 309-298-3111
http://www.wiu.edu

Communications, journalism, media arts

INDIANA

Anderson University
Anderson, IN 46012
phone: 765-641-4080
fax: 765-641-3851
http://www.anderson.edu

Communications

Ball State University*
Muncie, IN 47306

phone: 765-285-8300
fax: 765-285-1632
http://www.bsu.edu

Broadcasting, communications, film arts, journalism, speech/debate/rhetoric, telecommunications

Butler University
Indianapolis, IN 46208
phone: 317-940-8100
fax: 317-940-8150
http://www.butler.edu

Broadcasting, communications, journalism, speech/debate/rhetoric, telecommunications

Calumet College of Saint Joseph
Whiting, IN 46394
phone: 219-473-7770
fax: 219-473-4259
http://www.ccsj.edu

Communications

De Pauw University
Greencastle, IN 46135
phone: 765-658-4800
fax: 765-658-4007
http://www.depauw.edu

Communications

Franklin College of Indiana
Franklin, IN 46131
phone: 317-738-8000
fax: 317-738-8274
http://www.franklincoll.edu

Journalism

Goshen College
Goshen, IN 46526
phone: 219-535-7000
fax: 219-535-7660
http://www.goshen.edu

Communications

Indiana State University
Terre Haute, IN 47809
phone: 812-237-2121
fax: 812-237-8023
http://www.isu.indstate.edu

Broadcasting, communications, film arts, journalism

Indiana University at Bloomington*
Bloomington, IN 47405-7000
phone: 812-855-0661

fax: 812-855-5102
http://www.indiana.edu

Audio technology, communications, journalism, speech/debate/rhetoric, telecommunications

Indiana University-Purdue University/Indianapolis
Indianapolis, IN 46202-5143
phone: 317-274-4591
fax: 317-278-1862
http://www.iupui.edu

Communications, journalism

Purdue University/West Lafayette
West Lafayette, IN 47907
phone: 765-494-4600
fax: 765-494-0544
http://www.purdue.edu

Advertising, communications, film arts, journalism, public relations, telecommunications

Saint Mary-of-the-Woods College
Saint Mary-of-the-Woods, IN 47876-0068
phone: 812-535-5212
fax: 812-535-4900
http://www.smwc.edu

Journalism

University of Evansville
Evansville, IN 47722-0329
phone: 812-479-2468
fax: 812-474-4076
http://www.evansville.edu

Advertising, communications, journalism, public relations, telecommunications

Valparaiso University
Valparaiso, IN 46383
phone: 219-464-5011
fax: 219-464-6898
http://www.valpo.edu

Broadcasting, communications, journalism

IOWA

Drake University*
Des Moines, IA 50311-4505
phone: 515-271-2011
fax: 515-271-2798
http://www.drake.edu

Advertising, broadcasting, communications, journalism, public relations, speech/debate/rhetoric

Grand View College
Des Moines, IA 50316-1599
phone: 515-263-2800
fax: 515-263-2974
http://www.gvc.edu

Broadcasting, communications, journalism

Iowa State University of Science and Technology*
Ames, IA 50011
phone: 515-294-4111
fax: 515-294-5108
http://www.iastate.edu

Advertising, communications, journalism, speech/debate/rhetoric

Marycrest International University
Davenport, IA 52804
phone: 319-327-9609
fax: 319-327-9620
http://www.mcrest.edu

Communications

University of Iowa*
Iowa City, IA 52242-1396
phone: 319-335-3847
fax: 319-335-1535
http://www.uiowa.edu

Broadcasting, communications, film arts, journalism, speech/debate/rhetoric

KANSAS

Fort Hays State University
Hays, KS 67601-4099
phone: 785-628-4000
fax: 785-628-4187
http://www.fhsu.edu

Communications, telecommunications

Kansas State University*
Manhattan, KS 66506
phone: 785-532-6011
fax: 785-532-6393
http://www.ksu.edu

Communications, journalism, speech/debate/rhetoric

Pittsburg State University
Pittsburg, KS 66762
phone: 316-235-4251
fax: 316-235-4078
http://www.pittstate.edu

Broadcasting, communications

University of Kansas*
Lawrence, KS 66045
phone: 785-864-3911
fax: 785-864-5221
http:///www.ukans.edu

Advertising, broadcasting, journalism, speech/debate/rhetoric

Washburn University
Topeka, KS 66621
phone: 785-231-1010
fax: 785-357-5176
http://www.wuacc.edu

Speech/debate/rhetoric

Wichita State University
Wichita, KS 67260
phone: 316-978-3045
fax: 316-978-3174
http://www.wichita.edu/online

Communications

KENTUCKY

Eastern Kentucky University
Richmond, KY 40475-3102
phone: 606-622-1000
fax: 606-622-8024
http://www.eku.edu

Broadcasting, journalism, public relations, speech/debate/rhetoric

Morehead State University
Morehead, KY 40351
phone: 606-783-2000
fax: 606-783-5038
http://www.morehead-st.edu

Advertising, communications, journalism, speech/debate/rhetoric

Murray State University*
Murray, KY 42071-0009
phone: 502-762-2387
fax: 502-762-2390
http://www.murraystate.edu

Advertising, broadcasting, communications, journalism, speech/debate/rhetoric

Northern Kentucky University
Highland Heights, KY 41099
phone: 606-572-5220
fax: 606-572-5566
http://www.nku.edu

Journalism, radio/TV technology, speech/debate/rhetoric

University of Kentucky*
Lexington, KY 40506-0042
phone: 606-257-9000
fax: 606-323-3168
http://www.uky.edu

Advertising, communications, integrated strategic communication, journalism, telecommunications

Western Kentucky University*
Bowling Green, KY 42101-3576
phone: 270-745-0111
fax: 270-745-6133
http://www.wku.edu

Advertising, broadcasting, communications, journalism, public relations, speech/debate/rhetoric

LOUISIANA

Grambling State University*
Grambling, LA 71245
phone: 318-274-6183
fax: 318-274-3194
http://www.gram.edu

Communications, speech/debate/rhetoric

Louisiana State University
Baton Rouge, LA 70803
phone: 504-388-2336
fax: 504-388-2125
http://www.lsu.edu

Communications, speech/debate/rhetoric

Louisiana Tech University*
Ruston, LA 71272
phone: 318-257-3036
fax: 318-257-2499
http://www.latech.edu

Journalism, speech/debate/rhetoric

Loyola State University
New Orleans, LA 70118
phone: 504-865-2011
fax: 504-865-3383
http://www.loyno.edu

Communications, communications technology, telecommunications

McNeese State University*
Lake Charles, LA 70609
phone: 318-475-5290
fax: 318-475-5291
http://www.mcneese.edu

Broadcasting, communications, speech/debate/rhetoric

Nicholls State University*
Thibodaux, LA 70301
phone: 504-448-4586
fax: 504-448-4577
http://www.nich.edu

Communications, journalism

Northwestern State University of Louisiana*
Natchitoches, LA 71497
phone: 318-357-4503
fax: 318-357-5567
http://www.nsula.edu

Advertising, journalism

Southeastern Louisiana University
Hammond, LA 70402
phone: 504-549-2000
fax: 504-549-5632
http://www.selu.edu

Communications

Southern University and A&M College*
Baton Rouge, LA 70813
phone: 225-771-4500
fax: 225-771-2500
http://www.subr.edu

Broadcasting, communications, journalism, speech/debate/rhetoric

University of Louisiana at Monroe*
Monroe, LA 71209
phone: 318-342-5252
fax: 318-342-1049
http://www.nlu.edu

Film arts, journalism, radio/TV technology

University of Louisiana at Lafayette*
Lafayette, LA 70504-2651
phone: 318-482-1000
fax: 318-482-6104
http://www.usl.edu

Advertising, broadcasting, communications, public relations, telecommunications

MAINE

University of Maine
Orono, ME 04469-5713
phone: 207-581-1561
fax: 207-581-1213
http://www.maine.edu

Communications, journalism, speech/debate/rhetoric

MARYLAND

Bowie State University
Bowie, MD 20715-9465
phone: 301-464-3000
fax: 301-464-7521
http://www.bowiestate.edu

Broadcasting, journalism, public relations

University of Maryland*
College Park, MD 20742
phone: 301-405-1000
fax: 301-314-1978
http://www.umcp.umd.edu

Broadcasting, communications, journalism

MASSACHUSETTS

Boston University
Boston, MA 02215
phone: 617-353-2300
fax: 617-353-9695
http://www.bu.edu

Advertising, broadcasting, communications, film arts, journalism, public relations

Emerson College
Boston, MA 02116-1596
phone: 617-824-8500
fax: 617-824-8609
http://www.emerson.edu

Advertising, broadcasting, communications, film arts, journalism, media arts, public relations, publishing, radio/TV technology, speech/debate/rhetoric

Simmons College
Boston, MA 02115-5898
phone: 617-521-2000
fax: 617-521-3190
http://www.simmons.edu

Advertising, communications, public relations

Suffolk University
Boston, MA 02108
phone: 617-573-8460
fax: 617-742-4291
http://www.suffolk.edu

Broadcasting, communications, journalism, public relations, speech/debate/rhetoric

University of Massachusetts Amherst
Amherst, MA 01003
phone: 413-545-0222
fax: 413-545-4312
http://www.umass.edu

Communications, journalism

MICHIGAN

Central Michigan University*
Mount Pleasant, MI 48859
phone: 517-774-3076
fax: 517-774-7267
http://www.cmich.edu

Broadcasting, communications, journalism

Eastern Michigan University
Ypsilanti, MI 48197
phone: 734-487-1849
fax: 734-487-1484
http://www.emich.edu

Advertising, broadcasting, communications, communications technology, film arts, journalism, speech/debate/rhetoric, telecommunications

Madonna University
Livonia, MI 48150-1173
phone: 734-432-5300
fax: 734-432-5393
http://www.munet.edu

Communications, journalism, technical and business writing, video

Michigan State University*
East Lansing, MI 48824-1046
phone: 517-355-8332
fax: 517-355-1647
http://www.msu.edu

Advertising, communications, journalism, telecommunications

Oakland University
Rochester, MI 48309-4401
phone: 248-370-2100
fax: 248-370-4462
http://www.oakland.edu

Communications, journalism

University of Michigan/Ann Arbor
Ann Arbor, MI 48109-1285

phone: 734-764-1817
fax: 734-936-0740
http://www.umich.edu

Communications, journalism, media arts, speech/debate/rhetoric

Wayne State University
Detroit, MI 48202
phone: 313-577-3577
fax: 313-577-7536
http://www.wayne.edu

Broadcasting, communications, film arts, journalism, public relations, speech/debate/rhetoric

MINNESOTA

Bemidji State University
Bemidji, MN 56601-2699
phone: 218-755-2040
fax: 218-755-2048
http://www.bemidji.msus.edu

Broadcasting, communications, journalism

Moorhead State University
Moorhead, MN 56563
phone: 218-236-2161
fax: 218-236-2168
http://www.moorhead.msus.edu

Advertising, broadcasting, communications, journalism, public relations, speech/debate/rhetoric

Saint Cloud State University*
Saint Cloud, MN 56301-4498
phone: 320-255-0121
fax: 320-255-2243
http://www.stcloud.msus.edu

Advertising, broadcasting, communications, journalism, speech/debate/rhetoric

Saint Mary's University of Minnesota
Winona, MN 55987-1399
phone: 507-452-4430
fax: 507-457-1722
http://www.smumn.edu

Audio technology, public relations, publishing, speech/debate/rhetoric, telecommunications

University of Minnesota/Twin Cities*
Minneapolis, MN 55455
phone: 612-625-2006
fax: 612-625-1693

http://www1.umn.edu/twincities
Film arts, speech/debate/rhetoric

Winona State University
Winona, MN 55987
phone: 507-457-5100
fax: 507-457-5000
http://www.winona.msus.edu

Advertising, broadcasting, communications, journalism, speech/debate/rhetoric

MISSISSIPPI

Jackson State University*
Jackson, MS 39217
phone: 601-968-2151
fax: 601-974-5800
http://www.jsums.edu

Communications, speech/debate/rhetoric

Mississippi State University
Mississippi State, MS 38677
phone: 662-325-2323
fax: 662-325-7360
http://www.msstate.edu

Communications

Mississippi University for Women
Columbus, MS 39701
phone: 662-329-4750
fax: 662-241-7481
http://www.muw.edu

Communications

Rust College
Holly Springs, MS 38635
phone: 601-252-8000
fax: 601-252-6107
http://www.rustcollege.edu

Communications, journalism

University of Mississippi*
University, MS 38677
phone: 601-232-7226
fax: 601-232-5869
http://www.olemiss.edu

Advertising, broadcasting, journalism, radio/TV technology

University of Southern Mississippi*
Hattiesburg, MS 39406
phone: 601-266-5000
fax: 601-266-5816
http://www.usm.edu

Advertising, broadcasting, communications, journalism, speech/debate/rhetoric

MISSOURI

Central Missouri State University
Warrensburg, MO 64093
phone: 660-543-4811
fax: 660-543-8517
http://www.cmsu.edu

Broadcasting, communications, film arts, journalism, public relations, speech/debate/rhetoric

Culver-Stockton College
Canton, MO 63435
phone: 217-231-6000
fax: 217-231-6611
http://www.culver.edu

Communications

Evangel College
Springfield, MO 65802
phone: 417-865-2811
fax: 417-865-9599
http://www.evangel.edu

Broadcasting, communications, journalism, speech/debate/rhetoric

Lincoln University
Jefferson City, MO 65101
phone: 573-681-5599
fax: 573-681-5889
http://www.lincolnu.edu

Journalism

Lindenwood University
Saint Charles, MO 63301
phone: 636-949-4949
fax: 636-949-4910
http://www.lindenwood.edu

Communications

Northwest Missouri State University
Maryville, MO 64468
phone: 660-562-1562
fax: 660-562-1121
http://www.nwmissouri.edu

Broadcasting, communications, journalism, public relations, speech/debate/rhetoric

Southeast Missouri State University
Cape Girardeau, MO 63701
phone: 573-651-2000

fax: 573-651-5936
http://www.semo.edu

Advertising, communications, journalism, public relations, radio/TV technology

Stephens College
Columbia, MO 65215
phone: 573-442-2211
fax: 573-876-7248
http://www.stephens.edu

Public relations

University of Missouri—Columbia*
Columbia, MO 65211
phone: 573-882-7786
fax: 573-882-7887
http://www.missouri.edu

Advertising, broadcasting, communications, journalism

Webster University
St. Louis, MO 63119
phone: 314-968-6900
fax: 314-968-7115
http://www.webster.edu

Advertising, audio technology, broadcasting, communications, film arts, journalism, media arts, public relations, video

MONTANA

The University of Montana—Missoula*
Missoula, MT 59812
phone: 406-243-0211
fax: 406-243-4087
http://www.umt.edu

Broadcasting, communications, journalism

NEBRASKA

Creighton University
Omaha, NE 68178
phone: 402-280-2700
fax: 402-280-2685
http://www.creighton.edu

Communications, journalism, speech/debate/rhetoric

Hastings College
Hastings, NE 68901
phone: 402-463-2402
fax: 402-461-7480
http://www.hastings.edu

Broadcasting, communications, journalism, speech/debate/rhetoric

Midland Lutheran College
Fremont, NE 68025
phone: 402-721-5480
fax: 402-721-0250
http://www.mlc.edu

Advertising, communications, journalism

University of Nebraska—Kearney
Kearney, NE 68849
phone: 308-865-8702
fax: 308-865-8987
http://www.unk.edu

Advertising, broadcasting, communications, journalism, speech/debate/rhetoric, telecommunications

University of Nebraska at Lincoln*
Lincoln, NE 68588-0417
phone: 402-472-3041
fax: 402-472-8597
http://www.unl.edu

Advertising, broadcasting, communications, journalism, speech/debate/rhetoric

University of Nebraska at Omaha
Omaha, NE 68182
phone: 402-554-2416
fax: 402-554-3472
http://www.unomaha.edu

Broadcasting, communications, journalism, speech/debate/rhetoric

NEVADA

University of Nevada, Las Vegas
Las Vegas, NV 89154
phone: 702-895-3011
fax: 702-895-3850
http://www.unlv.edu

Communications

University of Nevada, Reno
Reno, NV 89557
phone: 775-784-1110
fax: 775-784-4283
http://www.unr.edu

Journalism, speech/debate/rhetoric

NEW HAMPSHIRE

Keene State College
Keene, NH 03431
phone: 603-358-2276

fax: 603-358-2767
http://www.keene.edu
Communications, journalism

NEW JERSEY

Rider University
Lawrenceville, NJ 08648-3099
phone: 609-896-5000
fax: 609-895-6645
http://www.rider.edu
Advertising, communications, journalism,
speech/debate/rhetoric

Rowan University
Glassboro, NJ 08028
phone: 609-256-4200
fax: 609-256-4929
http://www.rowan.edu
Broadcasting, communications, journalism, speech/debate/rhetoric

Rutgers, The State University of New Jersey/University College—New Brunswick
New Brunswick, NJ 08903
phone: 732-932-8093
fax: 732-932-1174
http://www.rutgers.edu
Communications, journalism

Seton Hall University
South Orange, NJ 07079
phone: 973-761-9000
fax: 973-761-9452
http://www.shu.edu
Communications

NEW MEXICO

Eastern New Mexico University
Portales, NM 88130
phone: 505-562-2178
fax: 505-562-2118
http://www.enmu.edu
Communications, journalism,
speech/debate/rhetoric

New Mexico Highlands University
Las Vegas, NM 87701
phone: 505-425-7511
fax: 505-454-3552
http://www.nmhu.edu
Communications

New Mexico State University
Las Cruces, NM 88003-8001
phone: 505-646-0111
fax: 505-646-6330
http://www.nmsu.edu
Communications, journalism

University of New Mexico*
Albuquerque, NM 87131
phone: 505-277-2446
fax: 505-277-6686
http://www.unm.edu
Communications, journalism, media arts,
technical and business writing

NEW YORK

Brooklyn Campus of Long Island University
Brooklyn, NY 11201-8423
phone: 718-488-1011
fax: 718-797-2399
http://www.brooklyn.liunet.edu/cwis/bklyn/bklyn.html
Broadcasting, communications, journalism, speech/debate/rhetoric

Canisius College
Buffalo, NY 14208
phone: 716-883-7000
fax: 716-888-2377
http://www.canisius.edu
Communications

Columbia University*
New York, NY 10027-7004
phone: 212-854-4150
fax: 212-854-7837
http://www.columbia.edu
Journalism (graduate only)

Cornell University
Ithaca, NY 14853-2801
phone: 607-254-4636
fax: 607-255-0659
http://www.cornell.edu
Communications

Fordham University
Bronx, NY 10458
phone: 718-817-4000
fax: 718-367-3426
http://www.fordham.edu
Broadcasting, communications, journalism

Hofstra University
Hempstead, NY 11549
phone: 516-463-6700
fax: 516-560-7660
http://www.hofstra.edu
Broadcasting, communications, film arts,
journalism, media arts,
speech/debate/rhetoric

Iona College
New Rochelle, NY 10801-1890
phone: 914-633-2502
fax: 914-633-2642
http://www.iona.edu
Advertising, communications, film arts,
journalism

Ithaca College
Ithaca, NY 14850-7020
phone: 607-274-3124
fax: 607-274-1900
http://www.ithaca.edu
Advertising, broadcasting, communications, film arts, journalism, media arts, public relations, speech/debate/rhetoric, technical and business writing, telecommunications, video

Marist College
Poughkeepsie, NY 12601
phone: 914-575-3226
fax: 914-575-3215
http://www.marist.edu
Communications, film arts, journalism

New York University*
New York, NY 10012
phone: 212-998-1212
fax: 212-995-4148
http://www.nyu.edu
Communications, film arts, journalism,
radio/TV technology,
speech/debate/rhetoric

Niagara University
Niagara University, NY 14109
phone: 716-286-8700, -8721
fax: 716-286-8710
http://www.niagara.edu
Communications

Saint Bonaventure University
Saint Bonaventure, NY 14778
phone: 716-375-2000
fax: 716-375-2005
http://www.sbu.edu
Journalism

Saint John Fisher College
Rochester, NY 14618
phone: 716-385-8000
fax: 716-385-8129
http://www.sjfc.edu

Communications, journalism

State University of New York at Buffalo
Buffalo, NY 14260
phone: 716-645-6900
fax: 716-645-6498
http://www.buffalo.edu

Communications, media arts

State University of New York/College at New Paltz
New Paltz, NY 12561
phone: 914-257-2121
fax: 914-257-3209
http://www.newpaltz.edu

Broadcasting, communications, journalism, speech/debate/rhetoric

Syracuse University*
Syracuse, NY 13244
phone: 315-443-1870
fax: 315-443-3946
http://www.syr.edu

Advertising, broadcasting, communications, film arts, journalism, media arts, public relations, publishing, speech/debate/rhetoric, video

Utica College of Syracuse University
Utica, NY 13502-4892
phone: 315-792-3111
fax: 315-792-3003
http://www.ucsu.edu

Communications, journalism, public relations, speech/debate/rhetoric

NORTH CAROLINA

Johnson C. Smith University
Charlotte, NC 28216
phone: 704-378-1010
fax: 704-378-1242
http://www.jcsu.edu

Communications

University of North Carolina at Asheville
Asheville, NC 28804
phone: 828-251-6600
fax: 828-251-6482

http://www.unca.edu

Communications

University of North Carolina at Chapel Hill*
Chapel Hill, NC 27599
phone: 919-966-3623
fax: 919-962-9149
http://www.unc.edu

Journalism, speech/debate/rhetoric

NORTH DAKOTA

North Dakota State University
Fargo, ND 58105
phone: 701-231-8643
fax: 701-231-8802
http://www.ndsu.nodak.edu

Communications

University of North Dakota
Grand Forks, ND 58202
phone: 701-777-3367
fax: 701-777-4857
http://www.und.edu

Advertising, communications

OHIO

Bowling Green State University*
Bowling Green, OH 43403
phone: 419-372-2531
fax: 419-372-6955
http://www.bgsu.edu

Broadcasting, communications, film arts, journalism, speech/debate/rhetoric

Kent State University*
Kent, OH 44242-0001
phone: 330-672-2444
fax: 330-672-2499
http://www.kent.edu

Advertising, broadcasting, communications, film arts, journalism, public relations, speech/debate/rhetoric, telecommunications

Ohio State University*
Columbus, OH 43210
phone: 614-292-6446
fax: 614-292-4818
http://www.osu.edu

Communications, journalism

Ohio University*
Athens, OH 45701
phone: 740-593-1000
fax: 740-593-0560
http://www.ohio.edu

Advertising, broadcasting, communications, film arts, journalism, speech/debate/rhetoric, telecommunications

University of Toledo
Toledo, OH 43606
phone: 419-530-4242
fax: 419-530-4504
http://www.utoledo.edu

Communications

OKLAHOMA

East Central University
Ada, OK 74820
phone: 405-332-8000
fax: 405-436-5495
http://www.ecok.edu

Advertising, communications, journalism, media arts, public relations, speech/debate/rhetoric

Northeastern State University
Tahlequah, OK 74464
phone: 918-456-5511
fax: 918-458-2326
http://www.nsuok.edu

Advertising, broadcasting, communications, journalism, speech/debate/rhetoric

Oklahoma Baptist University
Shawnee, OK 74804
phone: 405-275-2850
fax: 405-878-2046
http://www.okbu.edu

Broadcasting, communications, journalism, speech/debate/rhetoric, telecommunications

Oklahoma City University
Oklahoma City, OK 73106
phone: 405-521-5050
fax: 405-521-5916
http://www.okcu.edu

Advertising, broadcasting, communications, journalism, speech/debate/rhetoric

Oklahoma State University*
Stillwater, OK 74078-1012

phone: 405-744-6858
fax: 405-744-5285
http://www.okstate.edu

Broadcasting, communications, journalism, speech/debate/rhetoric

University of Central Oklahoma
Edmond, OK 73034
phone: 405-974-2000
fax: 405-341-4964
http://www.ucok.edu

Advertising, broadcasting, communications, journalism, speech/debate/rhetoric

University of Oklahoma*
Norman, OK 73019
phone: 405-325-2251
fax: 405-325-7124
http://www.ou.edu

Advertising, broadcasting, communications, film arts, journalism, public relations, video

OREGON

Southern Oregon University
Ashland, OR 97520
phone: 541-552-7672
fax: 541-552-6329
http://www.sosc.edu

Broadcasting, communications

University of Oregon*
Eugene, OR 97403
phone: 541-346-3111
fax: 541-346-0682
http://www.uoregon.edu

Journalism

PENNSYLVANIA

Bloomsburg University of Pennsylvania
Bloomsburg, PA 17815
phone: 570-389-4316
fax: 570-389-4741

http://www.bloomu.edu

Communications, speech/debate/rhetoric

Duquesne University
Pittsburgh, PA 15282
phone: 412-396-6000
fax: 412-396-5644
http://www.duq.edu

Advertising, audio technology, broadcasting, communications, journalism, media

arts, public relations, speech/debate/rhetoric

Indiana University of Pennsylvania
Indiana, PA 15705-0001
phone: 724-357-2100
fax: 724-357-6281
http://www.iup.edu

Communications, journalism, media arts

Lehigh University
Bethlehem, PA 18015
phone: 610-758-3000
fax: 610-758-4361
http://www.lehigh.edu
Journalism

Pennsylvania State University/University Park Campus*
University Park, PA 16802
phone: 814-865-5471
fax: 814-863-7590
http://www.psu.edu

Advertising, broadcasting, communications, film arts, journalism, speech/debate/rhetoric

Point Park College
Pittsburgh, PA 15222-1984
phone: 412-391-4100
fax: 412-392-3902
http://www.ppc.edu

Communications, film arts, journalism, video

Shippensburg University of Pennsylvania
Shippensburg, PA 17257
phone: 717-477-7447
fax: 717-477-4016
http://www.ship.edu

Journalism, media arts, speech/debate/rhetoric

Temple University*
Philadelphia, PA 19122
phone: 215-204-7000
fax: 215-204-5694
http://www.temple.edu

Broadcasting, communications, film arts, journalism, speech/debate/rhetoric, telecommunications

RHODE ISLAND

University of Rhode Island
Kingston, RI 02881

phone: 401-874-1000
fax: 401-874-5523
http://www.uri.edu

Communications, journalism, speech/debate/rhetoric

SOUTH CAROLINA

Benedict College
Columbia, SC 29204
phone: 803-253-5143
fax: 803-253-5167
http://bchome.benedict.edu

Journalism

University of South Carolina at Columbia*
Columbia, SC 29208
phone: 803-777-7000
fax: 803-777-4103
http://www.sc.edu

Advertising, broadcasting, journalism, media arts, public relations, speech/debate/rhetoric

Winthrop University*
Rock Hill, SC 29733
phone: 803-323-2211
fax: 803-323-2464
http://www.winthrop.edu

Communications, speech/debate/rhetoric

SOUTH DAKOTA

Black Hills State University
Spearfish, SD 57799
phone: 605-642-6011
fax: 605-642-6762
http://www.bhsu.edu

Broadcasting, communications, communications technology, journalism, speech/debate/rhetoric

South Dakota State University*
Brookings, SD 57007
phone: 605-688-4171
fax: 605-688-5034
http://www.sdstate.edu

Communications, journalism

University of South Dakota
Vermillion, SD 57069
phone: 605-677-5011

fax: 605-677-4250
http://www.usd.edu

Communications, speech/debate/rhetoric

TENNESSEE

East Tennessee State University*
Johnson City, TN 37614-0717
phone: 423-439-4317
fax: 423-439-7540
http://www.etsu-tn.edu

Broadcasting, communications, journalism, speech/debate/rhetoric

Middle Tennessee State University*
Murfreesboro, TN 37132-0001
phone: 615-898-2300
fax: 615-898-5682
http://www.mtsu.edu

Advertising, broadcasting, communications, journalism, speech/debate/rhetoric

University of Memphis*
Memphis, TN 38152
phone: 901-678-2401
fax: 901-678-4287
http://www.memphis.edu

Communications, journalism

Tennessee Technological University
Cookeville, TN 38505
phone: 931-372-3888
fax: 931-372-6250
http://www.tntech.edu

Journalism, technical and business writing

University of Tennessee at Chattanooga*
Chattanooga, TN 37403
phone: 423-755-4111
fax: 423-755-4695
http://www.utc.edu

Communications

University of Tennessee, Knoxville*
Knoxville, TN 37996
phone: 423-974-1000
fax: 423-974-6341
http://www.utk.edu

Advertising, broadcasting, film arts, journalism, speech/debate/rhetoric

University of Tennessee at Martin*
Martin, TN 38238-5099

phone: 901-587-7546
fax: 901-587-7550
http://www.utm.edu

Communications

TEXAS

Abilene Christian University
Abilene, TX 79699-9000
phone: 915-674-2000
fax: 915-674-2130
http://www.acu.edu

Advertising, broadcasting, communications, journalism, speech/debate/rhetoric

Angelo State University
San Angelo, TX 76909
phone: 915-942-2041
fax: 915-942-2078
http://www.angelo.edu

Communications, journalism

Baylor University*
Waco, TX 76798-7353
phone: 254-710-3435
fax: 254-710-3436
http://www.baylor.edu

Broadcasting, communications, journalism, speech/debate/rhetoric, telecommunications

Hardin-Simmons University
Abilene, TX 79698
phone: 915-670-1206
fax: 915-670-1527
http://www.hsutx.edu

Communications

Midwestern State University
Wichita Falls, TX 76308
phone: 940-397-4000
fax: 940-397-4672
http://www.mwsu.edu

Communications

Prairie View A&M University
Prairie View, TX 77446-0188
phone: 409-857-2618
fax: 409-857-2699
http://www.pvamu.edu

Broadcasting, communications, journalism, speech/debate/rhetoric

Sam Houston State University
Huntsville, TX 77341

phone: 409-294-1111
fax: 409-294-3758
http://www.shsu.edu

Journalism, speech/debate/rhetoric

Southern Methodist University
Dallas, TX 75275
phone: 214-768-2058
fax: 214-768-2507
http://www.smu.edu

Advertising, broadcasting, film arts, journalism, media arts, public relations

Southwest Texas State University
San Marcos, TX 78666-4606
phone: 512-245-2111
fax: 512-245-8044
http://www.swt.edu

Advertising, broadcasting, communications, journalism, speech/debate/rhetoric

Stephen F. Austin State University
Nacogdoches, TX 75962
phone: 409-468-2011
fax: 409-468-3489
http://www.sfasu.edu

Broadcasting, communications, journalism, speech/debate/rhetoric

Texas A&M University*
College Station, TX 77843
phone: 409-845-3211
fax: 409-845-5408
http://www.tamu.edu

Journalism, speech/debate/rhetoric

Texas A&M University—Kingsville
Kingsville, TX 78363
phone: 361-593-2111
fax: 361-593-2195
http://www.tamuk.edu

Communications

Texas Christian University*
Fort Worth, TX 76129
phone: 817-257-7000
fax: 817-257-7322
http://www.tcu.edu

Advertising, broadcasting, communications, film arts, journalism, media arts

Texas Southern University
Houston, TX 77004
phone: 713-313-7011
fax: 713-313-4317
http://www.tsu.edu

Communications, journalism,
speech/debate/rhetoric

Texas Tech University*
Lubbock, TX 79409-3082
phone: 806-742-3385
fax: 806-742-1085
http://www.ttu.edu

Advertising, broadcasting, journalism,
public relations, speech/debate/rhetoric,
telecommunications

Texas Wesleyan University
Fort Worth, TX 76105-1536
phone: 817-531-4422
fax: 817-531-4231
http://www.txwesleyan.edu

Communications

Texas Woman's University*
Denton, TX 76204-5828
phone: 940-898-2181
fax: 940-898-2188
http://www.twu.edu

Advertising, communications

Trinity University
San Antonio, TX 78212
phone: 210-999-7206
fax: 210-999-8164
http://www.trinity.edu

Communications, journalism,
speech/debate/rhetoric

University of Houston
Houston, TX 77204
phone: 713-743-1000
fax: 713-743-9633
http://www.uh.edu

Communications, journalism, radio/TV
technology, speech/debate/rhetoric

University of North Texas*
Denton, TX 76203
phone: 940-565-2000
fax: 940-565-2370
http://www.unt.edu

Communications, film arts, journalism,
radio/TV technology

University of Texas at Arlington
Arlington, TX 76019
phone: 817-272-2222
fax: 817-272-3435
http://www.uta.edu

Advertising, broadcasting, communications, journalism, speech/debate/rhetoric

University of Texas at Austin*
Austin, TX 78712
phone: 512-475-7440
fax: 512-475-7475
http://www.utexas.edu

Advertising, film arts, journalism,
speech/debate/rhetoric

University of Texas at El Paso
El Paso, TX 79968
phone: 915-747-5000
fax: 915-747-5848
http://www.utep.edu

Communications, journalism,
speech/debate/rhetoric

University of Texas—Pan American
Edinburg, TX 78539-2999
phone: 956-381-2011
http://www.panam.edu

Communications

West Texas A&M University
Canyon, TX 79016
phone: 806-656-2020
fax: 806-656-2071
http://www.wtamu.edu

Communications, speech/debate/rhetoric

UTAH

Brigham Young University*
Provo, UT 84602
phone: 801-378-4636
fax: 801-378-6016
http://www.byu.edu

Advertising, broadcasting, communications, film arts, journalism, public relations

University of Utah*
Salt Lake City, UT 84112
phone: 801-581-7200
fax: 801-585-6255
http://www.utah.edu

Communications, film arts,
speech/debate/rhetoric

Utah State University
Logan, UT 84322
phone: 435-797-1079
fax: 435-797-4077

http://www.usu.edu
Journalism

Weber State University
Ogden, UT 84408-1505
phone: 801-626-6000
fax: 801-626-6747
http://www.weber.edu

Communications, speech/debate/rhetoric

VERMONT

Saint Michael's College
Colchester, VT 05439
phone: 802-654-2000
fax: 802-654-2591
http://www.smcvt.edu

Journalism

VIRGINIA

Emory & Henry College
Emory, VA 24327
phone: 540-944-4121
fax: 540-944-6935
http://www.ehc.edu

Communications, journalism

Hampton University*
Hampton, VA 23668
phone: 757-727-5405
fax: 757-727-5084
http://www.hamptonu.edu

Communications

James Madison University
Harrisonburg, VA 22807
phone: 540-568-6211
fax: 540-568-3332
http://www.jmu.edu

Communications, media arts,
speech/debate/rhetoric

Liberty University
Lynchburg, VA 25402
phone: 804-582-2000
fax: 804-582-2617
http://www.liberty.edu

Communications

Norfolk State University*
Norfolk, VA 23504
phone: 757-823-8600

fax: 757-823-9119
http://www.nsu.edu
Communications, journalism

Radford University
Radford, VA 24142
phone: 540-831-5371
fax: 540-831-5138
http://www.radford.edu
Broadcasting, speech/debate/rhetoric

University of Richmond
Richmond, VA 23173
phone: 540-831-5371
fax: 540-831-5138
http://www.richmond.edu
Journalism, speech/debate/rhetoric

Virginia Commonwealth University*
Richmond, VA 23284
phone: 804-828-0100
fax: 804-828-9175
http://www.vcu.edu
Communications

Virginia Polytechnic Institute and State University
Blacksburg, VA 24061
phone: 540-231-6267
fax: 540-231-3242
http://www.vt.edu
Communications

Virginia Union University
Richmond, VA 23220
phone: 804-257-5600
fax: 804-257-5808
http://www.vuu.edu
Journalism

Washington and Lee University*
Lexington, VA 24450-0303
phone: 540-463-8400
fax: 540-463-8045
http://www.wlu.edu
Journalism

WASHINGTON

Central Washington University
Ellensburg, WA 98926-7550
phone: 509-963-6001
fax: 509-963-3022
http://www.cwu.edu

Broadcasting, communications, journalism, speech/debate/rhetoric

Gonzaga University
Spokane, WA 99258
phone: 509-328-4220
fax: 509-324-5780
http://www.gonzaga.edu
Broadcasting, journalism, public relations, speech/debate/rhetoric

Pacific Lutheran University
Tacoma, WA 98447
phone: 253-531-6900
fax: 253-536-5136
http://www.plu.edu
Communications

Seattle University
Seattle, WA 98122-4340
phone: 206-296-6000
fax: 206-296-5656
http://www.seattleu.edu
Communications, journalism

University of Washington*
Seattle, WA 98195-3740
phone: 206-543-2660
fax: 206-543-9285
http://www.washington.edu
Communications, speech/debate/rhetoric, technical and business writing

Walla Walla College
College Place, WA 99324
phone: 509-527-2327
fax: 509-527-2397
http://www.wwc.edu
Communications, speech/debate/rhetoric

Washington State University
Pullman, WA 99164-2520
phone: 509-335-5586
fax: 509-335-4902
http://www.wsu.edu
Advertising, broadcasting, communications, journalism, speech/debate/rhetoric

WEST VIRGINIA

Bethany College
Bethany, WV 26032
phone: 304-829-7000
fax: 304-829-7142

http://www.bethany.wvnet.edu
Communications, journalism

Marshall University*
Huntington, WV 25755
phone: 304-696-2360
fax: 304-696-2732
http://www.marshall.edu
Advertising, broadcasting, communications, journalism

West Virginia University*
Morgantown, WV 26506-6010
phone: 304-293-3505 (ext. 5413)
fax: 304-293-3072
http://www.wvu.edu
Advertising, broadcasting, communications, journalism, public relations, speech/debate/rhetoric

WISCONSIN

Marquette University*
Milwaukee, WI 53201-1881
phone: 414-288-7302
fax: 414-288-5227
http://www.marquette.edu
Advertising, broadcasting, communications, journalism, public relations

University of Wisconsin—Eau Claire*
Eau Claire, WI 54702-4004
phone: 715-836-2637
fax: 715-836-3820
http://www.uwec.edu
Advertising, broadcasting, communications, journalism

University of Wisconsin—La Crosse
La Crosse, WI 54601
phone: 608-785-8000
fax: 608-785-8940
http://www.uwlax.edu
Communications, speech/debate/rhetoric

University of Wisconsin—Madison
Madison, WI 53706
phone: 608-262-3961
fax: 608-262-1429
http://www.wisc.edu
Communications, journalism

University of Wisconsin—Milwaukee
Milwaukee, WI 53201
phone: 414-229-1122

fax: 414-229-6258
http://www.uwm.edu

Communications, film arts

University of Wisconsin—Oshkosh*
Oshkosh, WI 54901
phone: 920-424-0202
fax: 920-424-1207
http://www.uwosh.edu

Broadcasting, journalism,
speech/debate/rhetoric

University of Wisconsin—River Falls*
River Falls, WI 54022-5001

phone: 715-425-3911
fax: 715-425-0658
http://www.uwrf.edu

Communications, journalism,
speech/debate/rhetoric

University of Wisconsin—Whitewater
Whitewater, WI 53190-1790
phone: 414-472-1234
fax: 414-472-1515
http://www.uww.edu

Communications, journalism, public relations, speech/debate/rhetoric

WYOMING

University of Wyoming
Laramie, WY 82071
phone: 307-766-1121
fax: 307-766-4042
http://www.uwyo.edu

Broadcasting, communications, journalism

APPENDIX II
USEFUL WEB SITES FOR WRITERS

The following list of 101 best web sites for writers has been reproduced courtesy of *Writer's Digest* magazine. Please check the actual site at http://www.writersdigest.com/101sites/ to make sure you get the most up-to-date version, since the site is periodically updated.

INTRODUCTION

Whether you're looking for answers to your research questions, writing camaraderie and critiques, or the winner of last year's Academy Award for best picture, the answers can be found on the Internet. Here are the sites every writer should bookmark or put in his or her favorites folder.

It's more varied than your local library's reference shelf, packed with information on familiar questions and the most obscure topics you can think of—it's the Internet. And it's all available at the click of a mouse.

The list of the 101 best web sites for writers was culled from our staff's favorite lists, other F&W Publications employees, and about 1,500 people who visited writersdigest.com in December [1999] and early January [2000]. While many people recommended association and organiza-

tion sites, we limited our selections in that category to sites that provided valuable information to members and non-members alike.

A few caveats you're probably already aware of if you've spent much time on the World Wide Web:

The answers you find are only as good as the source. *Bartlett's Quotations,* for example, is a more reliable place to check a quote than a high school senior's term paper, but both are likely to show up in a search engine query.

Watch the date that the site or specific page was updated. Just as library reference materials become outdated, so do Web sites. There's a sense that if it's on the web, it must be current. Not so. Hundreds if not thousands of individuals, schools, and companies decided in the past three years they had to have a Web presence, only to let sites molder after a few months.

Don't let the web totally replace your interaction with your family, friends, writers' group, or other support network. While the Internet is a wonderful resource for research and interaction, it can't replace person-to-person contact.

That said, use the categories listed below to narrow your search and start bookmarking!

SEARCH ENGINES

SearchIQ
http://www.searchiq.com
"If you've never used a search engine, go to this site first. You'll not only get tips on how to run a successful search, you'll also find a list that ranks various engines by the types of searches they do best."
—Amanda Boyd, *Writer's Digest* managing editor

Alta Vista
http://www.altavista.com
"I love the natural-language question feature, where you can just type in 'What year did Batman first appear?' It seldom works precisely as promised, but your answer (1939) is usually lurking in the first screen of results."
—David A. Fryxell, F&W Publications magazine editorial director

Dogpile
http://www.dogpile.com
"This monster checks dozens of other search engines, newswires and newsgroups with one click. Dogpile is the fastest way I know to find out just how much Internet information exists on a topic."
—Melanie Rigney, *Writer's Digest* editor

Ask Jeeves Inc.
http://www.askjeeves.com
This "natural language" search engine fields questions posed as, well, questions. You can dispense with the Boolean search strings and find what you're looking for. "One of the most fun parts of this site is that it lists interesting questions users have posed to it. 'Who invented the laser?' Good question. 'Where can I learn Icelandic slang?' Even better question—

probably even more interesting than its answer."
—Bill Brohaugh, new media director, F&W Publications

DejaNews
http://www.dejanews.com
DejaNews allows you to search Internet newsgroups, those discussion forums that cover everything from home-brewing to laptop repair. You can also post to newsgroups through the site.

Hotbot
http://www.hotbot.com
Consistently rated by computer magazines as the best overall search engine, Hotbot came from the folks who originally brought you *Wired* magazine. Its advanced search lets you search by date, domain, varying page depth, even whether a page contains certain types of media.

Yahoo!
http://www.yahoo.com
Yes, it's been around forever (or at least, forever in cyberspace terms) and its search capabilities aren't the best. But the category listings are a big help when you want to find all the magazines about collecting toy cars, or all the places you can go to find ZIP codes.

Starting Page
http://www.startingpage.com/
**   index.html**
As with Yahoo!, you search by category rather than by words. The site is easy to navigate; you don't need to go as deep as you do in Yahoo! to get where you need to be.

DICTIONARIES

Oxford English Dictionary's Word of
**   the Day**
http://www.oed.com/wordofday.htm
Word of the Day is part of a prototype for an on-line subscription service, but the daily words are free. "What a wonderful way to learn more about the language, or to be totally confused by it. Learn, for instance, the dozens of ways we've spelled 'vouchsafe' since the 14th century and then try to pass your next spelling test."
—Bill Brohaugh, new media director, F&W Publications

A Web of On-Line Dictionaries
http://www.facstaff.bucknell.edu/
**   rbeard/diction.html**
"This site has dictionaries for every language imaginable, courtesy of the folks at Bucknell University."
—Dawn Ramirez, *Writer's Digest* associate editor

Semantic Rhyming Dictionary
http://www.link.cs.cmu.edu/dougb/
**   rhyme-doc.html**
Stuck for a rhyme? This site is the answer. You can ask for a perfect rhyme or some variation thereof (last syllable only, for example) and the site will even suggest ways to get from Word A to Word B (for example, angry is synonymous with wild, which triggers animals, which triggers eat, which triggers hungry).

NetLingo: The Internet Language
**   Dictionary**
http://www.netlingo.com
Perplexed by those strange characters—such as ;-)—that people put in E-mail to you? Think a gopher belongs in the ground? This one's for you.

A Glossary of Literary Terms and a
**   Handbook of Rhetorical Devices**
http://www.uky.edu/ArtsSciences/
**   Classics/Harris/rhetfo rm.html**
Great index, and don't forget to take the self-test.

GENERAL REFERENCE

Information Please Almanac
http://www.infopls.com
"Can they really be giving away all this info for free? Like having a stack of reference books inside your computer."
—David A. Frxyell, F&W Publications magazine editorial director

iTools
http://www.itools.com
A terrific assortment of tools, from language and library aids on the Research-It area of the site to search engines on the Find-It side.

World Factbook
http://www.odci.gov/cia/publications/
**   factbook/index.h tml**
Everything you need to know, from population to exports, about every country from Afghanistan to Zimbabwe. "A wonderful resource for developing contemporary fictional settings or for nonfiction research. Just be careful, this book is a publication of the Central Intelligence Agency."
—Melanie Rigney, *Writer's Digest* editor

Internet Public Library
http://www.ipl.org
The University of Michigan has staked out this ambitious claim and so far, seems to be delivering. The reference section sends the user to appropriate sites for information on areas ranging from arts and humanities to associations. There's even an experimental "ask a question" desk.

Encyberpedia
http://www.encyberpedia.com/ency.htm
An impressive portal connecting to on-line encyclopedias and other troves of knowledge.

Symbols.com
http://www.symbols.com

If you can't remember whether > means "greater than" or "less than," this is the place for you.

Virtual Reference Desk
http://www.refdesk.com
This reference desk has links by the dozen on a blizzard of topics, from today's stock quotes to ZIP codes to sports. One problem: Jam-packing those many topics into one home page means the type gets very, very small, and sometimes you need to go deep before you find what you want.

The Phrase Finder
http://www.shu.ac.uk/
**   web-admin/phrases/**
The folks at Sheffield Hallam University in England have compiled 5,000 common phrases, indexed them, and provided the meanings and origins of the phrases. What's more, they have a list of misconceptions about how some phrases originated.

Library of Congress
http://lcweb.loc.gov/homepage/lchp/html
It's almost like being there yourself. The site provides access to the Library of Congress's catalogs and other research vehicles, including full text access to bills under consideration in the U.S. House of Representatives and Senate.

E-Conflict World Encyclopedia
http://www.emulateme.com
Interesting collection of worldwide data, from flags to national anthems to current weather. Helpful in creating a realistic setting for fiction or short stories.

Roget's Thesaurus
http://humanities.uchicago.edu/forms_
**   unrest/ROGET.html**
Sometimes, it's easier to open a book than go to the Web, but heck, if you've got it bookmarked, why not?

The Polling Report
http://www.pollingreport.com/
A great place to find recent public opinion poll results to buttress your nonfiction article, generate fiction ideas, or both. The site features results from leading U.S. polling firms on politics, business, social issues, news events, sports, and entertainment.

The World Wide Web Acronym and
**   Abbreviation Server**
http://www.ucc.ie/acronyms/acro.html

See this site if you've got the acronym but don't know what it stands for, or vice versa.

Metric/imperial conversion
http://www.frenchproperty.com/ref/
    convert.htm

Quick, how many degrees Celsius is 80 degrees Fahrenheit? How many ounces in a liter? How many meters in a mile? This is the place to find out.

Time Zone Converter
http://www.timezoneconverter.com

Lets you know what time it is or will be any time in the world. Handy for overseas interviews.

InfoNation
http://www.un.org/Pubs/Cyber
    SchoolBus/infonation/
    e_infonation.htm

InfoNation is a two-step database that allows you to view and compare the most up-to-date statistical data for the member states of the United Nations.

555-1212.com
http://www.555-1212.com

Enter the city and find out the area code, or enter the area code and get a list of the cities it includes.

ZIP Code Lookup and Address Information
http://www.usps.gov/ncsc/

Look up a ZIP code, find out what codes go with what cities, or check out the Postal Service's preferred abbreviations. And since you're here, check out the complete schedule of rates and fees, track an express mail package, or calculate your postage cost.

Bartlett's Quotations
http://www.columbia.edu/acis/bartleby/
    bartlett/

It's the 1901 edition, but the Shakespeare citations in particular are quite complete.

Pulitzer Prize winners
http://www.pulitzer.org/navigation/
    index.html

A look at honorees of the past 80 years, and the works of recent winners.

Nobel Prize winners
http://nobelprizes.com/nobel/nobel.html

Lists of all winners, including the literature category.

Elements of Style
http://www.columbia.edu/acis/bartleby/
    strunk/

Not to worry if your copy's out of reach. Columbia University has put the 1918 edition on-line.

SPECIALIZED REFERENCE

International Trademark Association
http://www.inta.org

How do you spell that trademark? Are those in-line skates Roller Blades or Rollerblades? Check the correct spelling of "nearly 4,000" trademarks and service marks, and get the correct generic term. (Oh, and if you're curious about the skates, it's the latter.)

Internet Movie Database
http://www.imbd.com

Need to know who won best supporting actor in 1953 (Anthony Quinn)? Or how much Star Wars has taken in at the box office ($461 million in the United States)? The Internet Movie Database has the facts on 160,000 titles.

Publishing Law Center
http://www.publaw.com/

Good links and articles about intellectual property and other legal issues.

Eponym
http://student-www.uchicago.edu/
    users/smhawkin/na mes/index.html

Don't know what to name your character? This site offers names from just about everywhere in the world from a spectrum of time periods.

medword.com
http://www.medword.com/index.html

Okay, it's really a site for medical transcriptionists. But you also can get access to drawings of various parts of the body, definitions of prescription drugs, and the Hippocratic Oath. Handy for figuring out what happens when a malady befalls one of your characters.

FindLaw
http://www.findlaw.com

A good portal if you're looking for myriad legal decisions as well as legal publishers and state and local bar association information.

Current Population Survey
http://www.bls.census.gov/cps/
    cpsmain.htm

A joint project of the U.S. Bureau of Labor Statistics and the Census Bureau, this site slices and dices labor force characteristics of the U.S. population on a monthly basis. Good source for trend story ideas.

MapQuest
http://www.mapquest.com

Door-to-door and city-to-city driving directions are available. Unlike many services, directions also are available in text form, and there are maps for selected cities abroad. Handy for checking how your fictional character gets from one place to another if you don't know the setting like the back of your hand, or for your own travels.

The Currency $ite
Historical Tables, Current Rates and Forecasts for World Currencies
http://www.oanda.com

On this site's Classic Converter, find out how many Finnish markka (or any of 163 other currencies) to the U.S. dollar for any given day since January 1, 1990. Also an easy way to find out the current names for the world's currencies.

Copyright holders
http://www.lib.utexas.edu/Libs/HRC/
    WATCH/about.html

The Writers, Artists and Their Copyright Holders searchable database is a project of the University of Texas and England's University of Reading. The writers and artists listed for the most part have archives in libraries or other archival facilities in the United States or United Kingdom.

MEDIA NEWS AND REFERENCE

BookWire
http://www.bookwire.com

BookWire is owned by Cahners Business Information, the company that brings you *Publishers Weekly*. The site is packed with book industry news, features, author interviews, and guides to literary events.

Electronic Newsstand
http://www.enews.com

They call themselves the ultimate magazine site, and while they're essentially

Amazon.com for magazines, there are two areas of the site you'll find especially interesting. Hot Copy highlights news from the magazine biz—redesigns, new editors, new departments. The Fab Five lists "the five articles you absolutely don't want to miss this week."

Writer Beware
http://www.sfwa.org/Beware/
  Warnings.html
This section of the Science Fiction and Fantasy Writers of America site leads you to info on and questions to ask about agents; book doctors; contests; vanity anthologies; copyright, electronic rights, and other issues; on-line publication; and subsidy and vanity publishers.

Books Out of Print
http://www.bowker.com/bop/home/
  BOPformsrch.html
You have to register to run a search, but it's free—and you'll get the full citation, including ISBN for those books that are so obscure even Amazon.com can't find them.

Drew's Scripts-o-Rama
http://www.script-o-
  rama.com/table.shtml
Here you can access drafts and finished scripts for movies and TV shows, look up movie transcripts, and jump to sites specific to a particular movie or TV show.

Any bookstore site
http://www.amazon.com
http://www.barnesandnoble.com
http://www.borders.com
http://www.bookweb.org/bookstores.com
These sites are terrific places to check on a book's title, author, publisher, ISBN, or pub date.

Mediafinder
http://www.oxbridge.com
A handy site for basic facts about 100,000 publications.

Editor & Publisher
http://www.mediainfo.com
This magazine's site has an extensive on-line media directory.

Yearbook of Experts, Authorities and Spokespersons
http://www.yearbooknews.com
If you're looking for authorities on a particular topic area or for idea fodder, this searchable site is the place for you. The yearbook's most recent edition included more than 14,000 separate topics covered by 1,480 individuals, associations, corporations, academics, and public interest groups.

Newswise
http://www.newswise.com
A comprehensive database of news releases from top institutions engaged in scientific, medical, liberal arts, and business research.

Media Resource Service
http://www.mediaresource.org
This service provided by the Scientific Research Society helps writers find reputable sources of scientific information at no charge.

ProfNet
http://www.profnet.com
Writers can get in touch with 6,000 news and information officers at colleges and universities, corporations, think tanks, national labs, medical centers, nonprofits, and PR agencies courtesy of this PR Newswire service.

Literary awards
http://www-stat.wharton.upenn.edu/
  ~siler/litlists/amfic t.html
Courtesy of the University of Pennsylvania's Wharton School, lists the winners of major U.S. literary awards since 1970.

Shaw Guides Writers' Conferences
http://www.shawguides.com/writing/
Get info on hundreds of conferences and workshops worldwide at this highly flexible site.

Top 25 Most Important Magazines in America
http://www.impressionmag.com/
  thelist.html
This list, compiled by a panel of publishing industry insiders and academics, includes such titles as *Time, People, The New York Times Magazine,* and *Martha Stewart Living.* Really.

THE WRITING LIFE

Writer's Digest
http://www.writersdigest.com

Call it shameless self-promotion, but once you check out our searchable database of guidelines, register for our newsletter, and take a peek at our Market of the Day, you might call it something else: a great site.

Critters Workshop
http://brain-of-pooh.techsoft.
  com/users/critters/ind ex.html
Everyone's a critic, including you, at the Critters Workshop site (for science fiction, fantasy, and horror writers only). "Critters" is short for "critiquers," and Critters Workshop is a cyber writer's group, with members exchanging manuscript critiques. "Others have tried this concept with varying success, but this manuscript exchange is well-run, and is quite stable."
—Bill Brohaugh, new media director, F&W Publications

Inkspot
http://www.inkspot.com
There's market information, writing tips, author and editor interviews, and networking opportunities. "Has all the information a writer needs no matter what genre you write in."
—Teresa Bell Kindred (writersdigest.com nomination)

Fiction Writer's Connection
http://www.fictionwriters.com
Plenty of help even for nonmembers, with access to articles, public forums, and interactive novels. "It is inspiring. The web page gives that special feeling that a writer needs to be producing works of fiction. It recognizes the need to give writers that chance."
—Gautam Shankar Banerjer (writersdigest.com nomination)

Word Museum
http://www.wordmuseum.com
"They have everything from interviews to articles to author pages. I always find something new there and I love love love their free contests!"
—Melissa Dupaul (writersdigest.com nomination)

The Fiction Network
http://www.fictionnetwork.net
"It is one of the few sites to showcase both novels and short stories. It has a wide variety. The talent level is high. The exposure is good. And it's free."
—David R. Mark (writersdigest.com nomination)

Inscriptions
http://come.to/Inscriptions
A free weekly e-zine for writers that features contests, articles, and jobs. "The information this site presents is sensible, accurate, and informative."
—Diane Steendahl (writersdigest.com nomination)

Writers' Computer Store
http://www.writerscomputer.com
The store offers software as well as books on writing for the big and small screen as well as more general issues such as story structure.

Master Freelancer
http://www.masterfreelancer.com
Another store jam-packed with products and services for freelance writers.

Amateur Poetry Journal
http://amateurpoetry.virtualave.net/
"Always good reading—tips, articles, and poetry. Chat room and workshop. Learn new forms of poetry not familiar and a challenge each week!"
—Gene Wiginton (writersdigest.com nomination)

Zoetrope
http://www.zoetrope-stories.com
Interesting cooperative concept. For every story or one-act play submitted, the author is asked to read and critique five. After 30 days, Zoetrope decides whether the work will be considered for publication. "The site allows writers from all over the world to post short stories and get widespread, thoughtful critiques of your work, as well as to see other people's work. It gives you a view of the slush pile that editors have to wade through; it gives you something to shoot for. It gives you a community of people who are struggling with the same issues, the same problems."
—Cynthia Hartwig (writersdigest.com nomination)

Artsforge's Wordforge
http://www.artsforge.com/wordforge. html
Among the site's appeals is the ability to write a story in conjunction with other on-line visitors. "The creativity and opportunity to write interactively with others is excellent."
—Judy McCann (writersdigest.com nomination)

Children's Writing Resource Center
http://www.write4kids.com
Free resources for children's writers from Children's Book Insider newsletter.

1st Books Library
http://www.1stbooks.com
Even if you don't believe traditional paper-and-ink books will go the way of the dinosaur, this company's got an interesting concept. You can download more than 1,400 virtual books, many of them at no charge.

PageOne
http://members.aol.com/FICTWRI/ pageone.html
Besides a regular newsletter, the site provides literary news and some neat features, including Novel Beginnings, the first paragraphs of books that visitors are reading. "It's free and always contains at least one really good inspiring thought that helps me go on with my writing."
—Elizabeth Hamlin (writersdigest.com nomination)

Writer's Loft
http://www.bbims.com/writersloft
It takes a long time to get to the application to join in the fun of the progressive workshops, but you assure us it's worth it. "Very creative atmosphere. Wonderful people. Many options."
—Pat Linkhorn (writersdigest.com nomination)

All Mixed Up
http://www.digilogic.com/allmixedup/
E-zine for writers. "This e-zine has offered a lot to the new unpublished authors, myself included, and the caring that Jessica Fogg puts into it is unbelievable."
—Marilyn Olson (writersdigest.com nomination)

odd prose
http://munshi.sonoma.edu/jamal/ oddprose.html
Don't beat yourself up over every grammar error or non sequitur. Just be glad you write better than these Sonoma State students.

Zuzu's Petals
http://www.zuzu.com
How can you not like a site named for the younger daughter in *It's a Wonderful Life*? The editors of Zuzu's Petals Quarterly

Online also offer discussion groups, 7,000 useful links, and an on-line bookstore. "The variety of resources makes it easy to find the latest about smaller publications. The work featured in the 'zine is good quality work, not wannabe writers' attempts."
—Linda Clare (writersdigest.com nomination)

Screenwriters & Playwrights Home Page
http://www.teleport.com/~cdeemer/ scrwriter.html
It's run by Charles Deemer, author of *Screenwright: The Craft of Screenwriting,* and it has lists of useful links and information for both screenwriters and playwrights.

Authorlink!
http://Authorlink.com/
As with many other sites, there's publishing industry news and a lot of links. What sets this site apart is the preview of evaluated manuscripts seeking editors or agents.

WritersNet
http://www.writers/net/index.html
Links to web pages of published authors, editors, publishers, and literary agents.

Momwriters
http://www.offthewallemporium.com/ momwriters. html
This site caters to men and women who take care of the kids or grandkids but still want to write.

One Woman's Writing Retreat
http://www.prairieden.com/
Nice assortment of links and discussions of topics such as "what keeps you writing?" "This site has it all: exciting links, helpful articles, and frankly, anything a new or an experienced writer needs! In my opinion, it's the best writing link I've found, and I've found many."
—Jillian Leslie (writersdigest.com nomination)

SharpWriter.com
http://www.sharpwriter.com
Good portal dictionaries, punctuation, encyclopedias, even information on writer's block.

The Inditer
http://www.inditer.com/
Interesting assortment of on-line stories and poems.

WRITERS' ORGANIZATIONS

Association of Authors' Representatives
http://www.bookwire.com/AAR/
"If you ask me a question about agents, I'll refer you to this site. There you'll find a list of AAR members, their canon of ethics, questions you should be asking potential agents, and a great list of links to other resources."
—Amanda Boyd, *Writer's Digest* managing editor

American Society of Journalists and Authors
http://www.asja.org
ASJA is kind enough to share with members and nonmembers alike its ContractsWatch information about terms and negotiation issues of interest to freelance writers.

Romance Writers of America
http://www.rwanational.com
In addition to members-only areas, the association makes available to everyone upcoming releases in the genre, links to best-seller lists, and links to authors and publishers. "RWA uses its website to disseminate information to members, readers, booksellers, publishers, and librarians. It's up-to-the-minute and accurate, and a great place to gather recent market news or promote your work."
—Natalie J. Damschroder (writersdigest. com nomination)

Authors Guild
http://www.authorsguild.org
The guild is the nation's largest society for published book authors and freelance writers. But anyone can access at least some information on copyright protection and contracts. Another neat feature is backinprint.com, an on-line bookstore featuring out-of-print editions available from the authors themselves.

Writers Guild of America
http://www.wga.org
In addition to members-only data and news about the guild, the site provides information about agents.

National Writers Union
http://www.nwu.org//index.htm
The trade union for 4,800 freelance writers of all genres. Besides members-only areas, there's a wealth of information about the union's work on political and legislative issues and a discussion of contract issues.

Internet Writers Guild
http://members.tripod.com/~IWG/
Noncommercial association of writers and artists who use the Internet to publish their work.

Small Publishers, Authors and Writers Network
http://www.spawn.org/
Publishing resources, including much helpful information about the electronic aspects of self-publishing.

African American Online Writers Guild
http://www.blackwriters.org
Discussion groups, links to African-American writers and emerging writers.

JUST FOR FUN

Salon Magazine
http://www.salonmag.com/
"Worth visiting for the Media columnists alone, this well-written, attractively produced Web magazine (too big to be just a zine) is the Web at its best: informative, intelligent and interesting."
—Amanda Boyd, *Writer's Digest* managing editor

Daily planner and address book
http://www.planetall.com

No charge to use these services. "One less bulky thing to carry around. Lots of neat little planning gadgets available."
—Ed Dockter (writersdigest.com nomination)

Neoplanet
http://www.neoplanet.com
If Netscape is the Democratic Party of browsers and Internet Explorer the Republicans, jump political ship and use Neoplanet as your Bull Moose Party browser. It's a good alternative to the Big Two—more agile, and easy to customize. "Using graphic-interface themes with names like Plazm, NeoCircus, Drive-in and Deco, you can govern the look of your browser within seconds. Nicer on the eyes."
—Bill Brohaugh, new media director, F&W Publications

Weather Channel
http://www.weather.com
This is the place to go when you've got a writing project that will keep you cooped up indoors for days. Either you can find out that the weather at home isn't so great, or you can see what you're missing. In addition to highs and lows and precipitation, there are specialized forecasts for parks and seashores, driving conditions, and pretty much anything else you can think of.

Dumb Lists
http://www.dumblists.com
It had to happen. This is for everyone who has friends who really are worried about the "Goodtimes" virus or who think someone actually did pay a gazillion dollars for that department store cookie recipe. Every day or so, these guys post one of the dumb lists that goes around the Internet. It will give you a smile when you're on deadline, or opening a rejection letter.

APPENDIX III
PROFESSIONAL, INDUSTRY, AND TRADE ASSOCIATIONS AND UNIONS

Note: Since many of these organizations operate on limited funds, please enclose a self-addressed, stamped envelope when querying for information. Not all organizations maintain full-time offices, so some cannot be reached via phone, fax, or E-mail. Contact information for some organizations changes when a new president or director is selected.

Several other useful lists of publishing-related associations may be found on-line. For example, try http://pma-online.org, compiled by Publishers Marketing Association, and http://absolutesway.com/pfp/html/pubassoc.htm, compiled by Places for Publishers.

The Academy of American Poets
584 Broadway
Suite 1208
New York, NY 10012
phone: 212-274-0343
fax: 212-274-9427
E-mail: poets@artswire.org
http://www.poets.org

Academy of Television Arts and Sciences
5220 Lankershim Boulevard
North Hollywood, CA 91601
phone: 818-754-2800
fax: 818-761-2827
E-mail: info@emmys.org
http://www.emmys.org

Advertising Club of New York
235 Park Avenue South, 6th floor
New York, NY 10003
phone: 212-533-8080
fax: 212-533-1929

Advertising Women of New York
153 E. 57th Street
New York, NY 10022
phone: 212-593-1950
fax: 212-759-2865
E-mail: awny@aol.com

All Songwriters Network
Dept. A95, Box 15711
Boston, MA 02215
phone: 617-576-8836
E-mail: asn@tiac.net
http://www.tiac.net/users/asn/index.htm

American Advertising Federation (AAF)
1101 Vermont Avenue NW, Suite 500
Washington, DC 20005-6306

phone: 202-898-0089
fax: 202-898-0159
E-mail: aaf@aaf.org
http://www.aaf.org

American Association of Advertising Agencies
405 Lexington Avenue, 18th Floor
New York, NY 10174-1801
phone: 212-682-2500
fax: 212-953-5665
http://www.aaaa.org

American Association of Newspaper Editors
See American Society of Newspaper Editors

American Association of University Professors
1012 14th Street NW, Suite 500
Washington, DC 20005
phone: 202-737-5900
fax: 202-737-5526
E-mail: aaup@aaup.org
http://www.aaup.org

American Book Producers Association
160 Fifth Avenue, Suite 625
New York, NY 10010-7880
phone: 212-645-2368
fax: 212-989-7542
E-mail: abpahdq@ibm.net

American Booksellers Association
828 South Broadway
Tarrytown, NY 10591
phone: 914-591-2665
fax: 914-591-2720
E-mail: info@bookweb.org
http://bookweb.org

American Business Women's Association
P.O. Box 8728
9100 Ward Parkway
Kansas City, MO 64114-0728
phone: 816-361-6621
fax: 816-361-4991
E-mail: info@abwahq.org
http://www.abwahq.org

American Federation of Government Employees (AFGE)
80 F Street NW
Washington, DC 20001
phone: 202-737-8700
fax: 202-639-6441
E-mail: paystobe@afge.org
http://www.afge.org

American Federation of State, County and Municipal Employees (AFL-CIO)
1625 L Street NW
Washington, DC 20036
phone: 202-429-1000
fax: 202-429-1293
http://www.afscme.org

American Federation of Teachers (AFT)
555 New Jersey Avenue NW
Washington, DC 20001
phone: 202-879-4400
fax: 202-879-4545
E-mail: online@aft.org
http://www.aft.org

American Federation of Television and Radio Artists (AFTRA)
260 Madison Avenue
New York, NY 10016
phone: 212-532-0800

fax: 212-545-1238
E-mail: aftra@aftra.com
http://www.aftra.org

**American Guild of Authors and
  Composers**
See Songwriters Guild of America

American Marketing Association
250 South Wacker Drive, Suite 200
Chicago, IL 60606
phone: 312-648-0536
fax: 800-950-0872
http://www.ama.org

American Historical Association
400 A Street SE
Washington, DC 20003
phone: 202-544-2422
fax: 202-544-8307
E-mail: aha@theaha.org
http://www.chnm.gjm.edu/aha

American Jewish Press Association
1828 L Street NW, Suite 720
Washington, DC 20036
phone: 202-785-2282
fax: 202-785-2307
E-mail: toby@dershowitz.com
http://www.ajpa.org

American Library Association (ALA)
50 East Huron Street
Chicago, IL 60611
phone: 312-944-6780
fax: 312-280-3255
E-mail: ala@ala.org
http://www.ala.org

American Management Association
1601 Broadway
New York, NY 10019-7420
phone: 212-586-8100
fax: 212-903-8168
E-mail: cust_serv@amanet.org
http://www.amanet.org

American Medical Writers Association
40 West Gude Drive, #101
Rockville, MD 20850
phone: 301-294-5303
fax: 301-294-9006
E-mail: amwa@amwa.org
http://www.amwa.org

**American Newspaper Publishers
  Association (ANPA)**
See Newspaper Association of America

American News Women's Club
1607 22nd Street NW
Washington, DC 20008
phone: 202-332-6770
fax: 202-265-6477
E-mail: anwc@sprynet.com
http://anwc.org

**American Society for Information
  Science**
8720 Georgia Avenue, Suite 501
Silver Spring, MD 20910-3602
phone: 301-495-0900
fax: 301-495-0810
E-mail: asis@asis.org
http://www.asis.org

**American Society of Business Press
  Editors**
107 W. Ogden Avenue
LaGrange, IL 60525-2022
phone: 708-352-6950
fax: 708-352-3780
E-mail: info@asbpe.org
http://www.asbpe.org

**American Society of Composers,
  Authors and Publishers**
1 Lincoln Plaza
New York, NY 10023
phone: 212-621-6000
fax: 212-724-9064
E-mail: info@ascap.com
http://www.ascap.com

American Society of Indexers
P.O. Box 48267
Seattle, WA 98148-0267
phone: 206-241-9196
fax: 206-727-6430
E-mail: info@asindexing.org
http://www.asindexing.org

**American Society of Journalists and
  Authors, Inc.**
1501 Broadway, Suite 302
New York, NY 10036
phone: 212-997-0947
fax: 212-768-7414
E-mail: staff@asj.org
http://www.asja.org

American Society of Magazine Editors
919 Third Avenue
New York, NY 10022
phone: 212-872-3700
fax: 212-888-4217
http://asme.magazine.org

**American Society of Newspaper
  Editors (ASNE)**
11690 Sunrise Valley Drive, No. B
Reston, VA 20191-1409
phone: 703-453-1122
fax: 703-453-1133
E-mail: asne@asne.org
http://www.infi.net/asne

American Theatre Critics Association
1011 Spring Street
Savannah, TN 38372-1227
phone: 615-665-0595
fax: 615-259-8057

**American Women in Radio and
  Television, Inc. (AWRT)**
1650 Tysons Boulevard, Suite 200
McLean, VA 22102-3915
phone: 703-506-3290
fax: 703-506-3266
E-mail: jduncan@awrt.org
http://www.awrt.org

Asian American Journalists Association
1765 Sutter Street, Suite 1000
San Francisco, CA 94115
phone: 415-346-2051
fax: 415-346-6343
E-mail: national@aaja.org
http://www.aaja.org

**Associated Business Writers of
  America, Inc.**
3140 South Peoria Street, #295
Aurora, CO 88014
phone: 303-841-0246
fax: 303-751-8593
http://www.nationalwriters.com

Associated Writing Programs
George Mason University
Tallwood House, Mail Stop 1E3
Fairfax, VA 22030
phone: 703-993-4301
fax: 703-993-4302
E-mail: awp@gmu.edu
http://www.web.gmu.edu/departments/
  AWP

**Association for Business
  Communication**
Baruch College, Department of Speech
17 Lexington Avenue
P.O. Box 1326
New York, NY 10010
phone: 212-387-1620
fax: 212-387-1655
E-mail: pamela_ouellette@baruch.cuny.
  edu

Association of American Publishers, Inc.
71 Fifth Avenue
New York, NY 10003-3004
phone: 212-255-0200
fax: 212-255-7007
http://www.publishers.org

Association of Authors & Publishers
6124 Highway 6 North PMB 109
Houston, TX 77084
phone: 281-340-0185
fax: 713-896-9887
E-mail: info@authorsandpublishers.org
http://www.authorsandpublishers.org

Association of Canadian Publishers
110 Eglinton Avenue West, Suite 401
Toronto, Ontario, Canada M4R 1A3
phone: 416-487-6116
fax: 416-487-8815
E-mail: info@canbook.org
http://www.publishers.ca

Association of Earth Science Editors
c/o Mary Ann Schmidt
554 Chess Street
Pittsburgh, PA 15205-3212
phone: 412-622-3287
fax: 412-622-8837
E-mail: schmidtm@clpgh.org
http://www-odp.tamu.edu/
    publications/AESE

Association of Learned and Professional Society Publishers
South House, The Street, Clapham, Worthing
West Sussex, BN13 3UU
United Kingdom
phone: +44 (0)1903 871 686
fax: +44 (0)1903 871 457
E-mail: sec-gen@alpsp.org.uk

Association for Women in Communications
1244 Ritchie Highway, Suite 6
Arnold, MD 21012-1887
phone: 410-544-7442
fax: 410-544-4640
E-mail: womcom@aol.com
http://www.womcom.org

The Authors Guild, Inc. (corporate member of The Authors League of America, Inc.)
330 West 42nd Street, 29th floor
New York, NY 10036
phone: 212-563-5904

fax: 212-564-8363
E-mail: staff@authorsguild.org
http://www.authorsguild.org

The Authors League of America, Inc.
    (includes The Authors Guild, Inc., and The Dramatists Guild of America, Inc., but see separate references for them)
330 West 42nd Street, 29th Floor
New York, NY 10036
phone: 212-564-8350
fax: 212-564-8363

Bay Area Independent Publishers Association
P.O. Box E
Corte Madera, CA 94976
phone: 415-257-8275
http://www.baipa.org

Book Builders of Boston
27 Wellington Drive
Westwood, MA 02090
phone: 617-266-3336
fax: 781-326-2975
E-mail: webmaster@bbboston.org
http://www.bbboston.org

Book Builders West
P.O. Box 7046
San Francisco, CA 94120-9727
E-mail: president@bookbuilders.org
http://www.bookbuilders.org

Broadcast Music, Inc. (BMI)
320 West 57th Street
New York, NY 10019
phone: 212-586-2000
http://bmi.com

Broadcast Promotion and Marketing Executives
See Promax International

Business/Professional Advertising Association (B/PAA)
21 Kilmer Road
Edison, NJ 08899
phone: 732-985-4441

Canadian Publishers' Council
250 Merton Street, Suite 203
Toronto, Canada M4S 1B1
phone: 416-322-7011
fax: 416-322-6999
E-mail: pubadmin@pubcouncil.ca
http://www.pubcouncil.ca

Computer Press Association
2 Apollo Way
Flanders, NJ 07836
phone: 973-252-4037
E-mail: zatorski@computerpress.org
http://www.computerpress.org

Construction Writers Association
c/o Sheila Wertz
P.O. Box 5586
Buffalo Grove, IL 60089-5586
phone: 847-398-7756
fax: 847-590-5241
E-mail: office@constructionswriters.org
http://www.constructionwriters.org

Copywriter's Council of America
Communications Tower
7 Putter Lane, P.O. Box 102
Middle Island, NY 11953-0102
phone: 516-924-8555
fax: 516-924-3890
E-mail: linickgrp@att.net

Council for the Advancement and Support of Education
1307 New York Avenue NW, Suite 1000
Washington, DC 20005-4701
phone: 202-328-5900
fax: 202-387-4973
E-mail: membership@case.org
http://www.case.org/

Council of Authors and Journalists
See Georgia Writers

Council of Biology Editors
60 Revere Drive, Suite 500
Northbrook, IL 60062
phone: 847-480-9080
fax: 847-480-9282
E-mail: CBE_HDQTS@aol.com
http://www.cbe.org/cbe

Council of Writers Organizations
12724 Sagamore Road
Leawood, KS 66209
phone: 913-451-9023
fax: 913-451-4866
E-mail: cwo@sound.net
http://www.councilofwriters.com

Dance Critics Association
c/o Stacey Prickett
412 Euclid Ave., Apt. 1
Oakland, CA 94610
phone: 510-834-2115
fax: 510-548-7488
E-mail: ammills@dancealloy.org

Direct Mail/Marketing Association, Inc.
See Direct Marketing Association

Direct Marketing Association
1120 Avenue of the Americas
New York, NY 10036-6700
phone: 212-768-7277
fax: 212-302-6714
E-mail: dma@the-dma.org
http://www.the-dma.org

District 65, United Auto Workers
See Local 2110, United Auto Workers

The Dramatists Guild of America, Inc.
(corporate member of The Authors
League of America, Inc.)
1501 Broadway, Suite 701
New York, NY 10036-9366
phone: 212-398-9366
fax: 212-944-0420
http://www.dramaguild.com

Editorial Freelancers Association
71 W. 23rd Street, Suite 1910
New York, NY 10010
phone: 212-929-5400
fax: 212-929-5439
E-mail: info@the-efa.org
http://www.the-efa.org

Education Writers Association
1331 H Street NW, Suite 307
Washington, DC 20005-4733
phone: 202-637-9700
fax: 202-637-9707
E-mail: ewa@crosslink.net
http://www.ewa.org

Federally Employed Women, Inc.
1400 Eye Street NW
Suite 425
Washington, DC 20005-2252
phone: 202-898-0994
fax: 202-898-0998
E-mail: execdir@few.org
http://www.few.org

Garden Writers Association of America
c/o Robert C. LaGasse
10210 Leatherleaf Court
Manassas, VA 20111
phone: 703-257-1032
fax: 703-257-0213
E-mail: info@gwaa.org
http://www.gwaa.org

Georgia Writers
2633 Foxglove Drive
Marietta, GA 30064
phone: 770-943-5699
fax: 770-943-0325
E-mail: gawriter@mindspring.com
http://www.mindspring.com/~gawriter

Greeting Card Association
1030 15th Street NW, Suite 870
Washington, DC 20005
phone: 202-393-1778
fax: 202-393-0336
E-mail: gca@rgminc.com
http://www.greetingcard.org

House Radio-Television Gallery
H321 US Capital
Washington, DC 20515
phone: 202-225-5214
E-mail: radiotv@mailhouse.gov
http://www.house.gov/radiotv/index.htm

The Independent Publishers Association of Canada
Bankers Hall
P.O. Box 22184
Calgary, Alberta, Canada T2P 4J1
E-mail: hadesa@cadvision.com
http://www.trickster.com/ipac

Information Industry Association
See Software & Information Industry
Association

International Association of Business Communicators (IABC)
One Hallidie Plaza, Suite 600
San Francisco, CA 94102
phone: 415-433-3400
fax: 415-362-8762
E-mail: leader_centre@iabc.com
http://www.iabc.com

International Black Writers and Artists
P.O. Box 43576
Los Angeles, CA 90043
phone: 323-964-3721
E-mail: ibwa_la@yahoo.com
http://members.tripod.com/~IBWA/home.htm

International Communications Association
3530 Forest Lane, Suite 200
Dallas, TX 75234
phone: 214-902-3632
fax: 214-902-6521
E-mail: intlcoma@onramp.net
http://icanet.com

International Newspaper Advertising and Marketing Executives
See Newspaper Association of America

International Newspaper Marketing Association
12770 Merit Drive, Suite 330
Dallas, TX 75251
phone: 972-991-5900
fax: 972-991-3151
E-mail: inma@inma.org
http://www.inma.org

International Newspaper Promotion Association
See International Newspaper Marketing
Association

International Radio and Television Society Foundation (IRTSF)
420 Lexington Avenue, Suite 1714
New York, NY 10170
phone: 212-867-6650
fax: 212-867-6653
http://irts.org

The International Radio and Television Society-Alpha Epsilon Rho
c/o Prof. Jamie M. Byrne
Millersville University
Department of Communications &
Theatre
Millersville, PA 17551
phone: 717-872-3996
fax: 717-871-2051
E-mail: jbryne@mu2.millersv.edu
http://www.irts.org

International Society of Weekly Newspaper Editors
c/o Chad Stebbins
Institute of International Studies
Missouri Southern State College
Joplin, MO 64801
phone: 417-625-9736
fax: 417-659-4445
E-mail: stebbins-c@mail.mssc.edu
http://www.mssc.edu/iswne

International Women's Writing Guild
P.O. Box 810
Gracie Station
New York, NY 10028-0082
phone: 212-737-7536
fax: 212-737-9469
E-mail: iwwg@iwwg.com
http://www.iwwg.com

Investigative Reporters and Editors, Inc.
School of Journalism
University of Missouri
138 Neff Annex
Columbia, MO 65211
phone: 573-882-2042
fax: 573-882-5431
E-mail: info@ire.org
http://www.ire.org

Journalism Education Association
Kansas State University
Kedzie Hall 103
Manhattan, KS 66506-1505
phone: 913-532-5532
fax: 913-532-5563
E-mail: jea@spub.ksu.edu
http://www.spub.ksu.edu/~jea

Kappa Tau Alpha
c/o Dr. Keith P. Sanders
100 Neff Hall
School of Journalism
University of Missouri
Columbia, MO 65211-1200
phone: 573-882-7685
fax: 573-884-1720
E-mail: ktahq@showme.missouri.edu

Local 2110, United Auto Workers
113 University Place, 6th Floor
New York, NY 10003
phone: 212-387-0220
fax: 212-529-1986
E-mail: uaw9a@connix.com
http://uaw.org

Magazine Publishers Association
See Magazine Publishers of America

Magazine Publishers of America
919 Third Avenue, 22nd Floor
New York, NY 10022
phone: 212-872-3700
fax: 212-888-4217
E-mail: infocentral@magazine.org
http://www.magazine.org

Music Critics Association of North America
7 Pine Court
Westfield, NJ 07090
phone: 908-233-8468
fax: 908-233-8468
E-mail: beethoven@prodigy.com

Mystery Writers of America, Inc.
17 East 47th Street, 6th Floor

New York, NY 10017
phone: 212-888-8171
fax: 212-888-8107
E-mail: mwa_org@earthlink.net
http://www.mysterywriters.net

National Academy of Songwriters
6255 Sunset Boulevard, Suite 1023
Hollywood, CA 90028
phone: 213-463-7178
fax: 213-463-2146
E-mail: nassong@aol.com
http://www.nassong.org

National Academy of Television Arts & Sciences
111 West 57th Street, Suite 1050
New York, NY 10019
phone: 212-586-8424
fax: 212-546-8129
E-mail: trudywc@aol.com
http://www.internetgroup.com/natas

National Association of Black Journalists
8701-A Adelphi Road
Adelphi, MD 20783-1716
phone: 301-445-7100
fax: 301-445-7101
E-mail: nabj@nabj.org
http://www.nabj.org

National Association of Black Professors
c/o Dr. S. Miles Woods, President
P.O. Box 526
Crisfield, MD 21817
phone: 410-968-2393

National Association of Broadcast Employees and Technicians— Communications Workers of America (NABET—CWA)
501 Third Street NW, 8th Floor
Washington, DC 20001
phone: 202-434-1254
fax: 202-434-1426
E-mail: nabetcwa@aol.com
http://www.nabetcwa.org

National Association of Broadcasters (NAB)
1771 N Street NW
Washington, DC 20036
phone: 202-429-5300
fax: 202-775-3520
E-mail: irc@nab.org
http://www.nab.org

National Association of Composers, USA
P.O. Box 49256 Barrington Station
Los Angeles, CA 90049
phone: 310-541-8213
fax: 310-373-3244
E-mail: nacusa@music-usa.org
http://www.music-usa.org/nacusa

National Association of Farm Broadcasters (NAFB)
26 East Exchange Street, Suite 307
St. Paul, MN 55101
phone: 651-224-0508
fax: 651-224-1956
E-mail: nafboffice@aol.com
http://nafb.com

National Association of Government Communicators (NAGC)
526 King Street, Suite 423
Alexandria, VA 22314
phone: 703-518-4369
fax: 703-706-9583
E-mail: alexgroup@alexandriagroup.com
http://www.nagc.com

National Association of Government Employees (NAGE)
159 Burgin Parkway
Quincy, MA 02169
phone: 617-376-0220
fax: 617-376-0285
E-mail: info@nage.org
http://www.nage.org

National Association of Greeting Card Publishers
See Greeting Card Association

National Association of Hispanic Journalists
National Press Building, Suite 1193
529 14th Street NW
Washington, DC 20045
phone: 202-662-7145
fax: 202-662-7144
E-mail: liz@nahj.org
http://www.nahj.org

National Association of Science Writers, Inc.
P.O. Box 294
Greenlawn, NY 11740
phone: 516-757-5664
fax: 516-757-0069
E-mail: diane@nasw.org
http://www.nasw.org

National Black Public Relations Society
6565 Sunset Boulevard, Suite 301
Hollywood, CA 90028
phone: 323-466-8221
fax: 323-856-9510
E-mail: tobinpr@aol.com

National Conference of Editorial Writers
6223 Executive Boulevard
Rockville, MD 20852
phone: 301-984-3015
fax: 301-231-0026
E-mail: ncewhgs@erols.com
http://www.ncew.org

National Education Association
1201 16th Street NW
Washington, DC 20036
phone: 202-833-4000
fax: 202-833-7767
http://www.nea.org

National Federation of Federal Employees
1016 16th Street NW, Suite 300
Washington, DC 20036
phone: 202-862-4400
fax: 202-862-4432
E-mail: nffejmp@aol.com
http://www.nffe.org

National Federation of Press Women, Inc.
P.O. Box 5556
Arlington, VA 22205
phone: 800-780-2715
fax: 703-534-5751
E-mail: Presswomen@aol.com
http://www.nfpw.org

National Federation of State Poetry Societies
P.O. Box 486
Arab, AL 35016
phone: 507-278-4200
E-mail: poetsue@aol.com

National League of American Pen Women
Pen-Arts Building
1300 17th Street NW
Washington, DC 20036
phone: 202-785-1997
fax: 202-785-1997
E-mail: pinkflyd@wam.umd.edu
http://members.aol.com/penwomen/
    pen.htm

National Newspaper Association
1525 Wilson Boulevard, Suite 550
Arlington, VA 22209
phone: 703-907-7900
fax: 703-907-7901
E-mail: thenna@aol.com
http://www.oweb.com/nna

National Newspaper Publishers Association
3200 13th Street NW
Washington, DC 20010
phone: 202-588-8764
fax: 202-558-5029
E-mail: nnpadc@nnpa.org
http://www.nnpa.org

National Press Club
National Press Building
529 14th Street NW, 13th Floor
Washington, DC 20045
phone: 202-662-7500
fax: 202-662-7512
E-mail: npcmembership@npcpress.org
http://npc.press.org

National School Public Relations Association
15948 Derwood Road
Rockville, MD 20855
phone: 301-519-0496
fax: 301-519-0494
E-mail: nspra@nspra.org
http://www.nspra.org

National Society of State Poetry Associations
See National Federation of State Poetry
    Societies

National Sportscasters and Sportswriters Association
P.O. Box 559
Salisbury, NC 28145
phone: 704-633-4275
fax: 704-633-4275

National Turf Writers Association
1244 Meadow Lane
Frankfort, KY 40601
phone: 502-875-4864
E-mail: dliebman@bloodhorse.com

National Writers Association
3140 South Peoria Street, #295
Aurora, CO 88014
phone: 303-841-0246
fax: 303-751-8593
E-mail: sandywrter@aol.com
http://www.nationalwriters.com

National Writers Club, Inc.
See National Writers Association

National Writers Union
113 University Place, 6th Floor
New York, NY 10003-4527
phone: 212-254-0279
fax: 212-254-0673
E-mail: nwu@nwu.org
http://www.nwu.org

Newspaper Association of America
1921 Gallows Road, Suite 600
Vienna, VA 22182
phone: 703-902-1600
fax: 703-917-0636
E-mail: naainfo@naa.org
http://www.naa.org

The Newspaper Guild (AFL-CIO)
501 3rd Street NW, 2nd Floor
Washington, DC 20001-2797
phone: 202-434-7177
fax: 202-434-1472
E-mail: lgildersleeve@cwa-union.org
http://www.newsguild.org

Organization of American Historians
Indiana University
112 North Bryan Street
Bloomington, IN 47408
phone: 812-855-7311
fax: 812-855-0696
E-mail: oah@indiana.edu
http://www.indiana.edu/~oah

Outdoor Writers Association of America
27 Fort Missoula Road, Suite 1
Missoula, MT 59804
phone: 406-728-7434
fax: 406-728-7445
E-mail: owaa@montana.com
http://www.owaa.org

PEN American Center
568 Broadway
New York, NY 10012-3225
phone: 212-334-1660
fax: 212-334-2181
E-mail: pen@pen.org
http://www.pen.org

The Poetry Society of America
15 Gramercy Park
New York, NY 10003
phone: 212-254-9628
fax: 212-673-2352
E-mail: poetsocy@panix.com
http://www.poetrysociety.org

Poets & Writers, Inc.
72 Spring Street
New York, NY 10012
phone: 212-226-3586
fax: 212-226-3963
E-mail: ef@pwonline.com
http://www.pw.org

Promax International
2029 Century Park East, Suite 555
Los Angeles, CA 90067-3285
phone: 310-788-7600
fax: 310-788-7616
http://www.promax.org

The Public Relations Society of
America (PRSA)
33 Irving Place, 3rd floor
New York, NY 10003-2376
phone: 212-995-2230
fax: 212-995-0757
E-mail: hq@prsa.org
http://www.prsa.org

Public Relations Student Society of
America
Same address and fax as PRSA above
phone: 212-460-1474
·E-mail: sikita.skinner@prsa.org
http://www.prssa.org

Publishers Marketing Association
627 Aviation Way
Manhattan Beach, CA 90266
phone: 310-372-2732
fax: 310-374-3342
E-mail: info@pma-online.org
http://pma-online.org

The Publishers Association of the South
4412 Fletcher Street
Panama City, FL 32405
phone: 850-914-0766
fax: 850-769-4348
E-mail: info@pubsouth.org
http://www.pubsouth.org

Quill and Scroll Society
(for high school students only)
University of Iowa
School of Journalism
Iowa City, IA 52242
phone: 319-335-5795
E-mail: quill-scroll@uiowa.edu
http://www.uiowa.edu/~quill-sc

Radio-Television Correspondents
Association (RTCA)
c/o Senate Radio-Television Gallery
U.S. Capitol, Room S-325
Washington, DC 20510
phone: 202-224-6421

Radio-Television News Directors
Association (RTNDA)
1000 Connecticut Avenue NW, Suite 615
Washington, DC 20036-5302
phone: 202-659-6510
fax: 202-223-4007
E-mail: rtnda@rtnda.org
http://www.rtnda.org/rtnda

Radio and Television News Directors
Foundation
(all information same as above except:)
E-mail: rtndf@rtndf.org

Religion Newswriters Association
c/o Debra Mason
88 Plum Street
P.O. Box 2037
Westerville, OH 43086-2037
phone: 614-891-9001
fax: 614-823-1841
E-mail: mason@rna.org
http://www.rna.org

Republican Communications
Association
Longworth Building, Box 550
Washington, DC 20515

Romance Writers of America
13700 Veterans Memorial Drive, Suite
315
Houston, TX 77014
phone: 281-440-6885
fax: 281-440-7510
E-mail: info.rwanational@aol.com
http://www.rwanational.com

Science Fiction Writers of America
See Science Fiction and Fantasy Writers
of America

Science Fiction and Fantasy Writers of
America
c/o Michael Capobianco, Pres.
532 La Guardia Place, No. 632
New York, NY 10012-1428
http://www.sfwa.org

SESAC
55 Music Square East
Nashville, TN 37203
phone: 800-826-9996
fax: 615-329-9627
http://www.sesac.com

Sigma Delta Chi
See Society of Professional Journalists

Small Press Center for Independent
Publishing
20 West 44th Street
New York, NY 10036
phone: 212-764-7021
fax: 212-354-5365
E-mail: smallpress@smallpress.com
http://www.smallpress.org

Small Publishers, Artists & Writers
Network
P.O. Box 2653
Ventura, CA 93002-2653
phone, fax: 805-643-2403
E-mail: execdir@spawn.org
http://www.spawn.org

Small Publishers Association of North
America
P.O. Box 1306
Buena Vista, CO 81211-1306
phone: 719-395-4790
fax: 719-395-8374
E-mail: span@SPANnet.org
http://www.spannet.org

Society for Scholarly Publishing
10200 West 44th Avenue, No. 304
Wheat Ridge, CO 80033
phone: 303-422-3914
fax: 303-422-8894
E-mail: ssp@resourcenter.com
http://www.sspnet.org

Society for Technical Communication
901 North Stuart Street, Suite 904
Arlington, VA 22203
phone: 703-522-4114
fax: 703-522-2075
E-mail: stc@stc-va.org
http://www.stc-va.org

Society of American Archivists
527 South Wells, 5th Floor
Chicago, IL 60607
phone: 312-922-0140
fax: 312-347-1452
E-mail: info@archivists.org
http://www.archivists.org

Society of American Business Editors
and Writers
c/o University of Missouri
School of Journalism
120 Neff Hall
Columbia, MO 65211-0838

phone: 573-882-7862
fax: 573-884-1372
E-mail: carolyn-guniss@jmail.jour.
    missouri.edu
http://www.sabew.org

Society of Architectural Historians
1365 North Astor Street
Chicago, IL 60610-2144
phone: 312-573-1365
fax: 312-573-1141
E-mail: info@sah.org
http://www.sah.org

Society of American Travel Writers
4101 Lake Boone Trail, Suite 201
Raleigh, NC 27607
phone: 919-787-5181
fax: 919-787-4916
E-mail: satw@olsonmgnt.com
http://www.satw.org

Society of Children's Book Writers
See Society of Children's Book Writers
    and Illustrators

**Society of Children's Book Writers and
    Illustrators**
8271 Beverly Boulevard
Los Angeles, CA 90048
phone: 323-782-1010
fax: 323-782-1892
E-mail: membership@scbwi.org
http://www.scbwi.org

Society of Professional Journalists
16 South Jackson
Greencastle, IN 46135-0077
phone: 765-653-3333
fax: 765-653-4631
E-mail: spj@linkzooo.net
http://www.spj.org

**Software & Information Industry
    Association**
1730 M Street NW, Suite 700
Washington, DC 20036-4510

phone: 202-452-1600
fax: 202-223-8756
http://www.infoindustry.org

Songwriters Guild of America
1500 Harbor Boulevard
Weehawken, NJ 07087-6732
phone: 201-867-7603
fax: 201-867-7535
E-mail: SongNews@aol.com
http://www.songwriters.org

Songwriters Resources and Services
See National Academy of Songwriters

Special Libraries Association
1700 18th Street NW
Washington, DC 20009-2514
phone: 202-234-4700
fax: 202-265-9317
E-mail: sla@sla.org
http://www.sla.org

United Auto Workers, District 65
See Local 2110, United Auto Workers

Women in Cable
See Women in Cable and
    Telecommunications

**Women in Cable and
    Telecommunications**
230 West Monroe Street, Suite 730
Chicago, IL 60606-4702
phone: 312-634-2330
fax: 312-634-2345
E-mail: wict@aol.com
http://www.wict.org

**Women in Communications, Inc.
    (WICI)**
See Association for Women in
    Communications

Women in Scholarly Publishing
c/o Dariel Mayer
P.O. Box 27228

Knoxville, TN 37927
phone: 423-546-6436
fax: 423-546-4466
E-mail: dmayer@utk.edu
http://www.wispnet.org

**Women's National Book Association,
    Inc.**
160 Fifth Avenue, Room 604
New York, NY 10010
phone: 212-675-7805
fax: 212-989-7542
E-mail: skpassoc@internetmci.com
http://bookbuss.com/wnba.htm

Writers Guild of America, East, Inc.
555 West 57th Street
New York, NY 10019
phone: 212-767-7800
fax: 212-582-1909
E-mail: info@wgaeast.org
http://www.wgaeast.org

Writers Guild of America, West, Inc.
7000 West Third Street
Los Angeles, CA 90048-4329
phone: 213-550-1000
fax: 213-782-4800
E-mail: wga@wga.org
http://www.wga.org

Writers Workshop
(seminars in business writing)
200 Marvin Way
Auburn, CA 95603
phone: 530-885-7260
fax: 530-885-8012

APPENDIX IV
MAJOR TRADE PERIODICALS

The following are some of the principal trade publications serving writers in various fields. For information on additional publications, consult these reference books at your public library: *Directory of Publications and Broadcast Media, Literary Market Place,* and *Writer's Market.* In addition, most trade and professional associations and unions publish periodicals for their membership.

ACADEMIC, INSTITUTIONAL

The American Historical Review
American Historical Association
Indiana University
914 Atwater
Bloomington, IN 47401
phone: 812-855-7609
fax: 812-855-5827
e-mail: ahr@indiana.edu
http://www.indiana.edu/~ahr/

American Libraries
The American Library Association
50 East Huron Street
Chicago, IL 60611-2795
phone: 800-545-2433
fax: 312-440-9374
http://www.ala.org/alonline

School Library Journal
245 West 17th Street
New York, NY 10001
phone: 212-463-6759
fax: 212-463-6689
e-mail: dwatson@cahners.com
http://www.bookwire.com/slj

ADVERTISING, PUBLIC RELATIONS

Advertising Age
Crain Communications Inc. Publications
220 East 42nd Street
New York, NY 10017-5806
phone: 212-210-0100
fax: 212-210-0200
http://www.adage.com

Adweek
BPI Communications, Inc.
1515 Broadway, 14th floor
New York, NY 10036
phone: 212-536-5257
e-mail: cwessel@adweek.com
http://www.adweek.com

American Advertising
American Advertising Federation
1101 Vermont Avenue NW, Suite 500
Washington, DC 20005-6306
phone: 202-898-0089
fax: 202-898-0159
e-mail: aaf@aaf.org
http://www.aaf.org

The National Business Wire Newsletter
Business Wire
44 Montgomery Street
San Francisco, CA 94104
phone: 415-986-4422
fax: 415-956-2803
e-mail: alexs@bizwire.com
http://www.businesswire.com

ENTERTAINMENT

Billboard
BPI Communications Inc.
1515 Broadway, 14th floor
New York, NY 10036
phone: 212-536-5240
fax: 536-5358
http://www.billboard.com

The Hollywood Reporter
5055 Wilshire Boulevard, 6th floor
Los Angeles, CA 90036-7171
phone: 323-525-2000
fax: 323-525-2377
http://www.hollywoodreporter.com

Variety
245 West 17th Street
New York, NY 10011
phone: 212-337-7001
fax: 212-337-6977
http://www.variety.com

INTERNET AND E-ZINES

There are thousands of e-zines out there, and the number is growing every day. New ones are born; old ones disappear. Try typing "writing e-zines" into your favorite search engine to get a good, up-to-date list and see which ones appeal to you. Many e-zines feature the work of new writers. Here is a tiny handful to get you started. Some are databases that allow you to search for other e-zines.

American Studies Web
http://www.georgetown.edu/crossroads/asw/lit.html

eZINESearch
http://homeincome.com/search-it/ezine/

Fictioneer
www.fictioneer.com

forwriters.com
http://www.forwriters.com/

LIFT
http://www.lifted.com

The Literary Arts WebRing
http://www.lit-arts.com/WebRing/RingIndex.html

Q-Youth
http://www.q-youth.com/

Xenith
http://www.xenith.net/

JOURNALISM

American Journalism Review
University of Maryland

College of Journalism
8701 Adelphi Road
Adelphi, MD 20783
phone: 301-405-2239
fax: 301-431-0097
e-mail: editor@ajrumd.edu
http://www.ajr.org

Columbia Journalism Review
704 Journalism Building
Columbia University
New York, NY 10027
phone: 212-854-1881
fax: 212-854-8580
e-mail: cjr@columbia.edu
http://www.cjr.org

Editor & Publisher
11 West 19th Street
New York, NY 10011
phone: 212-675-4380
fax: 212-691-7287
e-mail: edpub@mediainfo.com
http://www.mediainfo.com

Presstime
Newspaper Association of America
1921 Gallows Road, Suite 600
Vienna, VA 22182
phone: 703-902-1600
fax: 703-917-0636
http://www.naa.org

Quill & Scroll
School of Journalism
University of Iowa
Iowa City, IA 52242
phone: 319-335-5795
fax: 319-335-5210
e-mail: quill-scroll@uiowa.edu
http://www.uiowa.edu/~quill-sc

Washington Journalism Review
See American Journalism Review

World Press Review
700 Broadway
New York, NY 10003
phone: 212-982-8880
fax: 212-982-6968
http://www.worldpress.org

MULTIMEDIA

MediaCentral
Cowles Business Media
4225 Baltimore

Kansas City, MO 64111
phone: 913-967-1838
http://www.mediacentral.com

MAGAZINE AND BOOK PUBLISHING

Folio: The Magazine for Magazine Management
Intertec
11 Riverbend Drive South
P.O. Box 4272
Stamford,CT 06807
phone: 203-358-9900
fax: 203-358-5823
http://www.foliomag.com

Independent Publisher
Jenkins Group, Inc.
121 East Front Street, 4th floor
Traverse City, MI 49684
phone: 231-933-0445
fax: 231-933-0448
e-mail: ipmag@bookpublishing.com
http://www.bookpublishing.com

Magazine & Bookseller
North American Publishing Co.
401 North Broad Street
Philadelphia, PA 19108
phone: 215-238-5343
fax: 215-238-5283
e-mail: editor@mb.napco.com
http://napco.com/mb/mb1.html

Publishers Weekly
245 West 17th Street
New York, NY 10011
phone: 212-463-6758
fax: 212-463-6631
http://www.publishersweekly.com

Small Press
See Independent Publisher

TECHNICAL WRITING

Technical Communication
Society for Technical Communication
901 North Stuart Street, Suite 904
Arlington, VA 22203-1854
phone: 703-522-4114
fax: 703-522-2075
e-mail: stc@stc-va.org
http://www.stc-va.org

Small Press Review
Dustbooks
P.O. Box 100
Paradise, CA 95967
phone: 530-877-6110
fax: 530-877-0222
e-mail: dustbooks@telis.org
http://www.dustbooks.com

WRITING, POETRY, DRAMA

The Drama Review
MIT Press
5 Cambridge Center
Cambridge, MA 02142
phone: 617-253-2889
fax: 617-577-1545
e-mail: journals-info@mit.edu
http://mitpress.mit.edu

Poets & Writers Magazine
Poets & Writers Inc.
72 Spring Street
New York, NY 10012
phone: 212-226-3586
fax: 212-226-3963
http://www.pw.org

The Writer
120 Boylston Street
Boston, MA 02116-4615
phone: 617-423-3157
fax: 617-423-2168
e-mail: writer@user1.channel1.com
http://www.channel1.com/thewriter

Writer's Digest
1507 Dana Avenue
Cincinnati, OH 45207
phone: 513-531-2222
e-mail: wdweb@fwpubs.com
http://www.writersdigest.com

APPENDIX V
BIBLIOGRAPHY

Accredited Journalism and Mass Communications Education 1993–94. Accrediting Council on Education in Journalism and Mass Communications.

Advertising Age. "Average Growth in Base Salary for 1999." Available on-line. URL: http://adage.com/dataplace/archives/dp297.html. Posted December 7, 1998. © Crain Communications Inc.

———. "Entry-Level Salaries." Available on-line. URL: http://adage.com/dataplace/archives/dp182.html. Posted December 1, 1998. © Crain Communications Inc.

———. "Executive Pay at Agencies." Available on-line. URL: http://adage.com/dataplace/archives/dp300.html. Posted December 7, 1998. © Crain Communications Inc.

———. "What to Expect for '99: Advertising Agency Salaries and Raises." Available on-line. URL: http://adage.com/dataplace/archives/dp302.html. Posted December 7, 1998. © Crain Communications Inc.

Angelo, Jean Marie and Rachel Drucker. "Editors Report Stalled Earnings." *Folio,* Aug. 1, 1993, pp. 41–46.

Association of Research Libraries. "1998–99 Annual Salary Survey Published." Available on-line. URL: http://arl.cni.org/stats/salary/1998–99/9899pr.html. Last modified January 26, 1999.

Avery, Dan, et al., "1999 Career Guide: 20 Hot Job Tracks." *U.S. News & World Report,* Vol. 125, no. 16, October 26, 1998, pp. 84–90.

Barron's Profiles of American Colleges, 23rd ed. Hauppauge, N.Y.: Barron's Educational Series, 1999.

Becker, Lee B. and Thomas E. Engelman. "Survey of Journalism and Mass Communications Graduates 1988: Summary Report July 1989." Columbus, Ohio: Ohio State University, and Princeton, N.J.: Dow Jones Newspaper Fund.

Becker, Lee B. and Gerald M. Kosicki. "Summary Results from the 1992 Annual Graduate Survey." Columbus, Ohio: Ohio State University.

Bernstein, Alan B., and Nicholas R. Schaffzin. *Guide to Your Career.* New York: The Princeton Review, 1977.

Bly, Robert W. and Blake, Gary. *Dream Jobs: A Guide to Tomorrow's Top Careers.* New York: Wiley & Sons, 1983.

Bolles, Richard Nelson. *Job-Hunting on the Internet,* 2nd ed. Berkeley, Calif.: Ten Speed Press, 1999.

Bone, Jan. *Opportunities in Cable Television Careers.* Lincolnwood, IL: VGM Career Horizons, NTC Publishing Group, 1993.

"Booming Website Salaries Reflect Growth of Industry." *HR Focus,* Vol. 74, issue 9, September 1997, p. 13.

"Booming Website Salaries Reflect Industry Strength." *HR Focus,* Vol. 75, September 1998, Issue 9, p. 4.

Bureau of Labor Statistics, U.S. Department of Labor. "Employee Benefits in Medium and Large Private Establishments, 1997." Available on-line. URL: http://stats.bls.gov/ebshome.htm. Posted January 7, 1999.

———. "Establishment Data Earnings, Not Seasonally Adjusted. Table B-17: Average hourly and weekly earnings of production or nonsupervisory workers on private nonfarm payrolls by major industry, in current and constant (1982) dollars." Available on-line. URL: ftp://ftp.bls.gov/pub/special.requests/ee/ceseeb17.txt. Downloaded on 9/4/99.

———. "Establishment Data Hours and Earnings, Not Seasonally Adjusted. Table B-15: Average hours and earnings of production or nonsupervisory works on private nonfarm payrolls by detailed industry." Available on-line. URL: ftp://ftp.bls.gov/pub/special.requests/ee/ceseeb15.txt. Downloaded on 9/4/99.

———. "Occupation Report Sorted by Percent Change in Total Employment, 1996–2006." Available on-line. URL: http://www.bls.gov/asp/oep/noeted/empoccp.asp. Downloaded September 25, 1999.

———. "Occupational Employment, Training, and Earnings: Occupation Report Sorted by Total Employment in 1996." Available on-line. URL: http://www.bls.gov/asp/oep/noeted/empoccp.asp. Downloaded on September 4, 1999.

———. *Occupational Outlook Handbook, 1998–99 Edition,* Bulletin 2500. Superintendent of Documents, U.S. Government Printing Office, Washington, D.C., 1998.

Busnar, Gene. *Careers in Music.* New York: Julian Messmer, 1982.

Butler, Susan Lowell. "What's Ahead for Communicators in the 90s." *The Professional Communicator,* Spring 1990, pp. 16–17+.

Carvajal, Doreen. "Middling (and Unloved) in Publishing Land: Authors with Less Than Stellar Sales Are Unwanted by Big Houses." *The New York Times,* August 18, 1997, p. D1.

———. "The More the Books, the Fewer the Editors: As Publishing Pressures Rise, So Do Errors." *The New York Times,* June 29, 1998, p. E1.

Career Information Center, 6th ed. Vols. 1, 3, and 13. New York: Macmillan Library Reference USA, 1996.

Carfagno, Jacalyn DePasquale. "We Got Jobs, and Pay Is Rising—A Little." *Columbia Journalism Review,* July/August 1998, Vol. 37, issue 2, p. 20.

Cassill, Kay. *The Complete Handbook for Freelance Writers.* Cincinnati, Ohio: Writer's Digest Books, 1981.

"Census Study Finds That Attending College Pays." *Black Issues in Higher Education,* Vol. 15, issue 22, December 24, 1998, p. 33.

Changery, Christopher M. "Newspapers March to New Beats." *Presstime,* Sept. 1989, pp. 24–26.

Chepesiuk, Ron. "The CNN Library." *Library Journal,* Sept. 15, 1992, pp. 31–33.

Click, J.W. and Baird, Russell N. *Magazine Editing and Production.* Dubuque, Iowa: Wm. C. Brown, 1974.

Colamosca, Anne. "Who's Left Out? Small Markets, Small Paychecks." *Columbia Journalism Review,* July/August 1999, Vol. 38, issue 2, p. 29.

Coleman, Lillian S. and Jennifer H. McGill. *Journalism and Mass Communication Directory,* Volume 11, 1993–1994. Columbia, S.C.: Association for Education in Journalism and Mass Communication.

The College Blue Book: Degrees Offered by College and Subject, 26/e. New York: Macmillan Reference USA, 1997.

Communicator, "RTNDA Salary Survey Statistics." Available on-line. URL: http://www.rtndf.org/issues/articles/ salstats.htm. Published jointly by Radio-Television News Directors Association and Radio and Television News Directors Foundation, © May 1999. All Rights Reserved.

Craft, Donna, and Terrance W. Peck, eds. *Profiles of American Labor Unions.* Farmington Hills, Mich.: Gale Research, 1998.

D'Agostino, Joseph A. "Wealthy Federal Workers Get Raise from Congress." *Human Events,* Vol. 55, issue 36, October 1, 1999, p. 5.

Darnay, Arsen J., and Helen S. Fisher. *Statistical Handbook of Working America: Statistics on Occupations, Careers, Employment, and the Work Environment,* 2nd ed. Detroit: Gale Research Inc., 1997.

Dodds, Robert H. *Writing for Technical and Business Magazines.* New York: John Wiley & Sons, Inc., 1969.

The Dow Jones Newspaper Fund, Inc. *1990 Journalism Career and Scholarship Guide.* Princeton, N.J.: 1989.

Editors of Federal Jobs Digest. *Working for Your Uncle.* Ossining, N.Y.: Breakthrough Publications, 1993.

Espinza, Galina. "Back to School?" *Money,* September 1998, Vol. 27, No. 9, p. 134.

Farrell, Christopher, et al. "A Rising Tide." *Business Week,* August 31, 1998, pp. 72–75.

Ferguson, Donald L. and Patten, Jim. *Opportunities in Journalism Careers.* Lincolnwood, Ill.: VGM Career Horizons, NTC Publishing Group, 1993.

Field, Shelly, *Career Opportunities in the Music Industry, 3rd ed.* New York: Facts On File, 1995.

Field, Syd. *The Screenwriter's Workbook.* New York: Dell, 1984.

Fischer, Carolyn A., ed. *Gale Directory of Publications and Broadcast Media: An Annual Guide to Publications and Broadcasting Stations, Including Newspapers, Magazines, Journals, Radio Stations, Television Stations, and Cable Systems,* 132nd ed. Detroit: Gale Research, 1999.

Fisher, Helen S. *American Salaries and Wages Survey,* 5th ed. Detroit: Gale Research, 1999.

Gerardi, Robert. *Opportunities in Music Careers.* Lincolnwood, Ill.: VGM Career Horizons, NTC Publishing Group, 1991.

Glanz, William. "Salaries Up for Website Workers." *Baltimore Business Journal,* Vol. 16, issue 9, p. 11.

Goeller, Carl. *Writing and Selling Greeting Cards.* Boston: The Writer, Inc., 1980.

Gould, Jay and Losano, Wayne. *Opportunities in Technical Communications.* Skokie, Ill.: VGM Career Horizons. National Textbook Co., 1980.

Greeting Card Association. "GCA Industry Fact Sheet." Available on-line. URL: http://www.greetingcard.org/ gca/facts.htm. Downloaded October 11, 1999.

Groome, Harry C. Jr., *Opportunities in Advertising Careers.* Louisville, KY.: Vocational Guidance Manuals, 1976.

Haas, Ken. *How to Get a Job in Advertising.* New York: Art Direction Book Co., 1979.

Haubenstock, Susan H. and David Joselit. *Career Opportunities in Art.* New York: Facts On File, 1988.

Heim, Kathleen and Myers, Margaret. *Opportunities in Library and Information Science Careers.* Lincolnwood, Ill.: VGM Career Horizons, NTC Publishing Group, 1992.

Heim, Kathleen and Peggy Sullivan. *Opportunities in Library and Information Science.* Skokie, Ill.: VGM Career Horizons, National Textbook Co., 1982.

Holm, Kirsten C., ed., and Donya Dickerson, asst. ed. *Writer's Market: 8,000 Editors Who Buy What You Write,* electronic 2000 ed. Cincinnati, Ohio: Writer's Digest Books, 1999.

Hosgrove, Holli, ed. *Encyclopedia of Careers and Vocational Guidance,* 10/e. Chicago: J.G. Ferguson, 1997.

Industry Standard, The: The Newsmagazine of the Internet Economy. "What Internet Professionals Make." Available on-line. URL: http://www.thestandard.net/articles/display/ 0,1449,3310,00.ht ml. Posted February 1, 1999.

Jacobs, Eva E., ed. *Handbook of U.S. Labor Statistics,* 2nd ed. Lanham, Md.: Bernan Press, 1998.

Jerome, Judson. *The Poet's Handbook.* Cincinnati, Ohio: Writer's Digest Books, 1980.

Johnson, Betty and Mary Esther Bullard Johnson. "Getting Ahead: A Profile of Black Media Managers." Published by the National Association of Black Journalists, Jan. 13, 1989.

Joyce, Cynthia. "Gabillions and Kazillions: The Small Screen Equals Big Bucks for the Writers and Producers Behind Hit TV Programs." *Salon/Media Circus.* Available on-line. URL: http://www.salonmagazine.com/ media/1997/10/29money.html. Posted October 29, 1997.

Jukabiak, Joyce, ed. *Specialty Occupational Outlook: Professions.* Detroit: Gale Research, Inc., 1995.

Kamerman, *Book Reviewing.* Boston: The Writer, Inc., 1978.

Katz, Bill, and Linda Sternberg Katz. *Magazines for Libraries,* 9th ed. New Providence, N.J.: R.R. Bowker, 1997.

Kissling, Mark. *1993 Writer's Market.* Cincinnati, Ohio: Writer's Digest Books, F & W Publications, 1992.

Knollenberg, Greg A. "Using the Internet to Crack the Greeting Card Market." Available on-line. URL: http://www.writerswrite.com/journal/feb98/gak4.htm. Downloaded September 24, 1998. © 1997, 1998 by Writers Write, Inc. All Rights Reserved.

Krantz, Les. *The Jobs Rated Almanac.* New York: World Almanac, Fharos Books, 1992.

Krefetz, Gerald and Philip Gittelman. *The Book of Incomes.* New York: Holt, Rinehart & Winston, 1981.

Lafky, Sue A. "Economic Equity and the Journalistic Work Force." Talk given for the Association for Education in Journalism and Mass Communication at Portland, Oreg. July 2–5, 1988; published in Sept. 1988 *Presstime.*

Lane, Susan. *How to Make Money in Newspaper Syndication.* Irvine, Calif.: Newspaper Syndication Specialists, 1985.

Leonard, Andrew. "Workers of the Web, Delight: For 'Word People,' the New Media Boom Means a Rare Chance to Make a Real Buck." *Salon/Media Circus.* Available on-line. URL: http://www.salonmagazine.com/media/1997/10/30money.html. Posted October 30, 1997.

Lloyd, Wanda. "Newsroom Salaries." American Society of Newspaper Editors Bulletin, Nov. 1993, pp. 14–15.

McCann, Nita. "Low Salaries Driving Print Journalism Grads Away from Newspapers." *Mississippi Business Journal,* September 23, 1996, Vol. 18, issue 39, pp. 9–10.

Mainstream Access, Inc. *The Public Relations Job Finder.* Englewood Cliffs, N.J.: Prentice-Hall, Inc., 1981.

Mainstream Access, Inc. *The Publishing Job Finder.* Englewood Cliffs, N.J.: Prentice-Hall, Inc., 1981.

Maki, Kathleen E., and Kathleen M. Savage, eds. *Professional Careers Sourcebook: Where to Find Help Planning Careers That Require College or Technical Degrees.* Compiled in cooperation with InfoPLACE, the Job, Career, and Education Service of the Cuyahoga County Public Library. New York: Gale Research, 1997.

Maurer, Christine, and Tara E. Sheets, eds. *Encyclopedia of Associations,* 34th ed. Detroit: Gale Research, 1999.

Maurer, Rolf, "B-to-B Editors See Biggest Gains." *Folio: The Magazine for Magazine Management,* Vol. 28, issue 10, August 1999, pp. 51–53.

Milliot, Jim. "Salary Survey: Top Guns at the Largest Companies Earn the Most, but Have the Most to Lose." *Publishers Weekly,* July 5, 1999, pp. 37–41.

———, and Susan Connolly. "Salary Survey: Bigger the Company, Bigger the Paycheck." *Publishers Weekly,* July 6, 1998, pp. 33–36.

Mitternight, Helen L. "Winning the Hearts—or at Least the Eyes—of the Online Audience." *Communication World,* Vol. 15, issue 4, March 1998, pp. 36–38.

Mogel, Leonard *Making It in the Media Professions.* Chester, Conn.: The Globe Pequot Press, 1988.

"*Money* Magazine's Best Places to Live, 1998." Cited in *Computerworld,* Vol. 32, issue 34, August 24, 1998.

"Money, Money." *Public Relations Tactics,* March 1999, p. 22.

Morgan, Bradley J. *Advertising Career Directory.* Detroit, Mich.: Gale Research, Inc., 1993.

———. *Book Publishing Career Directory.* Detroit, Mich.: Visible Ink Press, Gale Research, Inc., 1993.

———. *Magazines Career Directory.* Detroit, Mich.: Visible Ink Press, Gale Research, Inc., 1993.

———. *Newspapers Career Directory.* Detroit, Mich.: Visible Ink Press, Gale Research, Inc., 1993.

Public Relations Career Directory. Detroit, Mich.: Visible Ink Press, Gale Research, Inc., 1993.

Moses, Lucia. "Marketing and IT Execs 'Net-ting' Nice Salaries." *Editor & Publisher,* July 31, 1999, Vol. 132, issue 31, pp. 14–15.

New Jersey Library Association. "Minimum Recommended Starting Salaries for Certified Professional Staff, 1999–2000." Courtesy of a public librarian.

Newspaper Guild-CWA, The, "Collective Bargaining Manual." Washington, D.C., April 1, 1999.

———. "The Information Superhighway." Washington, D.C., July 1995.

"1999 Salary Guide: Salary Guide Outlines 1999 Compensation Levels and Hiring Trends for Administrative Professionals." Available on-line. URL: http://www.officeteam.com/career/salary.html. Downloaded September 20, 1999.

Ostmann, Sharon. "Facts For Sale." *APME,* Aug./Sept. 1992, pp. 3–5.

Pattis, S. William. *Opportunities in Magazine Publishing Careers.* Lincolnwood. Ill.: VGM Career Horizons, NTC Publishing Group, 1992.

Peek, Robin, and Paula J. Hane. "Access for Everyone—Sort of: Web Accessibility Guidelines Aim to Remedy Usage Limitations." *Information Today,* Vol. 16, issue 6, June 1999, pp. 48–49.

"Publishers Weekly Salary Survey." *Publishers Weekly,* April 25, 1994, pp. 36–38.

"PRJ's Fourth Annual Salary Survey." *Public Relations Journal,* June 1989, pp. 17–21.

Psivack, Jane F., ed. *Careers in Information.* White Plains, N.Y.: Knowledge Industry Publications, Inc., 1982.

Reed, Robert M. and Maxine K. *Career Opportunities in Television, Cable and Video.* 3rd ed. New York: Facts On File, 1986.

Ross, Tom and Marilyn. *The Complete Guide to Self-Publishing.* Cincinnatti, Ohio: Writer's Digest Books, 1985.

Rowe, Chip. "Easy E-zines." *Writer's Digest,* Vol. 76, issue 9, September 1996, pp. 64–5.

R. R. Bowker, *Ulrich's International Periodicals Directory,* 37th ed. New Providence, N.J.: R. R. Bowker, 1999.

Russman, Linda deLaubensfels. "WICI Job & Salary Survey Results." *The Professional Communicator,* Spring 1990, pp. 18–22.

Scherman, William H. *How to Get the Right Job in Publishing.* Chicago: Contemporary Books, Inc., 1983.

Shaffer, Susan E. *Guide to Book Publishing Courses.* Princeton, N.J.: Peterson's Guides, 1979.

Smith, Kelly, et al., "Salary Roundup." *Money,* September 1998, Vol. 27, No. 9, pp. 133–134.

"Special Report: Trends in Organizational Communications." *Communication World,* March 1999, Vol. 16, issue 4, p. 42. [no individual author listed]

Statesman, Alison, "Survey: Internships Provide an Advantage." *Public Relations Tactics,* September 1997, Vol. 4, issue 9, p. 8.

Statistical Service Center, for the Book Industry Study Group. "Press Release: 21st Edition of Book Industry Trends 1998: Study Calls Online Bookselling the Issue of the Year." Available on-line. URL: http://www.bisg.org/bisg/trends-98.html. Downloaded October 9, 1999.

Stone, Vernon. "Minorities and Women in Television News." Available on-line. URL: http://web.missouri.edu/~jourvs/tvminw.html. Downloaded September 20, 1999.

———. "Paychecks and Market Baskets: Broadcast News Salaries and Inflation in the 1990s." Available on-line. URL: http://web.missouri.edu/~jourvs/sals90s.html. Downloaded September 20, 1999.

———. "Supply, Demand and Entry-Level Pay in Television News." Available on-line. URL: http://web.missouri.edu/~jourvs/entrypay.html. Downloaded September 20, 1999.

———. "Women Break Glass Ceiling in TV News." Available on-line. URL: http://web.missouri.edu/~jourvs/tvfnds.html. Downloaded September 20, 1999.

Stone, Vernon A. "Pay Gains Top Cost Of Living." *The Professional Communicator,* Feb. 1994, pp. 68–70.

Tebbel, John. *Opportunities in Journalism.* Skokie, Ill.: VGM Career Horizons, National Textbook Co., 1977.

Tortorello, Nicholas J. and Elizabeth Wilhelm. "Eighth Annual Salary Survey." *Public Relations Journal,* July 1993, pp. 10–19.

U.S. Department of Labor. *Report on the American Workforce.* Washington, D.C.: U.S. Department of Labor, 1997.

———. "Women of Hispanic Origin in the Labor Force." No. 97–2, February 1997. Available on-line. URL: http://www.dol.gov/dol/wb/public/wb_pubs/hisp97.htm. Downloaded September 24, 1999.

U.S. Department of Labor, Bureau of Labor Statistics. *Occupational Outlook Handbook 1982–83.* Washington, D.C.: U.S. Government Printing Office, 1982.

U.S. Department of Labor, Bureau of Labor Statistics. *Occupational Outlook Handbook 1994–95.* Washington, D.C.: U.S. Government Printing Office, 1994.

Wall Street Journal Interactive Edition. "Entertainment Industry." Available on-line. URL: http://public.wsj.com/careers/resources/documents/19980323-entertainment-tab.htm. Downloaded October 20, 1999. © 1999 Dow Jones & Company, Inc. All Rights Reserved.

———. "Internet Professionals." Available on-line. URL: http://public.wsj.com/careers/resources/documents/19980619-internetpros-tab.htm. Downloaded October 20, 1999. © 1999 Dow Jones & Company, Inc. All Rights Reserved.

———. "Librarians." Available on-line. URL: http://public.wsj.com/careers/resources/documents/19980825-library-tab.htm. Downloaded October 20, 1999. © 1999 Dow Jones & Company, Inc. All Rights Reserved.

———. "Nonprofit Organizations and Trade Association Professionals." Available on-line. URL: http://public.wsj.com/careers/resources/documents/SB87770566741085 6500.htm. Downloaded October 20, 1999. © 1999 Dow Jones & Company, Inc. All Rights Reserved.

———. "Service Managers." Available on-line. URL: http://public.wsj.com/careers/resources/documents/19991013-se rvicemgr-tab.htm. Downloaded October 20, 1999. © 1999 Dow Jones & Company, Inc. All Rights Reserved.

———. "Special Librarians." Available on-line. URL: http://public.wsj.com/careers/resources/documents/19990928-li brarians-tab.htm. Downloaded October 20, 1999. © 1999 Dow Jones & Company, Inc. All Rights Reserved.

Weaver, David and Wilhoit, G. Cleveland. "Who Are We?" *Quill,* Jan./Feb. 1993, pp. 45–47.

Weiner, Leonard. "Upward Mobility: The Ultimate Job-Hopper's Guide." *U.S. News & World Report,* Vol. 125, no. 16, October 26, 1998, pp. 62–68.

"Where the Money Is: *PW's* Second Annual Publishing Salary Survey." Survey conducted by Mary Connors, commentary by John F. Baker. *Publisher's Weekly,* Sept. 29, 1989, pp. 17–21.

Wibking, Angela. "Firstword: Money for Webmeisters." *Nashville Business Journal,* Vol. 14, issue 29, pp. 1–2, July 17, 1998.

Williams, Gurney III. *Writing Careers.* New York: Franklin Watts, Inc., 1976.

Wilson, Jean Gaddy. "Special Report." *Presstime,* Oct. 1986, pp. 31–37.

Wright, John W. *American Almanac of Jobs and Salaries,* 3rd ed. New York: Avon Books, 1987.

Zeller, Susan L. *Your Career in Radio and Television Broadcasting.* New York: Arco Publishing, Inc., 1982.

Zipkowitz, Fay. "Fewer Graduates But Salaries Climb." *Library Journal,* Oct. 15, 1993, pp. 30–36.

INDEX